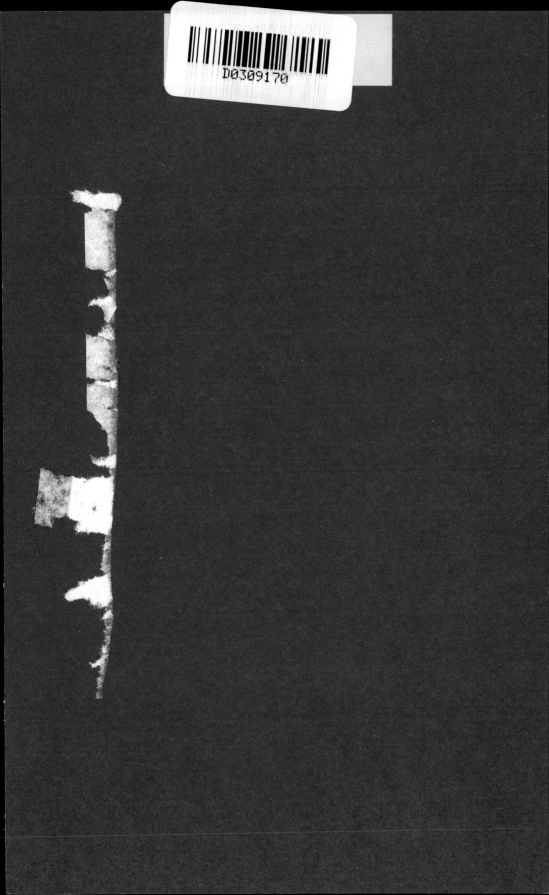

WORTH FIGHTING FOR

ALSO BY LISA NIEMI SWAYZE

The Time of My Life
(with Patrick Swayze)

WORTH FIGHTING FOR

LOVE, LOSS, AND

MOVING FORWARD

LISA NIEMI SWAYZE

**SIMON &
SCHUSTER**

London · New York · Sydney · Toronto · New Delhi

A CBS COMPANY

First published in Great Britain in 2012 by Simon & Schuster UK Ltd
A CBS COMPANY

1 3 5 7 9 10 8 6 4 2

Simon & Schuster UK Ltd
1st Floor
222 Gray's Inn Road
London
WC1X 8HB

www.simonandschuster.co.uk

Simon & Schuster Australia, Sydney
Simon & Schuster India, New Delhi

Permission to reprint lyrics to 'Since You've Asked' courtesy of
Wildflower Records, a Judy Collins Company (ASCAP)

A CIP catalogue copy for this book is available
from the British Library.

ISBN: 978-0-85720-838-5 (hardback)
978-0-85720-839-2 (trade paperback)
978-0-85720-841-5 (ebook)

Designed by Dana Sloan
Printed and bound by CPI Group (UK) Ltd, Croydon, CR0 4YY

Dedicated to the one I love
Gone from my sight, close to my heart

CONTENTS

WORTH FIGHTING FOR

Patrick and I are wed, with Father Welch presiding.

Chapter 1

FAIRY TALE

THE MOMENT I reached for my notebook to start working on this book, I was flooded with an emotion that I've tried to keep at bay for some time now. It's a wave of feeling composed of endless tears, reminding me that I haven't remotely cried enough.

The emotion that washes over me brings the distant past to an instant present. And the details scream out in my mind and heart: every time I pushed down my feelings, every time I smiled when my world was tumbling down around me, and every time I heard a piece of bad news and reacted positively, laughing with mock bravery when I should have been dissolved in tears.

There is a high price to be paid for the privilege of caring for your loved one when he's dying, but it's one I wouldn't have traded for anything. I always said that I'd have plenty of time to cry later. When Patrick first got his diagnosis it looked like he might have only weeks to live. Then it was months. And then, luckily, we passed a year. And we kept going. . . . Twenty-one months is a long time to battle for your loved one against a foe like cancer. It's a long time to "hold up." And now, I've been spit out on the other side of the fight, alone, trying to figure out how I'm going to go on with my life.

Hot and cold.

Right now I'm running hot and cold.

As I write this in May of 2010, it's been over six months since I lost Patrick, and right now, at this particular moment, I either despise the bad times he and I had together, or worship the good we had. No in-between.

So, at this particular moment, I worry how can I talk about us, him, in an objective way. One that gives an accurate, albeit can't-help-but-be-emotional-here-and-there idea of what really happened, who he really was, who I have been, and who I am now. 'Cause I tell you, I am a different person now. One who has been thrown into the fire and forged. One who got stripped of all the nice things that sheltered me from the world, and from myself.

It's been hard living out here in the cold. I look for a life raft anywhere, and there's none to be found. No usual anchors to ground me. No more comfortable illusions. But this person I am is real, painful in its growing spurt, the growing spurt that's happened without my husband . . . but real. And because I am real there are possibilities.

Now, this isn't the way to start a book, but . . . I guess I'm having an angry day, one of those days that happens sometimes since the loss of my Buddy ("Buddy" was his lifelong nickname). And, yes . . . I guess I am sad.

I think I was hoping to wrap my experience with him up with a nice little bow. And remember it that way. At arm's length. So, if I seem a little caustic right now, it's just my attempt to have an arm's-length view of the story I'm telling. And unfortunately, I know that my being snarky is an attempt to not feel the loss. Because . . . when I talk about him (as I'm doing here) . . . I miss him so much. So terribly. So completely that I worry how I'm going to get to the next moment.

Wait a minute . . .

. . . there.

I made it to the next moment.

And *that's* how you get through the bad moments of *grief.* You do it one at a time.

And now I want to talk about him. About who he was when he was here on this earth. My beautiful man. I want to tell this story before I get too far away from it and forget what the journey of the last couple years was really like. 'Cause we do forget. It's only real when you experience it. After that, as time goes on, it becomes merely the recounting of a story.

—

YOU KNOW, it's funny because there's always so much talk about divorce statistics. When you get married you can't help but be aware that there is an approximately 50 percent chance it will end in divorce. There are data about how many couples divorce in their twenties, their thirties, and so on, how many heterosexual couples, how many homosexual. There are television series starring divorced men and women, books written about divorce and by the divorced, major movies made, let alone all the divorced people you run into in everyday life, right? And then there are the children of divorced parents, the books the children write when they grow up, the movies subsequently made, the kids that are carted off to one parent or another, or even kidnapped. There is so much information out there about what happens when marriages don't work out.

But no one ever talks about what happens when marriages *do* work out.

What happens when you *stay together*? If this is something that's been the source of great discussions, it's not really been on my radar. The short answer to what happens when marriages work out is that the lucky couple lives happily ever after. That's the fairy tale. But we're not living in a fairy tale, are we?

No one talks about the "till death do us part" that comes at the end of the traditional wedding vows. What it means, *what it really means*. I think it's funny now how many people have changed that line to "as long as we both shall live" or "for all the days of our lives." While I agree that the "death" word is a little gruesome-sounding, the two alternatives are full of loopholes. I mean, one can cherish someone's memory—after one kicks him out of the house. I knew without a doubt, when things were so terrible between Patrick and me in 2003 that I moved out for a year, that I would unequivocally love him always and to the end of time, but I was *still* going to divorce his ass if things didn't change in our relationship. (Luckily they did.) The other wedding vow alternatives also give me a laugh: "for all eternity" (really, you can really promise that?), and one with an even more obvious escape loophole, "through whatever life may bring us." But hey, it's honest. No one wants to be stuck in a bad marriage.

—

"TILL DEATH do us part." That's what Patrick and I said in our vows when we got married. I had already made sure "to honor and obey" was stricken from the record. Somehow I missed "till death do us part." I was eighteen years old, I knew death existed, but it was still a *concept*, something far, far in the future. So far that I didn't have to worry about it.

We had the greatest priest marry us, Father Welch. Father Welch was a friend of the Swayze family. Patrick's mom, Patsy, had actually done some musical theater with him back in the day and said that he had a crazy sense of humor. She told us how one day the Father came up to her, "Hey Patsy, I have a great idea for the show," he enthused, "Let's have a really elegant lady in a fancy ball gown come on the stage, then when she gets to the chair, she hikes up her dress, sits down like a farmhand, and starts plucking a chicken! Isn't that great?" I looked at Patrick and deadpanned, "He sounds great."

And Father Welch was great. During my interview with him, which I found out was required for a Catholic wedding, I balked at saying yes to the questions about converting to the Catholic religion, raising children, and birth control. He'd wave a hand and write in, "yes," "yes," "yes," saying that all these questions were going to change in a few years anyway so it didn't matter. I find it hilarious that I was so honest and sincere that it was difficult for me to let him put in the "yes" answers, and yet, I didn't once mention that I didn't really believe in the institution of marriage, and furthermore, fully expected this one to end up as one of the divorce statistics. And that I was okay with that.

The whole idea of marriage had come about in an abrupt way. It wasn't like Patrick and I had talked about marriage. We had talked about the future, though mostly in terms of what we wanted to do as dancers, where we wanted to dance, and with whom. I just wanted to dance. Patrick wanted to dance with me. And it made me nervous.

We had been living together in our tiny, one-bedroom brownstone apartment with dark yellow-gold walls in New York City for about nine months. I had just returned from doing a dance performance and visiting my family in Houston for a few days, where I had a conversation with my very liberal, open-minded mother in which she raised a surprisingly conservative point, and said, "You know . . . without the commitment of marriage, all you and Buddy are doing is 'playing house.'" *Yeah, and . . . ?* Back in New York, I made the mistake of relaying this exchange to Patrick. He just kind of . . . stopped for a moment. Three days later,

we were in the middle of a tickling fight on our futon couch when
he paused, his arms around me.

"What?" I asked curiously.

His face flushed. "Why don't we do it? Why don't we get
married?"

I froze. And tried to buy time, clumsily attempting to negoti-
ate a lengthy engagement, "Yeeahh, we could do that . . . we could
get married . . ."

I had left home only nine months before. I wasn't ready to
move straight from there into another home. I had places to go,
people to see, things to do! I wanted to dance! I didn't even *believe*
in marriage to begin with, although I planned to revisit my stance
on that subject in another twelve years or so when I reached thirty.

"When?" he was warming up to the idea, "When do you
think we should do it?" He was not only warming up to the idea,
he wanted to close the deal right then and there.

"Uhm, how about . . . in the fall of next year?" That was a
year and a half away. I figured I'd have plenty of time to figure a
way out by then.

His face fell. And he began to look mortally wounded.

"Don't you think that would work?" I defended. "Why?
Why . . ." I softened, "What were *you* thinking?" *Never dreaming
that he would say* . . .

"I think if we're going to do it, we should just do it right away.
Like next month," he said with conviction. "What do *you* think?"
And he nervously looked me straight in the eye while he waited
for my reaction.

Guess who won?

———

WE WERE so different from each other, and yet, so much alike.
I was fourteen years old when I first laid eyes on him at Hous-

ton Music Theater when his mom's dance school and company merged with the theater group I was working with. How could you not notice him? He was tan, buff, and had a dazzling smile. And his reputation for being a Casanova and having a big ego had preceded him. This wasn't helped by the fact that my first contact with him came when we passed each other coming in and out of the theater, and he reached over and pinched me on the butt. "Hey there, cutie!" he said in a both friendly and mischievous tone. *"Oh, brother."* I rolled my eyes as he passed me.

Although I had a rich and deep internal life, on the outside I was painfully shy and had excruciating difficulty being around people. I just didn't know how to talk to them, not the slightest idea. I hate using that word "shy," because it indicates that I was *always* that way. I wasn't when I was in a situation I was familiar with. I always marveled how I could bust it up plenty loud and good with my brothers at home, but at school, never utter a word or raise my head or hand. I was so socially withdrawn that I would plot and plan how I was going to walk from point A to point B across a room in public long before I actually did so. Honestly, I wouldn't make a move until I'd figured out how to do it and be as invisible as possible lest I draw attention and have someone look at me, or say something. I wasn't just a wallflower; I was an expert, practiced wallflower. Not such an easy thing to master when you're skinny and strikingly fair, with a shock of unusually white blonde hair. And yet, this shy girl is the same girl who opened up on stage like gangbusters, who felt she could reach out and touch the deepest parts of people.

Buddy, on the other hand, was gregarious. He carried himself shoulders back, head high, with the confidence of the popular guy, and one who was very comfortable with that position. Me, I was hanging with the longhaired, misfit, doper crowd. It was natural that any friends I did have were people who also didn't fit in. And we hid behind our cigarettes, pot, and differentness. I wasn't so noticed with them and it was okay to be weird. In contrast, Buddy looked like a cliché of the All-American, clean-cut, clean-living star athlete of school and home. He was almost . . . *too perfect*. And it wasn't that I hated that about him, I was never quick to judge people. If anything, I gave them too much latitude. It's just what I observed. If anything, I felt a little sorry for him. For all his being so perfect looking, and perhaps because of it, he didn't fit in either.

One thing about being so quiet is that while everyone else is busy doing something or talking—you are watching. *Really watching* (beware the ones who are quiet!). You can see things that might not be apparent to others. Being painfully shy, I was always quick to see others' pain, although I never let on that's what I saw. Behind Buddy's quick grin, I saw nervousness. Behind his bravado, I saw a pain I thought that even he didn't really know about (that's my fourteen-year-old self speaking). Behind his awkward teasing and small talk, I sensed a deep insecurity and need. One thing I knew for certain . . .

This guy wasn't my type.

And later, when I shifted to dancing full-time with his mom, he asked me out.

Of course I accepted.

—

OUR FIRST dates were not very successful . . . to put it mildly. They consisted mostly of him chatting on to fill every possible silence and me barely talking at all as we cruised along in his bright yellow Opel GT. He loved that car!

A sample of our conversation:

Patrick: "My first car, I built from the ground up, I got most of the parts from my uncle's automotive shop, he had gotten this big shipment of used Dune Buggies for old-folks homes and took them apart for parts, so I got to get whatever I needed from him, of course my Dad came in and helped me with some things. And then there was football practice, which was taking most of my time after school, and then I had to hustle to dance class so there wasn't a lot of time to make extra money, and then there was a paper route I threw from three to four o'clock in the morning. But I manage to get to dance class every chance I get. So, you are looking to go to New York and dance?

(pause)

"Yes."

(pause)

(pause)

Patrick: "That's good 'cause you really have the talent. No, really, I wouldn't just say that. You know Bob Joffrey, who I've known all my life, says that if I really work on my feet, you know how you can get that little arch just above the metatarsal. It's the hardest thing, and then getting the foot to do that little wing. . . . It's not so easy for a guy to get, but my feet are looking pretty good . . ."

And on and on. It was strange because the dates were so uncomfortable and yet . . . not uncomfortable at all. Of course I'd been told that all the girls wanted him and he could have his pick (so they said, and it was probably true). But he didn't intimidate me, mostly because 1) I was not looking to lay any claim to him, 2) I had his number. I knew he appeared to be a flirt and to have a big ego. But I knew what he felt like inside. And though our first few dates were pretty terrible, there was a powerful attraction between us, and we kept coming back, even though we still didn't trust each other. I was still wary of his self-centered, Casanova reputation, and he was still wary of my "bad girl" doper rep. And then, one day that mistrust melted away. It actually happened when he wrote me a letter from New York telling me that he thought he had fallen in love with a fellow dancer at Harkness Ballet. My reaction surprised me—I was happy for him. I discovered that I really cared about him. And the depth of my feeling surprised me.

You know, some people talk about how they knew when they met the love of their life. I didn't know that Patrick was going to be the love of my life. I wouldn't have even dared to suppose that. But I did have a premonition, a strong sense that there was destiny between us. Maybe it was that we'd have a more meaningful relationship before we parted, or . . . I didn't know exactly what. But I knew there was going to be *something*. And I was confident in it. From the beginning, even while I still had my guard up, I saw something deep inside him that I thought was pure gold. It belied all the things that were said about him and who he was, it belied even the things he said about himself. And then one night, right before our relationship made a turn and we started to trust, I had a dream about him. It was like a moving picture, moving, but still life. He was seated on something akin to a windsurfer board, a small sailboat floating on a big, beautiful, blue lake . . . bright, clear, golden light shining on him . . . a breeze gently blowing through his hair. And he was sitting naked, feet folded up in front on him. And though he was beautiful, it wasn't that it was sexy . . . he was pure. And he smiled at me with one of the most beatific smiles I've ever seen.

I woke up with wide eyes! Now, I've been writing down and paying attention to my dreams since I was twelve years old. I was shocked at this vision of him in my dream. I knew then, without a shred of doubt, that I liked him. I really, really liked him.

So, when he asked me to marry him, when for some crazy reason I was still holding on to the idea that he "wasn't my type," that, and a few other things that concerned me about committing to him for the rest of my life . . . *I was not prepared to let him go.* And I didn't feel I could say "no" without losing the relationship, or hurting him badly.

"Oh, well," I thought, *"I need to go through with this. We can always get divorced later."*

And on June 12, 1975, as I stepped out into my family's small backyard in Houston, Texas, the group of family and friends standing scattered in the grass, Father Welch standing calmly center with his Bible, my father proudly offering his arm to me at the back door to lead me out, out to face a fuzzy Patrick, Patrick standing stiff and still in his light blue suit, fuzzy not only because he seemed somewhat paralyzed, but as I grasped his hands and we held tight, tears had pushed their way into my eyes . . . and they started to stream down my cheeks.

—

AND WE were off to the races! From being dancers, we went to working in the theater, from theater we moved to Los Angeles for film. There were heartbreaks and struggles, along with adventure, enthusiasm, and sweet little victories. It was tough at times, but we were resilient, and we always made it somehow. We were living and pursuing our dreams.

It was during this time that I started to learn how to talk to people. I started with things as simple as saying to a grocery cashier, "It's a nice day today." Then I graduated to more challenging conversation. Practice, practice, practice.

How ironic is it that this quiet, introspective girl got thrown into the public eye on a level that few people have to deal with? When Patrick first did the miniseries *North and South* and then hit it big with *Dirty Dancing*, the lid blew off our lives and there were not only multitudes of people and decisions to make, but he *and* I were thrown into a high-profile world that included doing press and on-camera interviews for national and international audiences. Gimme a break! Patrick was always pulling me from the shadows that I moved in so well. Actually, early on, before he had made any kind of name for himself, his first manager suggested that he not even mention he was married, to which Patrick emphatically and without hesitation said, "No way. I'm *proud* to be married." Not many other ambitious actors would have made that choice. He always insisted that I be a part of everything he did and included me in every interview possible. He wanted people to *see me*. We were a team. I learned how to give an interview with the best of them (Patrick being my main example!).

At the same time, the fact that I was so quiet and guarded came in handy in this new, highly public life. A life in which there were many things you did not tell. To anyone. Ever. Not sharing your deepest thoughts, your painful problems, or any unhappiness was considered an asset to a public image, but it reinforced the worst of my lonely struggles and feelings that I was always on my own to sink or swim.

Along with success comes another set of problems. I've always said, "If you really want to test someone, give them what they really want." Getting want you want removes the idea that once you get it, everything will be great. Try living with that. Lots of people can't deal with it. And as down-to-earth a person as Patrick could be, he got lost in that conundrum more than a few times. Added to the fact that he spiraled downward when his father died, taking on the booze that his dad had imbibed for many years. And alcohol and he did not mix very well.

So many challenges. And so many adventures. With our new lives we got to travel, do incredible things, enjoy fascinating work, have access to situations people only dream about and be crazy in love with each other as we learned, grew, and gained valuable experience. We also fought, pushed ourselves beyond stress, and tested the limits of our relationship. From Patrick I learned bravery, knowing that nothing is impossible, and the startling ability to push beyond the boundaries of what you think your limits are.

I don't know how—but we always hung in there together. Close as close could be. A friend once described us as symbiotic twins, something I thought possibly was not a compliment. But through thick and thin we stayed fast, which only made it all the more painful when in 2003 I moved out after his drinking had escalated to a breaking point. I know I had reached mine. It had been a good ten years in coming, and I felt I was breaking in half. It had gotten to the point where I knew something had to stop or someone was going to die. It was that terrible. I was gone a year. And after he stopped drinking, and there was some hope that things could be manageable again, I moved back in.

But our reunion was not going to solve all of our problems. And little by little, my faith in the relationship crumbled further into despair. I'd find myself waking up in the middle of the night crying, not stopping for hours. I had given up on the hope that Patrick's and my relationship could turn around and truly be what it was meant to be, and I felt like I was witnessing the living death of our marriage at that point.

My friend Lynne, who had been there for me in some of the hardest times, always reminded me that miracles could happen. I didn't believe that was possible with Patrick and me. There was too much history. Sometimes you just go too far down that road of destruction. There ends up being too much hurt, you become too entrenched in your positions to ever break free. Again, for the final time, I was ready to leave, for good. I hadn't moved my stuff out yet, but in my heart, the door had closed and I was already gone. And then . . .

A miracle happened.

Honestly.

A lady psychic came to visit us—yes, that's right, a lady psychic—and it was the catalyst that turned our relationship around overnight. Whether this woman was truly psychic or just incredibly intuitive, or both, she saw what was going on and, unlike many, wasn't afraid to say what she saw and *not back down*. Mercilessly, but with care, she wasn't going to let us *not see*. And what happened, I wouldn't have believed was possible if I hadn't been through it myself. It was as if both of us were ready to walk through that door together at the same time. It was nothing short of magic. I felt like for the first time in years Patrick saw me, *really saw who I was,* who he fell in love with. And though I was still afraid, I still wanted him more than anything on the planet. We saw that. And we opened ourselves to each other and took that leap together. Hand in hand.

The change was profound. And when a few weeks later, we broke into a terrible argument, Patrick stopped in the middle of the argument and held me tight, tears coming into his eyes, and he said, "I will do anything. I *never* want us to go back to the way it was." My heart melted, and I squeezed him back. We were finally learning what to do, to have what we wanted so much. And every time he showed me love, every time he was kind to me, every time he smiled at me, it erased the parts of our history I thought could never heal. Crazy, huh? You can heal with love. Just sometimes too much stuff gets in the way of that love.

When we were first together we had always joked about how a relationship was not supposed to be easy, that it wasn't like we were Prince Charming and Snow White. All "roses and daffodils," as we said. And God knows it had been work. But here we both were, over three decades later, and we had just witnessed a fairy tale come true. It took over thirty years, but it was better than roses and daffodils. He had me. And I had something even better than the man of my dreams.

Then . . .

—

NEW YEAR'S 2008, we were visiting friends in Aspen and raised a glass of champagne for a toast over dinner. Patrick grimaced a little when he swallowed it down, but he didn't say anything. Throughout our trip and our stay at our ranch in New Mexico, he was hitting the Tums pretty regularly. But I didn't worry; he'd always had a sensitive digestive system.

Back in Los Angeles a week later, he came to me on a Sunday afternoon, "Do my eyes look yellow to you?" He hadn't been feeling well and had bad indigestion. I had also noticed he had eaten little to nothing in the last two or three days. I peered into his eyes curiously, moved him into better light to make sure. "Yes, yes, they *do* look yellow." I called Celinda, our housekeeper for over twenty years, over to confirm, "Yes. Yellow." She nodded in her definitive way. I looked at him . . . "Let's get you in to the doctor first thing tomorrow," but Patrick assured me that there was no rush. I'm not an alarmist, and wasn't trying to be one now, but I shook my head, "No . . . better to go. This is not normal. Let's get you in." *So what,* I thought. *We get it checked out and that'll be that.*

—

THERE'S A word in the Finnish language that the Finns hold in very high regard—"Sisu." I've known of this word since I was a youngster, and being of Finnish heritage, I was told that this "Sisu" was in my blood and a part of my DNA. My family's roots on both sides are Finnish, and I am the second generation born in the United States. I always thought that my family was a little strange. That is, until the first time I visited Finland. Everyone there was just like my family! I realized that we weren't crazy; we were just a Finnish family living in Texas, U.S.A. Hell yeah! And while I learned from Patrick how to be braver and to believe nothing was impossible, I had also learned how to be tougher than the rest as I grew up as the only girl with five strapping brothers (and no, I was not spoiled being the only girl). But that toughness and pluck was nothing compared to the "Sisu" I had been always been told was my birthright.

"Sisu" basically means courage. But it's more than just having guts. Loosely translated into English it means strength of will, determination, perseverance, and acting rationally in the face of adversity. For example: a riding student falls off a horse, she doesn't cry and gets back on the horse. If she falls again, and keeps getting back on, she is showing Sisu. Several Finnish athletes have shown their Sisu, like Lasse Virén, who in the Munich Olympics fell during the 10,000-meter running event, but got up and won the event, breaking the world record. In 1939, a powerful Russia invaded Finland with three times as many soldiers, thirty times as many aircraft, and one hundred times as many tanks. By the time it was over, the Russians had suffered heavy losses and succeeded in taking only 11 percent of Finland's territory. Unbelievable.

Sisu is not a momentary courage, but a particular brand of doggedness, one that is capable of facing down death itself. Knowing that you have lost and still continuing to fight . . . that shows Sisu.

The next two years would test my Sisu beyond anything I had ever imagined.

Chapter 2

THE DIAGNOSIS

Early January 2008, fresh from morning skiing.
A few short weeks before Patrick's diagnosis.

J ANUARY 14, 2008. By the time we got to the doctor's office it was late afternoon on Monday and fast approaching office closing hours. I had driven Patrick in since he had an upset stomach and wasn't feeling very well. Dr. Davidson's was a forty-five-minute drive from our house, longer with traffic, and was located just around the corner from Cedars-Sinai Hospital.

We sat waiting in one of Dr. Davidson's examining rooms, Patrick messing with his settings on his iPhone, me thumbing through a magazine and thinking about the inconvenient traffic we'd face on the way home. Davidson, a small, sincere man who could flash a dazzling smile at will, came back into the room. He waved a piece of paper in his hand, Patrick's blood results. He wasn't smiling.

"Uhm . . . your bilirubin is high," he said.

"My . . . what did you call it? Bilirubin?" Patrick asked. We had never heard of a bilirubin and frankly, we both thought the word was a little hilariously silly-sounding.

"Yes." Davidson nodded, explaining that bilirubin was a pigment in the bile juices that gives your stool its brown color . . . *ah, that makes sense, Patrick's stool had turned pale in color* . . . and this bile/pigment is usually eliminated through the bile duct in the liver. That is, unless something stops it from flowing through and it backs up.

Dr. Davidson gave us the number. "It's showing at 13.3."

"Is that high?" I asked.

He nodded. I could see from his concerned doctor's demeanor that this number was indeed very high, but he didn't linger on this information, focusing instead on, "I'm going to call Mark Taper Imaging over at Cedars-Sinai and see if I can get you in for a CT scan right away." And he went to contact them.

Patrick and I looked at each other. We were impressed that this seemed serious enough for the doctor to get Patrick in for a scan, even though it was after hours. At the same time, we weren't going to get too worried about something that might be nothing. Like years ago, when Patrick had a couple of oval brown marks on the lower part of his leg. They looked like motorcycle burns, like what happens if you wear shorts and touch your calf to the hot cylinder and scorch the skin. But these oval marks didn't go away after a while. Although Patrick isn't a huge hypochondriac, he worried that *this might be cancer.* He worried and worried for three years. And I heard about it and heard about it. Finally, I begged him to go to the doctor and ask him what it was so I didn't have hear him keep fretting about it. He went. It was nothing but an errant blemish.

At Mark Taper Imaging a half hour later, we were whooshed through the lobby and into a back room before the few people still around recognized us. An hour later, Patrick had the CT scan, and we were back in the car on the way home. We called Dr. Davidson to see if he had gotten the results yet.

He had.

The scans showed a 5 by 4 centimeter mass on the head of Patrick's pancreas. That's approximately 2 by 1½ inches.

And an alarm sounded inside our heads.

What? What does this mean? Dr. Davidson was hesitant to guess until further investigation. But we pushed.

"We-e-l-l-l, it *could* be cancer," he said.

"And . . . what else?" hoping there was more.

"You could have acute pancreatitis. Which could be caused by heavy alcohol use," he ventured.

I didn't like the tone of Dr. Davidson's voice. He was usually very friendly and engaging, but from the time he got Patrick's blood results back, he had been quite serious and professional. Though I did my best to ignore it, I heard in his voice that he was afraid, more than afraid that Patrick had cancer. I was hoping for the better scenario—that it was pancreatitis due to alcohol consumption. That gave me something to grab on to. Patrick had slowly started to drink again a little here and there, and who knows, who knows . . . maybe a lot more when I wasn't around.

In figuring out what this thing was, this mass, the next step was for Patrick to have an ERCP (endoscopic retrograde cholangiopancreatography), a procedure in which a scope is inserted down your throat, through your stomach, to reach your bile duct; there the doctor inserts a stent that will open up the bile duct, thus letting bile flow, relieving his jaundice and pale stool and bringing his bilirubin count down. *Okay* . . . Also while they are in there, they will take a look at the mass, aka "the tumor," and they'll get a biopsy. *Great, great, then we'll know!* The only problem was that this wasn't going to happen for another five days.

"Five days?"

We were not happy. We already knew that *this might be cancer.* Five days of not really knowing was . . . ridiculous! I knew that Patrick was upset and tense, although he didn't say too much about it. I jumped on the Internet, trying my best to find evidence one way or the other (mostly looking for the noncancer alternatives), but the information was so broad at that point, I just gave up.

We just kept the most positive outlook possible while we waited. Funny that you would hope that a diagnosis would involve alcohol abuse, that you would pray for it even . . . rather than have it be a diagnosis of cancer.

The days went by and finally . . . it was early on a bright Saturday morning when we showed up at the gastroenterology department on the seventh floor at Cedars-Sinai Hospital. It was a busy day there because it just so happened that a big conference of GI doctors had assembled for that weekend. In order to get Patrick in for the ERCP as quickly as possible, we chose to go ahead and do it during the conference, otherwise it would have been *another five days* before he could get an appointment. We couldn't bear waiting any longer. Basically, this conference consisted of a couple of days in which gastrointestinal doctors gathered from all over the country to perform, to watch the procedures, and to exchange information. Though we worried about there being so many people and the risk of Patrick's privacy being compromised, we saw the situation as a big, big plus. Patrick was going to have some of the best doctors from all over the country looking at this. We felt lucky that we were going to have so many expert minds involved.

The ERCP would involve three doctors in one room who would insert a scope down Patrick's throat into his insides with a camera attached, and in the room next door, what the camera saw would be viewed by twenty or so doctors. There was great excitement and energy in the department, people hurrying around with cables strewn through the rooms hooking up to recorders and monitors. I thought it was kind of ironic, I mean, Patrick is used to being on camera, right? But this was like some crazy sitcom, "We're shooting live! Get ready!" But there's something so personal, so oddly intimate, in a different way, about having a group of people looking literally *inside you*. There's no celebrity, no doubt about your humanity when you're traveling down a person's esophagus, down into the deep regions of his gut.

Patrick and I laughed and chatted with the nurses as he was prepped for the procedure. I took a deep breath and held his hand throughout, and when it was time for him to be wheeled in, I kissed him lightly on the lips and smiled at him, just in case. "I love you," I told him. Already getting woozy, he returned with a dopey smile, "I love you."

—

THEY COULDN'T get the stent in.

Dr. Lo and the other doctor who actually performed the procedure took me into a nearby private office afterward and explained that the area around his pancreas was so crowded and blocked that they couldn't get through to insert their little piece of metal and open it up.

And another thing . . .

"He has pancreatic cancer." They were solemn. "Everything we saw points to this. The blockage, the mass is consistent with . . ." I don't know which one was saying this to me, or whether both said it together; it all ran together at that point. I just remember the information kind of freezing in my brain. I heard it, but I could feel it freezing . . . because it had no reality attached to it.

"Are you sure? How can you be sure?" I had to ask.

"We're 98 percent certain," they said with a look that indicated they were sorry to say it. They filled me in with some information about the disease, where it was placed with Patrick. Adenocarcinoma, the head of the pancreas . . . that it can be aggressive . . .

"Maybe the biopsy can come back negative?" I hoped.

One doctor took a breath, as if he was considering saying, *"There's always a chance."* But he thought better of it and let his breath go, "No. . . . It's just going to confirm what we already saw."

"That's right," the other nodded.

"We're so sorry . . ."

—

I WAS feeling an odd rush of different thoughts: *Oooh, I don't want to cry, not now, not now. Should I cry? I don't know what to do. Why do I feel nothing? Am I looking stupid? Am I hearing what they're saying? I feel okay, but can I trust myself to really hear this information?* I didn't know how to feel what I was feeling. The word "cancer" brought instant terror, but terror that was uninformed and confusing, so much so that I couldn't even identify it as terror at this point. I looked around as we talked . . . it was a normal day, like any other normal day. And yet, I had just been given this huge news . . .

"Would you mind," I blurted out, "Would you mind getting on the phone with my sister-in-law, Maria, in Houston and explaining this to her? She's an oncologist there . . ." *I didn't trust myself to hear them properly.*

"Of course."

I found Maria's number in my cell phone and dialed her, my fingers tingly and removed. My oldest brother, Ed, picked up. "Ed!" I tried to sound casual but to the point, "Is Maria there? I need to talk to her." A doctor's husband, he didn't ask any questions, he just said, "Sure, I'll get her." And he handed the phone over.

Maria's voice was bright and buoyant, "Hello, Lisa!"

I explained where I was, that Patrick had just had an ERCP, that they had just diagnosed him with pancreatic cancer and I needed to let the doctors explain to her what was going on because I didn't trust myself to remember it all.

Maria was suddenly quiet, "Okay, sure . . . put them on the phone."

I handed the phone over to Simon Lo. I felt that I was calm and in control, that I was handling this. Then why was my voice shaking? Why was it so cold in the room?

—

PATRICK WAS recovering slowly from the endoscopic procedure, and doing so poorly. Most people bounce right out, but not him. It's possible that the amount of air they had to pump through him to attempt to get the stent in was now causing him pain. I joined him at his bedside as he started to come around, my hand resting lightly on his shoulder. He grimaced and then emitted a groan. He was still woozy and recovering from the anesthesia. I was recovering also, but not from the drugs. I was trying to get my footing, trying to figure out what the next step was. How do I tell him this news? How do you tell someone he's been diagnosed with cancer?

His abdominal pain from the procedure was so intense that the doctors had him stay overnight in the hospital, and we moved into a room. He was still dopey and now had new pain medication on top of that. I didn't feel like I could tell him, not when he wasn't fully conscious. *How can he assimilate information like this when he was incredibly medicated and in pain?* I decided to wait until morning. *Yeah, that's what I'll do . . . I'll wait . . .*

What a dreadful night. Living with this horrible knowledge all to myself was an incredibly awful thing. I felt as though *I* was the one who had crawled into a coffin and closed the lid. I could hear the nails being banged into the top. And it was very dark and lonely there. And as I lived with this knowledge, I didn't feel too terrible about not telling him right away. I felt that it actually was a good thing that I hadn't told him yet, and in a way, it became my gift to him. I knew how I felt having this new, terrible knowledge, and I couldn't imagine how he'd feel once he knew, too. I mean, *he was the one who had cancer.* I counted . . . if I waited until morning, he'd have eight more hours of innocence. Eight hours was a lot of time. A lifetime, in this case. Also . . . I suppose I didn't tell him because I didn't want to go into that future just yet. I knew that, inexorably, on a dime, our lives had turned. And they'd never, ever, be the same from this day forth. Once he knew, there was no going back. We'd be on our way.

—

IWOKE up on the lumpy hospital cot the next morning, dressed in the same clothes I had been wearing since the previous morning, and brushed the hair out of my face with my hand. Dr. Nissen, a young surgeon we hadn't met before, was sitting at the foot of Patrick's bed talking to him. Patrick was alert and awake. I panicked that the doctor was going to say something and tried to straighten myself up and get my bearings as fast as I could. But I was too late. Patrick was looking confused. The doctor looked at me. I'm sure I looked scared.

"He doesn't know?" he was asking me.

My stomach turned. I shook my head. "I didn't tell him yet."

"During your ERCP they found you have pancreatic cancer," he told Patrick. *So much for picking the right time.*

Patrick looked quickly at me, alarm rising in his eyes. I just met his eyes as steadily and calmly as I could. Dr. Nissen continued explaining what he could provide as a surgeon, that surgery provided the best chance of survival, but they had to confirm that the cancer had not yet spread to other organs.

We were nodding. I could see Patrick taking in this information evenly, and he definitely appeared attentive. But he was as stunned as I was. As he told me later, inside he was thinking . . .

"I'm a dead man."

I think both of us had that kind of deer-in-the-headlights look the entire day. We kept calm and composed, as we had learned to do under pressure, as an overwhelming slew of doctors came in and out of the room, most of whom we had never seen before. For the next couple of days, doctors were assembled who could address any and every possible aspect of the disease, from surgery, to attempting another stent in the next week, to chemotherapy and treatment options, to setting up his PET scan for the following day. There were discussions about how to alleviate the intense discomfort he still had, about different hospitals that offered treatment, risks of infections, pain management . . . One thing that was hard to take was that no doctor sugarcoated the disease. Every single one of them told us there was no cure, and that we had some decisions to make quickly—sooner rather than later. Though it was hard to hear, I respected them for being so honest. I would rather hear the truth. I can do something with the truth. I can't do anything with a lie, even if it is a little fib. Patrick felt the same. We held on to the hope that the disease had not spread and Patrick could go into surgery, a major, complicated surgery called a Whipple Procedure. They remove most of the pancreas and parts of other organs, thus increasing his chance of survival past two years by 35 percent. What was the life expectancy without the procedure?

"How long have I got?" Patrick was brave enough to ask Dr. Hoffman, one of the doctors and an oncologist/cancer doctor who could provide treatment locally in LA.

"It depends. Maybe a couple weeks, maybe a couple months," replied Dr. Hoffman evenly. "I won't kid you. This disease is extremely aggressive."

Later that first day, Patrick turned to me and sighed ruefully. I could tell there was emotion under the sigh, but he was without self-pity when he remarked, "You know . . . whenever I heard that someone had pancreatic cancer, my first reaction was, 'Well, *he's outta here.*'"

I couldn't reply, I could only listen.

Patrick and I had been married for more than thirty-two years and had been through the worst and best life could bring us. But nothing could prepare us for this diagnosis. Nothing could prepare us for the hours of just doing our best to take in new information regarding further tests, possible procedures that could be done if the disease hadn't spread, and the possible outcomes, of which there were pitifully few. Okay, to be straight, if his cancer had indeed spread, we were being told that there was only one real possible outcome, and it's not the good one.

It was a good twelve hours after Patrick first heard his diagnosis when all the doctors and nurses finally dwindled out of the room for the day. The staff shift changed, it quieted, and he and I were finally alone.

After we revisited and recapped the day and all the information we had received, we fell silent. What could you say? I crawled into the bed with him and laid my head on his shoulder. And started to cry. And then, softly through my sobs, I begged him, "Please . . . I can't do this. Please, don't make me do this." I had been through thirty-two years of ups and downs with him, been through a yearlong breakup, jumped out of airplanes, survived fame, failure, off-airport landings, a miscarriage, drunken arguments, rehab, horses, dogs, cats, laughter, shouts, and tearful embraces. And now I was begging him to not ask me to do this one last thing. As if he had a choice about changing his reality. It was a nonsensical request, and I knew it. But I so did not want it to be true. And at that moment, and after all we'd been through, I felt finally beaten. I wondered if I could ever get up again.

But that was that day.

Giving Patrick a hug that clearly says, "I'm not letting you go anywhere!"

Chapter 3

IT AIN'T OVER TILL IT'S OVER

I WOKE UP THE next morning, and somehow, I had taken a look in my little storage room for any emergency reserve strength and found enough to get through the next twenty-four hours. We found that the disease had spread to his liver. This was not the news we wanted to hear. It meant no best-case scenario. It was worst-case scenario.

But we don't know everything yet. Don't panic. Hold steady.

We were not going to scare off that easily, we were still going to research for information and answers . . .

Patrick was hanging in there. He was steady, keeping a level head, but I knew he hoped as much as I did that we would find some answers. After another visit to the seventh floor, Dr. Lo successfully placed the stent that got Patrick's bile duct open again, and we were checked out of the hospital to go back home. Patrick was tentative.

"It's like . . . going home is going to make it real." He looked brave, but there was a hint of dread in his voice.

Even home was different now. Not the same place at all. It

had now been transformed into a command center, dedicated to finding the best possible course of action for Patrick. Notepads, Internet research, phone calls, strategic planning . . . From day one, we had begun a journey of education, planning, and stubborn optimism against the disease that would prove to be the fight of our lives.

—

OUR GUIDING light as we navigated through these tricky waters of doctors, hospitals, and treatments was my older brother Ed's wife, sister-in-law and oncologist Dr. Maria Scouros. I had been on the phone with her every day since we got the diagnosis. How lucky was it that we had her? I can't imagine what a disadvantage it puts other people at to not have someone like her to help. Her resources and the people she knew were phenomenal, and she was able to provide us with information about the most cutting-edge treatments and technology that was out there. She was an educated sounding board. And she didn't scare off. She was aggressive, and positive! And she knew how fast this disease could spread.

"Whatever you decide, you guys, I want you to be in treatment in the next two weeks," she ordered. That meant we had to compile information quickly and start meeting doctors—now. "Okay. When you're meeting doctors," she continued, "if they say they want to make you comfortable, I want you to turn around and *walk out the door.* Because we're not here to make you comfortable, we're *here to make you better!*" She said it fiercely and I'll never forget it, and nobody could be on board with that kind of attitude more than Patrick, who was born a warrior!

It became clear that the treatments out there for pancreatic cancer were just not good enough to stop the disease. We had to get into a study, a clinical trial wherein new treatments are administered and documented. We had to think outside the box. Be daring. That pointed us in the direction of Stanford, which had a new drug in its second phase of study (good), an angiogenesis drug that was the new thing (also good). They also had the new technology of cyberknife, an incredible new robotic machine that delivered radiation therapy with amazing, unheard-of accuracy. (Who knew?) Maybe Patrick could combine the new chemotherapy drug with the cyberknife zapping the spot in his liver?

—

THREE DAYS later, we were excited to be at Stanford Cancer Center in Palo Alto, California, meeting Dr. Koong, director of the cyberknife program, and Dr. George Fisher, director of clinical trials at the cancer center. Although Albert Koong was very helpful, it was established very early on that Patrick was not a candidate for cyberknife therapy. His disease had spread; it would be a pointless exercise to chase spots and lesions. Radiation therapy was valuable only if it had a chance of arresting the disease, which this would not. As far as the clinical trial was concerned, Dr. Fisher actually steered us toward programs nearer to home, mentioning that he felt Patrick could get as good treatment from doctors there as he could from him.

"What? But we want to go here!" I wanted to whine.

Our hopes were being dashed. We were so excited about what they had to offer, and here we were being told that they had nothing for us. I stifled all the little cries and protests that were circling my brain and focused on scribbling all the information we were given on my big, yellow legal pad. Dr. Fisher, like the others, recommended that Patrick not waste time. That he think about what he wanted to do with the time he might, or might not, have remaining. And then he got up to take a call and left the room . . .

I looked over at Patrick, who was getting visibly upset. Controlling his emotions, he forced an ironic grin, "Wow! All I feel now is doom and gloom. That I'm dead."

Dr. Koong looked at him, friendly, unruffled, "Dr. Fisher is very, very good. Trust me. He's just being . . . I don't know if this is the word . . . but modest."

Does that mean he can help Patrick and that we should not give up on getting treatment here? Or . . .

Dr. Fisher came back into the room. And even though we were both fighting back a spiral into depression, we didn't want to waste our time. We thought of every possible question we wanted answered before we left. The piece de résistance was, "You have to qualify for the PTK study," Dr. Fisher informed us, "One of the requirements is that your bilirubin level be 1.3 or below. Unfortunately, your labs show it at 6.7. So, that right there disqualifies you."

—

HIS BILIRUBIN was still high? After Dr. Lo successfully put in the stent, this count came down dramatically within twenty-four hours and then appeared to bounce back up again with the next set of labs. Back in LA, I asked, "Could the labs be wrong? This doesn't make sense!" No, the labs could not be wrong, I was told. The only other explanation was that the stent had *already clogged again.*

On top of that, Patrick was rapidly heading toward needing stronger pain medication. His indigestion was intense, and he refrained from eating, saying he felt like his stomach was full.

And as if things weren't crazy enough . . . we were supposed to fly to Germany the following week for a televised awards show. It wasn't exactly a time we wanted to be traveling internationally.

—

SINCE WE had received Patrick's diagnosis, I felt as if I had been plunged into a nightmare that I couldn't wake up from. But also, there was a strange thing that started to happen to me after we got past those first few days in the hospital. I felt a new kind of energy, like I was being infused with a kind of rush of grief-stricken adrenaline. Maybe it's the same, albeit a much smaller version, as what people must feel when they go into battle. And certainly in our own way, that's what Patrick and I were doing—going to war. I could feel this grief stripping me down to my bare self . . .

> *Nothing like tragedy to peel away the layers that we impose on ourselves. Like articles of clothing. "Oh! This one is about pleasing other people" and "Oh! This one is about getting acknowledgment" (an undergarment to the previous layer . . .) and "Yes . . . this one is about holding resentments & blame" and "This one is about my 'idea' of what I think I should do . . ." "Who I should be?" "This is about my fear." "This is about my hope." And the fact of the matter is . . .What I want has nothing to with any of the above.What I want exists on its own without all those connections—to me, or anything else. My true heart's desire (if I could call it that) is more like a river, and I can either express it, or not.*
>
> *It couldn't care less what my little mind thinks about it. I can either turn away from it, or go for the ride.*
>
> *February 1, 2008*

I can live out here, on my own, without all the comforts of "who I am," "what I do," and "what I feel." I loved Patrick. And that dwells in another world, all its own. I can live out here . . . I can live out here, with him.

I also felt the physical evidence of this adrenaline when I worked out in our dance studio. I felt stronger than I had in a long time. As if I were eighteen, my leg whooshed up with effortless intention. Magic. I sat down to play piano, and I was faster and more adept than ever . . . I had this feeling as if I could leap over buildings in a single bound simply . . . because I could. I felt an incredible ability to overcome. That, or crash and burn big-time! For real, I had an incredible obstacle ahead of me. Both Patrick and I did . . . it was, how do we find a way to make him live? Yeah, just a little thing. And it was like my body was powering up for this, streamlining for the task ahead and leaving unnecessary encumbrances behind.

My true heart's desire . . .

Maybe it was the terrible grief I was already feeling that was pumping new energy through my veins, or maybe it was really that this grief was pulling off the layers of clothing to reveal the "authentic" me under the cloak of all the things, all the personalities I've tried so hard to be.

One thing for sure. I didn't need to be bothered with any of that stuff now. I was traveling light.

—

THIS TRIP to Germany had been in the works for a few months now. Patrick was being presented the Goldene Kamera's Award for International Star. It was a prestigious award, and beyond that, it would help the movie and the people who were involved in the movie that Patrick had just shot in Austria, called *Jump*. We were booked and set to go. If he backed out now, it would send up a big red flag. We worried about keeping his health problem secret. Although Patrick had times of extreme discomfort, other times he was able to function extremely well. He'd always had a high pain threshold and was tough when it came to handling discomfort. We decided to go, and turn around and come right back the next day to continue pursuing his treatment. But first . . . we needed to address his clogged drain.

"Go to Stanford and have them look," Maria encouraged. "We need to get the bilirubin down." We still hadn't given up on Patrick's qualifying for the Stanford study. As was pointed out to us, Stanford was like a well-oiled piece of machinery where all departments worked in close union with each other. We wanted Stanford to be our home. Also, surprisingly and wonderfully, they had no problem accommodating Patrick on Saturday, thus giving him more time to recoup before jumping on an international flight to Germany the following Monday.

We flew up to Stanford, and on that Saturday, Dr. Jacques Van Dam put a scope down into Patrick's stomach. And found it full of food. Patrick was right about feeling full. Jacques cleaned it out as best he could and recommended Patrick stay overnight, and they would try again in the morning.

Early the next morning, nurses woke us to take Patrick's blood. A short while later, Van Dam and Dr. Fisher came into the room. We were tense about the upcoming procedure. Nothing seemed to go according to plan, and we kept getting surprised by further complications. And now *both* doctors were back in the room.

But Dr. Van Dam smiled, "Go home."

We were confused.

Dr. Fisher elaborated, "Dr. Van Dam ran the labs on your blood this morning. Your bilirubin level is down to 1.6."

We were elated! It was the first time in two weeks that I'd seen Patrick really smile like his old self! Up to that point, I was complaining about how many times people had to take Patrick's blood for labs. Every time we turned around . . . and we had just gotten new blood work done on Friday. And now I saw why they did it, why everyone wanted their own labs. I would never complain again! The stent was working after all. We could only guess that it must have unclogged itself all on its own. It was a mysterious thing, but we were going to take it.

As soon as we got home to LA that evening, I went to the pharmacy to fill a prescription for Patrick. Patrick and I had been on the phone discussing the upcoming Germany trip with Dr. Fisher—the pros and cons, and what could happen. To make sure we were covered on the trip, I made a list of things to bring for Patrick to eat, and Dr. Fisher prescribed a heavier pain medication that Patrick would take if it came to that. It would be morphine.

I walked into my local Rite-Aid with the slip. The lady behind the counter at the pharmacy took a look and shook her head, "I can't fill this. It needs to be on a secure form. It's a narcotic."

I was there to get a job done. Get the medication. I asked her, "What do we have to do to fill it? We're going out of the country tomorrow." And I found out that I couldn't have the doctor call her, he couldn't fax it . . . I had to present the secure prescription form in person. I was beside myself, and running out of options.

"Unless . . ." the lady offered helpfully, "Unless it's a terminal situation. We make exceptions in cases of those patients who are terminally ill."

I stopped . . .

I didn't want to say it, hadn't wanted to say it . . . Then I had to, to this unfamiliar lady . . .

"Yes, he's terminal. He has pancreatic cancer." As soon as I said it, hot, unwilling tears sprung into my eyes. I tried to quickly wipe them away, adding as brightly as I could, "But you know, we try not to think that way, you know. We like to think that there's hope and we're going to beat this thing. And . . ."

"I understand," she nodded kindly, and whisked the slip away.

While I waited, I cruised the aisles of Rite-Aid and choked back the sobs that wanted to gush out of my throat. I hadn't expected this to happen. I had been so good about keeping it together, keeping positive. A grief so deep it was unbearable threatened to overtake me. In a Rite-Aid, next to the Dr. Scholl's section. I managed to keep it together until they called my name over the loudspeaker, and I collected the morphine and left.

I wish I could get away
Is there a place where I can get away from myself?
Somewhere where they don't even know my name.

February 2008

"They're just going to have to understand. We can't discuss it now, but when they know later on what was happening, they will more than understand." I was canceling the Germany trip with our publicist, Annett Wolf. In the end, we decided that it was just too much. What a relief. Now we could take the next days to concentrate on getting treatment started for Patrick. But things were not going to be easy . . .

After the great news at Stanford over the weekend, we were crushed to find that new labs showed that his bilirubin level had risen again, knocking him out of the Stanford program once again. I know it was tough on Patrick to Ping-Pong around like this. I could not accept that this could be so. And if it was so, what are we, what is someone going to do about it? I wished it, prayed it, to force it to turn around so he could get the treatment and the chance we all wanted for him. I felt like the little train that could "will" this into being, "I think I can, I think I can, I think I can . . ."

Again, it was that rush of grief-stricken adrenaline. This heightened awareness that was so focused on him. And it kept me going. Kept me positive in the face of adversity. Whatever this inner strength and clarity was—I embraced it. And I knew I could keep it up for as long as it took.

The clock was ticking, and we needed to start treatment, even if it wasn't his first choice of therapy. Even so, I knew that the fight wasn't over yet. Somehow, some way, this was going to be positive. It was going to be positive until . . . it wasn't going to be positive. And we weren't going to go there yet.

We finally conceded. We needed to move to our Plan B. And we showed up at Dr. David Hoffman's at Tower Oncology in Beverly Hills to start Patrick's first chemo treatment. We showed up with smiles, nervous anticipation, and . . . positive energy.

"Please do one more set of labs before you start," I asked. "Just to make sure." Patrick had just had labs done the day before. But I, we, needed that one last time before we forever sealed off the possibility of his getting into the Stanford clinical trial.

"Of course," Dr. Hoffman said, "We would do that anyway." He was great.

We waited, talked, and held each other's hand, building our courage for the treatment that he would begin in just minutes.

Dr. Hoffman came back into the room. And he grinned.

"No treatment today. We ran the labs," and then he added the magic words, "Your bilirubin is 1.3."

1.3! 1.3! That's the number that qualifies for the Stanford trial!

We bid adieu with warm, happy handshakes and went home to collect our flight bag and head to the airport to fire up our airplane and go to Stanford. On the way, I called the lab where we had gotten all the high bilirubin results. It wasn't hard to figure out at that point that it was the only place that ever showed high counts. Those mistakes came very close to having harsh consequences for Patrick—he almost had surgery, and he nearly had to forgo his first choice of treatment against this deadly cancer.

"Just to let you know, your lab work was wrong. You may want to check it," I told them. There was disbelief on the other end of the line. "I'm just letting you know . . ." I said. And I'm sure they did check what the problem was, and did correct it, but they never even offered an apology. No "I'm sorry."

It was late in the day, and the treatment center at Stanford was empty except for a grinning Dr. Fisher and the nurses who would be administering treatment. It was a sweet victory. We were full of joy, and for that day, we felt like we had been granted . . . hope. It was an exciting day. A very, very exciting day.

In the cockpit of our King Air 200. (Photo by Lisa Dickey)

Chapter 4

UNCHARTED
TERRITORY

I T WAS EXACTLY two weeks after Patrick had been discharged from Cedars-Sinai that he sat on the bed in the treatment room at Stanford Cancer Center, ready to receive his first chemotherapy. Patrick's brother, Donny, came with us for moral support, and we were all chatty and happy, with Patrick's feet propped up comfortably on the bed while Donny and I squeezed in chairs nearby, trying to stay out of the way. The nurses took blood for new labs, thank you . . . while we were introduced and interviewed by the doctors and the RN running the program. In this flurry of activity and conversation, Patrick was hooked up to a small plastic bag that hung next to him on a metal tree. When there was a small break in the conversation, I asked nurse Kathy, with casual curiosity, what was now flowing into the veins in his arm.

She looked a little surprised, "Oh. That's the Gemzar."

"Already?"

Donny and I looked at each other with amazement, then started talking over each other, exclaiming, "No kidding!" "That's the Gemzar?" "He's been getting chemotherapy for ten minutes now and we didn't even know it?" "Who'd have believed it?!" Somehow this notion just thrilled us. We had always thought of chemotherapy as having such sinister connotations, like it's the big, bad boogeyman. Here Patrick was receiving it, and the event was so benign we didn't even notice!

Patrick smiled at our pleasure. But later he told me, "I *definitely* knew when the chemotherapy started. Not that it . . . felt really bad, but . . ." and then he found the right words, "I knew that there was some *really weird, heavy duty stuff* going into my veins."

But of course, he was way too cool to comment on it. So he smiled and kept talking with everyone like nothing was happening. Nothing at all.

Every moment I got, I visualized that this drug going into his veins was made of light and good. That it would pour into his body like a brilliant knight and vanquish this enemy. Patrick's getting chemotherapy was not an awful or scary thing. It was cause for celebration.

His medication, or protocol as they called it, would be the study drug PTK, also called Vatalanib, which was easily taken in pill form twice a day, coupled with Gemcitabine, or Gemzar for short. This would be given intravenously once a week for three weeks, with one week off. If all went well, meaning if the treatment showed that it was effective and he was not getting worse, he would start the whole cycle all over again.

———

THERE'S A reason why people fight so hard to get better, to cure illnesses. Why doctors keep researching, developing new treatments. And there is a reason why there are all these experimental studies concerning a disease that, in this stage, proves fatal—because at some point *someone will get better.* That day will come. Why shouldn't Patrick be the first one? We knew it was a long shot. But any victory against this disease would be a victory. Even if it just meant he'd have more time.

I had the greatest hopes for our fight against this cancer. But, as we were told, this diagnosis brought with it a probable death sentence. In my personal, private time, I had to deal with my own suffering. While we were determined to be realistic about it and not cover our heads in fear or denial, we held out the hope that things would be different for Patrick. Still, with this kind of disease, you can't help but be thrown into a kind of grieving process. Starting from day one I couldn't stop this feeling, this terrible sense of the loss I was facing, the loss that everyone said was coming. And every day I agonized in private. I'm amazed how strong and positive and "on point" I seemed to be in dealing with the daily ins and outs of his treatment and living our lives to the best of our ability. And I truly believed in the power of being positive. But in my personal moments, I felt like I was living in a nightmare that I couldn't wake up from. I marveled that I had enough focus to drive a car, because I felt so numb and so in pain.

What did I do to try to deal with this? Just tried to remember to breathe, and to get through each twenty-four hours. Sometimes . . . just the next hour.

There was a big learning curve that came along with all of this. And coupled with the emotional stress, sometimes the strain of learning so much new information so quickly made me feel like my brain was at the snapping point, like it was ready to explode. I remember going to sleep and repeating the name of one of Patrick's nausea medications over and over and over. I repeated in my mind the right way to say it, "O-*dan*-se-tron" and the wrong way to say it, "O-de-*nes*-tron." "O-*dan*-se-tron." "O-de-*nes*-tron." Over and over, as if Patrick's life depended on my pronunciation of this word! Aaarrgh! It was like I had a glitch in my circuitry. Like the black cat in the movie *The Matrix* that keeps repeating over and over. Fortunately, though, this particular medication was the first of *three* nausea medications he could take, so we ended up calling it simply "Number One." That worked for me!

Needless to say, I had copious lists. I had my yellow legal pad with notes from every conversation concerning his illness and the list of possible alternative directions. I also made and printed out a detailed graph of his medications so I could fill in and track what he had taken and when. This last item was very valuable. The medications were complicated, important, and could be difficult to remember, as there were up to twelve items on his daily list and the dosage varied from once to four times a day. I was secretly pleased when the folks at Stanford saw my spreadsheet and were impressed. Every week they happily asked to copy it for their files. I felt like kid showing off a good report card, like I deserved an apple or a gold star.

—

I WAS frustrated with the lack of nutritional advice other than the normal mainstay regimens. Patrick had already dropped weight, and it was his job to put on and keep on weight for the fight ahead. The problem was that his stomach was still feeling full, he had absolutely no appetite, and he had to be careful about certain foods (leafy vegetables, sticky, elastic foods) that could clog the stent that was working within him. I kept wanting to find the magic answer, when in reality, I needed to reinvent the wheel for his personal nutrition. It made me laugh, because everyone was thinking he was on some kind of macrobiotic or high antioxidant diet when in reality, I was happy that he ate anything. Anything at all! Ice cream, great! Calories, calories, was the word of the moment, with protein coming in a close second. We had to make every bite count! It's weird when you've spent years looking at the calorie, fat, and carb totals on packages in the supermarket and suddenly find yourself putting foods back on the shelf because they don't have *enough* calories for your liking. I also experimented, blending everything into a puree. Even blending yellowtail sushi for him, and guess what it tasted like—yellowtail sushi. The chicken pot pie was not as successful, and I would not recommend it!

We also had to be careful not to go off on extreme diets that would interfere with his digestive system, or deluge his system with vitamins. It's a catch 22—your body loves to consume healthy vitamins, but the cancer does, too. You may think you're making your body able to fight the cancer, but in reality, you're just feeding the cancer. And sugar—cutting him off from sugar entirely wasn't good either. The body needs sugar to function. If we severely limited his sugar intake, his body would eventually take proteins from his body to produce sugar on its own. And he needed those proteins! He had already lost some muscle mass and was struggling to keep what he had. He didn't need to lose more! I had to appreciate the merciless, insidious nature of cancer—it destroys your appetite while it's feeding off the nutrients in your body. It's no wonder that many people "go" so fast. Patrick knew this. He forced himself to nourish himself, even if it was the last thing he wanted to do. I'm so glad he made the effort, I would have been pretty upset otherwise.

Anyway, I digress. As you can see, nutrition was a daily and passionate obsession. I finally found a protein shake supplement that was actually 1,250 calories per serving (although I had to cut it in half because it was too thick at the full portion). I blended it with raw cashews and other nuts and seeds, and he drank it for a while, until like everything else, he couldn't bear it anymore, and I had to find something new and different! In the end, eating still came down to old-fashioned balance. Counting calories and protein, yes, but eating as balanced a diet as he could.

—

DURING ALL this jockeying around and trying to get our bearings, flying up to Stanford for treatment and organizing ourselves here at home, we were able to keep his diagnosis a secret. One thing we knew for sure—we didn't want everyone knowing and blowing this thing up into huge proportions, which meant that very, very few people could know. At the same time, it was important that some did. I knew that there were some things that Patrick probably didn't feel free to express to me. Knew he needed someone he could say these things to, someone he could trust. That person was his brother, Donny, and Donny came in with full support. For me, it was my friends, Lynne and Kay. As I already mentioned, Patrick had issues with alcohol over the years, and one of the best things I ever did for myself and for our relationship was join Al-Anon, the twelve-step program that gives support to people who are dealing with a loved one's or friend's drinking problem. Both Lynne and Kay had been my sponsors in the program at one time or another, and I knew beyond a shadow of a doubt that I could entrust my feelings and any information to them and it would be consigned to what they called "The Vault." Kay, herself, had just lost her mother the previous year to Alzheimer's, and taking care of her and losing her had been very tough for her. She knew a bit of the territory I was treading.

"I know Al-Anon has all these tools and these guidelines to live your life by." Kay nodded firmly when I told her what was going on. "But as of now, all the rules are *out the window*!" She was right, and I felt bolstered by her support.

Our sister-in-law, Jessica, worked for us and needed to know why all these doctors were calling, along with her husband, and my brother, Paul, who was over at our house practically every day.

Everyone loved Patrick. And though he liked to push his limits and take chances, he appeared to be indestructible. He could be larger than life and adorable. That this could happen to him was beyond comprehension. It was tough for the few who knew what was going on, and there were tears at times. But they were wonderful enough to not burden Patrick with their tears, they were there to help and support him in any way they could. They knew our energies were going toward finding a solution, if one could be found.

And then there were the few people in our professional lives: our lawyer, agent, and manager . . . all people we've known for over twenty-five years and call our friends. And when Patrick started treatment, we all determined that the network, A&E, and Sony Studio had to be told. Just a little over a month before, in Chicago, Patrick had shot a pilot for a television series named *The Beast*, in which he plays a darkly unorthodox but brilliant FBI agent. A&E and Sony were in the midst of deciding whether to go ahead with a full season of *The Beast*. This little piece of news just might have some bearing on their decision. So Patrick and I invited the show's producers and writers over to the ranch for a meeting.

We sat in the living room, fireplace lit and warming the room, and after our hellos and how are yous were done, Patrick announced that he had pancreatic cancer. It was like a silent bomb had just been dropped. He went on to explain his diagnosis, what the protocol was . . . his chances . . .

We moved outside into the fresh air and sat on the patio. Everyone kept their spirits up and did their best to be positive, although this news had clearly shaken everyone. One of the producer/writers had to take a walk by our pool for a moment, his tough exterior dissolving privately into tears. There was sensitivity to the situation as we brainstormed on how to proceed with all of this, what everybody felt . . . what we wanted . . . what they wanted . . . and where we go from here. When all had been talked about, Patrick stood up,

"Well, let's call Sony and A&E," and he clapped his hands together like a coach.

"Now?" they were a little taken aback.

"Yeah."

"Why not?" I said. This was not exactly something we wanted to hang on to into the next week. Time in every way for us was at a premium. And there was no time like the present.

I got a speakerphone and pulled it outside, and once everyone was on the phone, Patrick stood, pacing back and forth with positive energy, and he told them the news. Bob DeBitetto at A&E in New York remarked later about the trepidation he felt going into the call, "When it's eight o'clock at night and ten to twelve people want to get on the phone with you, you know something big is happening. But I had no idea . . . *no idea* that this was what it was going to be." They were shocked. Needless to say, Patrick's health scare made for many future phone calls between all. And I have to say, Sony TV and A&E's reaction was amazing. They reacted like human beings instead of businesspeople, and they decided to hang in there with Patrick. They were going to wait and not make any decisions until we saw how he responded to treatment.

Patrick still wanted to do the series.

Do you know how crazy that might have sounded to people who knew even the least bit about pancreatic cancer? But he was not about to plan a future that was dictated by cancer, a future in which he had already given up. He was determined that he was going to go on and live his life, and cancer was not going to tell him how to do it.

It's a fearful thing, facing cancer, but Patrick entered this fight with dignity, courage, and strength. Donny remembers witnessing a phone conversation that happened that first week we were out of the hospital. As a formality, the doctor called us to confirm that the biopsy taken from his tumor during the ERCP was indeed pancreatic cancer. Of course we still held that little bit of hope that it would come back negative, even though we had been told *not* to hope. How could we not?

We were gathered around the speakerphone in our kitchen to hear this news. Donny watched Patrick closely when he heard the results . . .

"There wasn't even a *flicker* of fear that crossed his face," Donny said with awe, "He just straightened and said, 'Well, I guess we move on to the next step.'"

And when the doctors were describing treatments and procedures that would have scared other people witless, Patrick's reaction was more one of lively curiosity, *"Wow, that's interesting. Let's see what that does. What do you think, Lisa?"* It was like he could step outside his body and look at it like an objective observer. He was *interested* in this fight. And I was equally engaged.

—

IT WAS tricky and difficult gearing our whole lives toward fighting this life-threatening disease. Functioning with this huge . . . thing . . . weighing on you at every moment of every day, and keeping it secret. Trying to act like everything was normal. It was cause for some additional pressure, and some great acting work from both of us. It was true that the fewer people who knew the better, but the effort of covering up something this enormous couldn't help but take its toll. It was a good thing that, in general, Patrick and I loved to stay at home on our ranch, to ourselves. We couldn't have done many public appearances, dinners with friends, and so on. It would have been asking too much of ourselves.

It was only four weeks after Patrick was diagnosed that I was scheduled to fly a charter to Las Vegas overnight. I could have canceled, but no, if we were going to "act normal," I needed to do it. I also would have left the charter company in the lurch if I had backed out at the last second.

In the last six months I had gotten my commercial flying license and trained to be a first officer at Sun Quest, the charter company we kept our plane with. I was very flattered that I was considered a "good stick" (as they say), and I wanted to fly professionally, not as a career, but because I thought I might learn more, have more opportunity to fly with and learn from other pilots and, who knows, maybe I'd fly a jet someday, which was a dream of mine. Okay . . . I loved to fly. So I flew the trip with our friend Yann, whom we've flown with many times. When we landed in Vegas, Yann suggested we stay by the airport.

"No, no," I said, "Let me call some friends . . ."

And soon we were checked into Planet Hollywood Hotel and Casino and I was looking out the enormous windows of the same suite that Patrick and I had stayed in just months before when we attended the opening of that same hotel and casino. My whole being felt like one, big, giant ache. I wondered what the heck I was doing there. What was I doing there without him? The view was fantastic, the suite was fabulous, and so silent. All I wanted to do was cry. I hadn't really gotten the chance to cry yet . . . but I couldn't. Yann's room was next door, and if he heard me, he'd wonder what was so terrible that I would be uttering these awful sobs. *What could be so terrible?* I had miscalculated. Why in the world would I want to be away from Patrick's side, even for one night? I couldn't wait to get home. And I never booked another overnight charter again.

—

OUR AIRCRAFT was a Beech King Air 200, and we loved it. And even though Patrick was fighting pancreatic cancer, he still wanted to fly and did so when he felt good and sharp enough to sit in the left seat (the pilot's seat). In order to do so, he'd carefully forgo any pain medication the whole night before we went up to Stanford. He'd fly up, and then I'd fly back because by that time he'd had quite a dose of drowsy-making nausea medication along with his chemotherapy. (It could be pretty interesting when he talked on the radio after all that medication! His responses were very, very slow.) I was afraid that it might be that some of the drugs Patrick was taking would disqualify him from flying entirely. But I couldn't find it in my heart to bring up this possibility and risk having his flying privileges taken away. Patrick was a man with a lot of pride.

I talked to another pilot friend about my dilemma. "How in the world could I ask him *not to fly?*" I asked. He looked at me and shook his head, understanding only as a guy can, "You can't."

When Patrick flew, he was a safe pilot. And that was the important thing. I also was always there with him in the cockpit. Later on, he would be the first to decline piloting the plane when he wasn't feeling well enough. And this was going to happen more and more . . . but for that time, we worked together like a great team. And flying was infinitely more comfortable for Patrick than driving in a car and being jostled around. The jostling and bumps hurt him. So being able to fly up to Stanford and land at the Palo Alto Airport, passing the handsome California mountains and Pacific Ocean on our left, the snow-capped Sierras on our right, with the beautiful San Francisco Bay sparkling ahead, was an incredible convenience and luxury for us. And it was a bonus to be doing something that we loved together.

We weren't *always* so amiable and tolerant in the cockpit during our flying careers. We could both be strong-willed, and perfectionists at times. When we were first flying, we'd get into huge arguments! Oh, my God! People had mentioned the problems that husband and wife might have flying together but . . . give me a break! I remember when I had been flying for two to three years, still fairly fresh as a pilot and doing quite well. I was flying in the left seat (captain) of our twin-engine Cessna 414, and Patrick was in the right seat (copilot). We were approximately three thousand feet in the air over the coast of Ventura, California, when an argument broke out. He was telling me what to do, I was telling him, no. And it escalated to where I pushed the yoke of the airplane away from me and said, "Okay! *You* fly the airplane!" He pushed the yoke away also, "No! *You* fly the airplane!" Me, "No, *you* fly . . ." You get the picture. I finally got sense enough to realize that *no one* was flying the airplane and that someone better calm down and take the wheel.

A couple of days later, when we were calmer, we sat down together and I said, "You know . . . this arguing in the cockpit is terrible. We can't keep doing this. It ruins everything. It makes me not want to fly anymore."

"I hate it, too." Patrick nodded solemnly in agreement.

And then I had an idea, the only one I could think of. "Hey! How about this? *I* love flying. *You* love flying. Why don't we just enjoy ourselves . . . *in spite of ourselves*?"

Patrick had just the glimmer of a smile as he considered that thought.

And that's what we did. For years and years after. Not that we didn't sometimes have disagreements. But they were disagreements, not full-blown arguments.

—

"Airplanes can take a lot of turbulence. Usually the pilot falls apart long before the airplane does. Just hang in there and fly the plane."

—*Captain Frank Kratzer*

When you're flying an airplane, situations like heavy turbulence, thunderstorms, or emergencies can be frightening. One thing that I like and find demanding about flying is that there's no place for fear in the cockpit. An airplane isn't like a car. You can't just pull it over to the side of the road while you figure things out. When you're in an airplane, you need to think. And fear can paralyze you, much as it can in a situation like we were in now with Patrick's illness—one that made us confront life and death on a day-to-day, sometimes moment-to-moment basis. On top of that, you're getting so much new information. You're learning how things work in the body, how the treatments work, why other treatments don't work, and getting a handle on the doctors' and nurses' everyday lingo. It's undoubtedly overwhelming for anyone. It'd be easy to freeze, it'd be easy to run away, to turn it over to someone else, or simply to fold.

I needed to hang in there. The prospects were so dim, I instinctively felt that I shouldn't just give over his care completely to the doctors, nurses, and hospitals, or to anybody else. Patrick wasn't the only one they were treating. They couldn't devote the kind of energy I was prepared to contribute to his health. They're also human beings, they can make mistakes, they can get overloaded with work themselves . . . I didn't want to take that big a chance. In other areas of my life, I could feel paralyzed, but not here. Not if I wanted to help him.

When I felt fear, I tried to do the same thing I did in an airplane—I nicely but firmly told it to sit in the seat behind me while I figure something out or addressed the task at hand. I was asking it to do that now. *Yes, I know you're there . . . but you're going to have to sit there until this is done. Then you can go crazy, but not now.* I had also trained and competed in aerobatics. You know, where you turn the airplane upside down and do loops and stuff? I felt that made me a better and safer pilot, because if something happened to the plane, I wasn't going to freak out. And if the worst happened, if I was going down, I was going to be flying, and I was going to keep a cool head while I didn't give up trying to save that plane right through to the end.

It's not often you get asked to face something so difficult, emotional, and potentially devastating as a life-threatening ill-ness. And every day I wished it were different. But you do your best, whatever that might be. *Whatever that might be . . .* So much of the time everything can feel like it's beyond human endurance. But you do it anyway. Why? Because it means life and death. You do it. And you keep your eye on the prize.

—

AS WE approached the end of Patrick's first cycle of four weeks of chemotherapy, we sat in the treatment room at Stanford and they took more blood to run a CA19-9 test. We had been on pins and needles to hear some kind of results. Anything. This would be a preliminary test, a teaser to the scans that would be taken in another month. That was the deal—Patrick needed to have at least two cycles before he had another set of scans done. "Give the treatment a chance to work," Dr. Fisher said. It was hard to be patient, but patient is what we had to be.

That day, Patrick looked at Dr. Fisher and marveled cau-tiously, "I feel . . . pretty good. It's the best I've felt since before I was diagnosed." We were all cautious, but couldn't help but feel that this was a good sign, that this might be a good indication that the treatment was having a positive effect. But new labs on his blood might say something different.

—

THERE'S ONE thing about facing possible death. There's no time like the present to be who you want to be. No holds barred, let's pull out all the stops, no reservations. I don't know what Patrick saw when he looked at me, but I know I admired how he was facing his illness. I'd been with him for over three decades and seen the worst and the best of who he could be. And now, faced with the worst that could happen, I saw a true hero emerge from him. Not like one of those in the movies, playing a part that everyone expected of him, no . . . this was better. It was a hero who was humble, brave, loving, kind, wise, and tough. It was as if *he* had also dropped his cloak and revealed his true self. And he was a hero. And if there was one thing I wanted to show Patrick, other than that I loved him, it was that if Death was going to come take him, Death would have to pry him out of my cold, clamped-on fingers. I was not going to let him go easily.

There was also no better time for us to be presented with a . . .

Unique . . .

Precious . . .

Opportunity.

We got to live now. We got to know what was important. Our souls embraced what was before us.

Fear can isolate you from each other. Everyone's worried about what the other person is feeling, what *they* themselves are feeling, what's the right thing to do, and in some cases, I'm sure many people even wonder what the heck does anything matter anyway at this point and give up. Facing possible death is a fearsome thing. Not only for the one who's intimately involved, but for everyone around that person. Cancer doesn't discriminate. It sets out to wipe out everyone in its path. Everyone. And this fear can draw a dividing line, not only within yourself, but with each other.

When I started flying aerobatics, it was interesting what the recovery procedure was for a spin. For decades, if you entered a spin, you died. There was no recovery. Until one person did the unthinkable . . . he survived. Even better, he had the presence of mind to remember what he did . . .

POWER OFF.

HANDS OFF.

Then, and only then . . . STEP LEFT, STEP RIGHT.

Isn't it interesting, the only way to gain control of the airplane was to let go . . . *Power Off . . . Hands Off* . . . It's like, you give up the airplane to itself and take yourself out of the equation. Could you imagine how hard it would be to do this, to relinquish control when you were in a life and death situation and just go with it?

In a way, this is what Patrick and I did with each other. We could have let fear and our struggles rule us. But we threw caution to the wind. We let go. We risked. We trusted. And we went on a ride into unknown, uncharted territories. Together.

The mere act of being with each other righted our course beyond anything that we could have imagined. And brought us closer than ever.

—

AFTER THE "one month" of chemo, Patrick's blood results came back.

When he started treatment, his CA19-9 number was 1,240. And now . . . it was down to 508!

Okay. If I can bore you for a second (trust me, these things aren't boring if they're happening to you!), the CA19-9 blood test measures molecules that contain a bevy of protein and carbohydrates. These are molecules that have fallen/shed off the surface of tumors and into the bloodstream, where they can be picked up by the CA19-9 test. The amount of these molecules roughly indicates the rate of tumor activity. It's not so accurate that you would stake a diagnosis on it, but it gives a very good indication of the trend of the disease—that is, is it getting worse or better? Patrick's CA19-9 dropping from 1,240 to 508 was significant, and according to the doctor, was . . .

"Almost *always* associated with favorable response to chemo." Dr. Fisher nodded.

It was precious, good news. These results so far, his feeling good, the lowered CA19-9, heartened us.

We still had another cycle to do before Patrick had new scans done, though, and we geared up for this second round, which would take place over the next month. And, although we never thought it was going to be easy, we had already been rewarded with victory. More than once! Which made what was going to happen next all the more ironic. Our lives were going to get harder to deal with. And soon.

Can you see what's here? If you can't, that's good.
It's the screen material I put on our fence to keep photographers
from taking pictures of us at home.

Chapter 5

EVERYBODY FINDS OUT

I T WAS ON a typical, sunny, Southern California Wednesday morning, March 5, 2008, that Patrick's mother, Patsy, now eighty years old, got up to answer the doorbell in her Simi Valley home. She was there that morning to answer the door because she had just retired the previous year after successfully teaching dance for over sixty years, and she was sitting at home now, wondering what to do with the rest of her life. It was a tough adjustment after being so busy and independent and always carrying such a heavy workload, and she was *bored to death*. But she did her best to bear it with the grace of someone who's spent her whole life demonstrating to thousands how to point their feet and hold their arms and shoulders with a dancer's elegance.

Her bones creaked a bit as she started to move, but then she bounced up with a sprite's agility as she always did, and made her way to the door. She opened it to find a man she didn't know standing there. A man from the tabloids.

"Mrs. Swayze?" he spoke.

"Yes?" Patsy queried.

"Mrs. Swayze, how do you feel about your son, Patrick, having pancreatic cancer?"

"Whaaat?"

Patsy was shocked; she sputtered that she didn't know anything about it. Stunned, she closed the door, made her way to the phone, and dialed Donny, panicking at the horrible fear rising inside her. "Donny?" she gasped, tears threatening to overtake her as he picked up the phone, "Donny? There was a man at the door . . . please tell me it isn't true . . ."

And that's how his mom found out.

Patsy was one of the people we had not told, and for a good reason. When she answered the door, she had adjusted the dark glasses she was wearing to make sure they stayed on properly. She was wearing dark glasses because she had just had *eye surgery* to help correct the terrible vision problems she was having. She needed to protect her eyes for at least a month. She had to avoid wind, dust, light, and she had to *not cry*. And of course, now she was doing everything we were trying to avoid—getting upset and *crying*. How was she going to not cry knowing her son had pancreatic cancer?

—

PATRICK SWAYZE HAS 5 WEEKS TO LIVE!

That's what the headline read on the *National Enquirer* that hit the stands that morning. Inside the article, it reported that Patrick's response to treatment had been "less than his doctors hoped for" and that he should "prepare for the end."

Wow. Pretty brutal. Inaccurate, yes. And brutal.

And unfortunately, it was no longer our private battle. The news was everywhere. Our phone was ringing with upset people, Patsy was crying, and we were deluged with well-wishers and emotion from friends and family, along with both tabloid and legitimate news entities wanting more information. We had known that if word got out it could blow up into something big. But this was assuming epic proportions. The news was everywhere, and a friend remarked that the kind of coverage that Patrick was getting was usually reserved for heads of state.

Within twenty-four hours of the word getting out, I put together an email to send out to worried friends, acquaintances, and family. I knew they'd be shocked and would want to know what was going on. Patrick and I wanted them to know we were thinking of them also:

> *Dear Friends,*
>
> *Many of you may have read or heard the terrible reports that Patrick has cancer and has weeks to live. It's unfortunate that this private matter has been released in this insensitive way, and we're sorry for how upsetting this might have been for many of you.*
>
> *The facts of the matter are:*
>
> *YES. Patrick has been diagnosed with pancreatic cancer.*
>
> *NO. There is no prognosis that he only has five weeks to live, or that doctors hold little hope.*

And then I included the press release we had quickly put together with Annett and Dr. Fisher. Annett, our publicist, was being deluged, and we had to say something to the press. Here is what we said:

> *Actor Patrick Swayze has been diagnosed with Pancreatic Cancer and is currently undergoing treatment. Patrick's physician, Dr. George Fisher, states, "Patrick has a very limited amount of disease and he appears to be responding well to treatment thus far. All of the reports stating the timeframe*

of his prognosis and his physical side effects are absolutely untrue. We are considerably more optimistic." Patrick is continuing his normal schedule during this time, which includes working on upcoming projects. The outpouring of support and concern he has already received from the public is deeply appreciated by Patrick and his family.

I also included an update on how we were addressing the disease:

You will be pleased to know that he is receiving the best, most cutting edge treatment and has an incredible support team of physicians. He is in absolutely the best possible hands. And besides, you know Patrick . . . if there's a way he will, and his will usually finds a way!

Your love and support mean a lot to both of us. We strongly believe in the power of positive energy and intention and appreciate any and all contributions of positive attitude, in whatever form that may take.

—

LETTERS AND emails started to pour in. To us, to our agent, our publicist. There were messages of wonderful support, but also, suddenly, there were people trying to use Patrick's name and health circumstance for their own gain—whether to raise money, or to lean on a drug company to get their own treatment, or to gain publicity for a movie. Representatives of one such film said Patrick backed out because of his illness, when in fact Patrick never even read the script and turned down the offer long before he was diagnosed. Unscrupulous reporters managed to get phone numbers, both listed and unlisted, for Maria, Ed and Donny, among other people, and the more unscrupulous of those lied about who they were, saying they worked for the *LA Times* or some other reputable entity, or that we were sanctioning the article, or even that it was to benefit pancreatic cancer research.

Of course the day the news broke . . . I was scheduled to fly a charter.

Crazy.

It was just a day trip, no more overnights, and I'd be back before dark. I already knew about Patrick's illness and had for some time, right? But the lid had just blown off the world as I knew it. I showed up at Sun Quest to fly the trip like it was any normal day. But it wasn't. On occasion I've had the ability to downplay the most incredible things that were happening in our lives, but this turned out to be a little much! The news about Patrick's health was all over the world, and I was going to fly a trip like I was any old first officer. It felt so strange, so strange to insist on acting normal when everyone around me was not normal. But what else was I going to do? Go home and hide my head? And for how long? Everyone at Sun Quest had heard the news and appreciated that somehow I still managed to show up. I felt a little sheepish, I mean, I had kept the reason for our trips to Stanford secret from them also. But they didn't feel the need to ask any questions, not one. They just let me know they were there if we needed them and that we had the use of their other planes to get to treatment in case ours had any down time, and we gratefully ended up taking them up on that offer on a few occasions.

Speaking of our airplane, 400KW. We were perplexed how photographers knew where we were. They were lurking in the bushes like guerilla soldiers when we took off at the airports, shooting over fences with a super-long lens, or even pretending to pose for a group photo outside another aircraft far, far away, when they were, in fact, shooting us. And of course they were taking less-than-flattering photos of Patrick. But then we discovered that online programs designed to track aircraft were following the flights of our airplane. All you do is enter the plane's tail number (the letters and numbers you see on the tail of the aircraft) and you can get information on when and where the plane is scheduled to depart, if the plane is in the air now, and its exact location, and when and where it's going to land. You can even get the plane's entire history for the past year. This is why we had photographers waiting at every airport where we landed. To remedy this, I had to file a request with the NBAA to block our tail number from these sites, then set up our own tracking account so that Sun Quest could still follow the movements of our plane. It took me about three weeks to put all this into action. But it got done.

There was also the issue of who leaked the news about Patrick's health. I don't know about Cedars-Sinai, but Stanford Hospital took it very seriously and launched a full and comprehensive investigation. So few people in our personal life knew about Patrick's cancer, and even the ones who did knew little of the specific details. The leak of information had to come from someone in the medical profession. Are you aware that if you work in the medical profession and you give out personal medical information it is a felony? A *felony*. There are reasons these laws exist. And it's not only to protect the patient's privacy. To divulge medical information can have a huge impact on someone's life and on those around him—it can cause job and financial ruin, bring down companies, devastate families, affect insurance issues . . . it can destroy, unnecessarily, patients' lives, and those of others. And for what? In our case, so someone could line his pockets with a little money.

The tabloids endlessly followed us, taking photos, reporting that Patrick's hair was thinning (not true), that he was smoking cigarettes (unfortunately true). They reported that he had lost more than twenty pounds and now his weight was 140. Okay now . . . let's get real . . . I had been struggling with my weight since I quit smoking three years previously and was hovering right around 140. I dieted, I exercised, I commiserated with my other friends in the same predicament, and no matter what I did, I couldn't shake this weight off. And all I can say is—Patrick was *never* down to 140 pounds, because if he ever was, if he was ever *lighter than me without even trying*, the disease wouldn't kill him, *I* would. (Did anyone laugh? I joked about this a few times to various people and I never got a laugh. I thought it was pretty funny. No . . . ?)

One thing we always tried to do was find some humor in the situations we were in, even if it was some pretty bad humor. Pancreatic cancer isn't exactly a hilarious subject, but leave it to Patrick to find something amusing. He was the self-proclaimed "King of Irreverence" and prided himself that "nothing is sacred or off-limits for me." And he had no problem with calling it in on himself, even in this situation, albeit with gallows humor. He and Donny got a great laugh over, "Nobody puts Patrick's pancreas in a corner," which played on the famous *Dirty Dancing* line. And though there is no doubt how incredibly sensitive Patrick was to people's suffering, we *did* chuckle that if he kept losing weight, his next job would be *Holocaust—The Musical.* That is of course, if I didn't get to him first.

—

SINCE PATRICK had had success with projects like *North and South, Dirty Dancing,* and *Ghost,* we had some experience dealing with celebrity and press in the last twenty-five years. And Patrick was always smart and very much a gentleman about how he handled it. If we were being chased by photographers in London or someplace, Patrick's solution would be to tell the driver to stop, he would get out and smile while they took a few photos, after which the photographers would just go away. Easy! In airports or appearances where we were going to encounter many, many people, too many to stop for . . . he would have bodyguards and escorts around him, but told them to go easy and not be aggressive. It's funny; the ones who are aggressive invite trouble. They give the crowd something to push against, so the crowd pushes back. Basically, we figured that all people want is some kind of connection. And both Patrick and I would try to achieve that as we moved through, smiling, looking people in the eye, and shaking as many hands as we could. And we could let the bodyguards be nice.

One of our first encounters with "extreme" celebrity happened after *Dirty Dancing* came out. We went to a record signing at Sam Goody in New York, where there were approximately three thousand people waiting in line around the block outside. It was a little frightening to see these people pushed up against the store's two-story, plate-glass windows. I thought surely they might come toppling through, making for a really major disaster. But like the saying goes, "Nobody panic and nobody gets hurt!" So, we acted like there was nothing out of the ordinary, nothing at all. Getting out through this crowd to the car only fifteen feet away was pretty exciting also. I had to focus aggressively and, without delay, get into the car and get the door closed.

Of course many women had the good taste to think my husband was sexy and gorgeous. And most fans we ran into were respectful, excited, and had great fun meeting him. And there were the few who shamelessly gave him smoky eyes and flirted with him and all but slipped him their phone number . . . right in front of me! I remained cool when this happened, I mean, I didn't feel threatened, but I wanted to wave my hand in front of their face and go, "Helloooo? I'm right here! Helloooo?" It was just bad manners! Some of these coquettish ladies were fairly famous, too. It was like they couldn't help themselves. People do strange stuff sometimes.

And then there were bodyguards, aides, and handlers who were so focused on Patrick that they put their arms out and separated me from him and forced me into the crowd, almost knocking me down, or preventing me from getting into the car! One time, a person leaned over to talk to Patrick and literally draped a coat over my head. Patrick emphatically and politely pointed out the rudeness. We soon learned that some people could be pretty stupid in these situations, and we learned how to deal with it. Patrick made sure that he impressed them from the get-go that I was to be treated with as much respect as he was. It was that, or he was going to be one ticked-off dude. And people learned very quickly. For him it was like, "You mess with her, you mess with me." We were a team, right?

Being recognized, followed, photographed, and asked for autographs . . . if you were going to be successful as an actor, this was something you could expect. And if you didn't want these things to happen—you didn't go out. There are great things about being well known; you're treated like a VIP, you're escorted around lines, people give you free goods, and you get treated to all sorts of things. The downside is that you have to pay for lawyers to keep people from suing you for things you've never done, pay for things you really don't need, and choose where you can go and where you can't if you want to have a life. And even that doesn't work out some of the time, but you take your best shot. There were many things we couldn't do with our friends because it just wouldn't work—like go to an amusement park, or go to a concert where you weren't cordoned off like a bunch of goats with the other celebrities.

And I'm not telling you all this so you think we were some kind of elitist couple. We weren't above picking up horse and dog poop. It was *other people* who were making us out to be an elitist couple.

I remember Patrick and I were at the White House for some big dinner with Bill and Hillary Clinton. I can't remember what for. Afterward they had a band and a dance floor. This was after the Monica Lewinsky scandal and things had finally died down to about as much as they were ever going to die down. I was dancing with Bill and chatting while Patrick was swinging Hillary around the floor. A photographer stepped in front of us to take our picture, and Bill immediately stiffened and stepped back formally while we kept dancing. I felt uncomfortable because I knew why he adopted the more distant pose. *He wasn't going to take any chance that a photo might be misconstrued.* I, being the brilliant conversationalist I am, said being a movie star was tough enough as far as what people say about you, but it's nothing compared to what they go through. "You just have to have a thick skin," he said, and mentioned that when he came into office, they asked the press to leave their daughter Chelsea alone, as she was a young girl who couldn't protect herself as they could, and the press honored that request.

My mom has the photos that were taken that evening. In the picture of me dancing stiffly with Bill, I look like an awkward third-grader with a double chin. Meanwhile Patrick and Hillary's photo looks like a promo shot for *Dancing With the Stars,* with Patrick dipping Hillary with flair, and Hillary listing delightfully, having just erupted into a lovely peal of laughter!

Thick skin . . . I thought we, I, had developed a pretty good, thick skin as far as the press and tabloids were concerned. I thought so . . . but the situation we were in now was a *little* different. I was going to find out how different as time went on.

Anyway, with celebrity, once you learn the ropes it's not so bad. I was always in awe at how some stars always seemed to have photographers catching them at all sorts of places, until I was on the receiving end of the attention with Patrick. The paparazzi are pretty easy to deal with and pretty easy to avoid. The people who were in the press all the time *wanted* to be in the press all the time, made sure they showed up at places with press, and probably even called and alerted the press on themselves. So, press is easy to avoid—unless it's something big, and particularly if it's devastating. Then it's hard, really hard to avoid being written about. It's even harder in this day and age where anyone, anywhere can snap your photo or take a video of you with a phone. I was to find that the professional paparazzi are very good at what they do. When everyone heard Patrick was sick, it was a double-edged sword—so many, many people cared so much, and because they cared so much, the tabloids wanted stories and bad pictures of Patrick even more. His life and his possible death meant money for them.

My brother Ed and his wife, Dr. Maria Scouros, visit us in LA.

Chapter 6

THE TROOPS ARRIVE

I'm a tough girl
I'm here to stay
I won't cry
And I won't run away.

—*March 2008*

IT HAD BEEN very tough keeping Patrick's illness a secret. We thought maybe there might be some relief now that the word was out, but after the news broke and everyone knew, we yearned for the simplicity of having to just look after ourselves. It was infinitely easier when all we had to focus on was getting Patrick better. Having so many people know, and having his illness reported so much, demanded attention and focus.

Maria, my brother Ed, and the two kids came to California to visit us. (Ed had taken the news very hard and wept openly on the phone when he first heard the news.) We visited our friends Warren and Jale who were in town in Laguna Beach, where Patrick indulged in eating clams and then paid for it by painfully throwing up the entire night. (This was before we knew that he needed to avoid any foods that might carry bacteria.) And there were other friends who came in to visit.

It was wonderful to see people, but hard at the same time. I knew why Ed and Maria were visiting. They knew how aggressive this disease could be. They knew it could be the last time they saw Patrick. I loved having them there, but it frightened me also. I wanted to accommodate people's feelings, but secretly, underneath it all, it was an additional emotional burden. Likewise with others who wanted to visit. We had one friend who jokingly threatened to jump over the gate, saying that come hell or high water, "I'm going to see Patrick!" But that was exactly what we didn't want. It sent the message, "YOU ARE GOING TO DIE and I'm GOING to see you before you do." There was even a family member who wept copiously on the way out of our house, falling to her knees in sobs two to three times before reaching the car. Patrick and I watched some of this scenario from the kitchen window. I couldn't help but be just a little ticked off and shook my head, and turned to Patrick and deadpanned, "I think *someone* might be losing their visiting privileges." I didn't want to cut anyone off . . . but I didn't want us to be put in the position of having to take care of everybody else. And I certainly wasn't going to give people free rein at the expense of Patrick's well-being. *He was the one going through it.*

—

I BOUGHT a wig, a cute little dark, reddish brown Victoria Beckham number, and I wore it when I went out shopping or to run errands. Since we were in the press so much, people's radar was sensitized, and I got recognized a lot. Or at least I noticed it more. And it wasn't that I didn't want to be recognized, not like Britney Spears shielding her face from prying eyes. And it wasn't that people were rude, just the opposite. It was just that—people cared. When I got out of the house for whatever reason, it was a break for me. I could get lost in the aisles of canned goods checking calories, or among rows and rows of shirts at T.J.Maxx. But when people recognized me, I would see this look of sympathy and care on their faces. They felt sorry for me. And how wonderful is it that they cared, but they reminded me of the one thing I was trying to forget for just an hour or two. Trying to forget that my husband could die. Could die soon.

It's so hard to know what to do when someone is ill. Do you call? Send a card? Flowers? Knock on their door? I was probably the worst at knowing what to do in the past so . . . *I didn't do anything.* I was so afraid that I wouldn't do the right thing that I did nothing at all. That's changed now. I know what it's like to be on the other side. Now, I pick up the phone. I call, and I offer my services if I'm able. But the message I leave goes something like this:

"Hi! Just checking in. Thinking of you. I'm here if you need me. Just call, any time. Love you." And hang up. Click.

And you don't even have to offer your help if you're not able. Just say, "Hi! Just called to say I'm thinking of you. Don't need to call me back . . ." If you do offer and are called back, be ready to listen to what they need. They might need help with groceries, a ride, or the laundry, or something crazy stupid or mundane. Or they might need to cry, bitch, or just talk like a normal person and have a few laughs. But don't expect a return phone call, *and don't ask for one.* There are many reasons why calling you back is hard, so hard. And you're looking to ease their difficulties and pain, right? Not add to them. Just remember that all you're offering is your love and support, not your personal baggage about death and loss. They've got enough to carry.

Anyway, it was already a full work and stress load. And we could handle only so much. We couldn't spend all our time responding to press and people's suggestions, letters, and requests, and weren't about to! Our plate was full. Every moment of every day counted in his treatment and that's what came first. Selfishly, selfishly, selfishly, my, our goal was that Patrick live. And when it came to that, everyone else was just going to have to deal with his or her own world. And every chance we got . . . it was like we had an invisible, Zenlike wall come down and shut the world out. We were on our ranch with the fresh air, our animals . . . and we focused on his daily treatment and on our resolve that things would continue to move us in a positive direction.

—

AND NOW. The flip side.

As with celebrity, there are pros and cons in every situation. Yes, Patrick's health no longer being a private battle made things more stressful and difficult, but it also brought some huge gifts.

While the tabloid headlines were busy reporting that Patrick says "Sad Farewell to Wife," "Plans His Funeral" (accompanied by photos of his father's and sister's graves), and touted so-called exclusive information about his "Final Days" as he "Prepares to Die," there was the flip side of all this negative attention. And that was in the number of good people in the world who came forward to lend their support. And in this dark cloud of everyone knowing, there was the silver lining of some very beautiful people.

It was unbelievable. The amount of genuine love and care that poured out to Patrick from all over the world was awesome and inspiring. There were so many people praying for him, and sending him supplements, information, offering services . . . and asking for nothing in return. With some exceptions (and there are always exceptions), the support coming Patrick's way was given freely and without strings. It was amazing and incredibly touching. Boxes and boxes of letters, supplies, tokens, and good wishes were funneled through our agent, our publicist, Stanford Hospital, friends, family . . . There was so much that I got my mom and a few family members to sort through it all and organize it into something that made sense so that Patrick and I could look at it.

In addition to cards, letters, prayers and meditations, sacred oils and waters, feathers, and a four-leaf clover encased in plastic that had gotten one man through World War II in one piece, there was a wide range of treatment suggestions. As wide a range as there were people who cared about Patrick and his battle with this formidable cancer. The number and diversity was truly surprising. There were healers with Reiki, Bioenergy, Naturopaths, Psychics, Gemstones, Reconnection, Visualization, Past Life Readings, Zenmasters, Shamans, and the Lord . . . who sent letters, prayers, and healings from Scotland, Brazil, Cardiff, Massachusetts, India, Las Vegas, Germany, Arizona, and so on. There were the more traditional suggestions such as the surgical Whipple Procedure, cyberknife, removing several organs to access the tumor and cancer growth and then putting them all back in again, Insulin Potentiation Therapy, Vitamin B-17, and a list of other chemotherapy drugs . . . coupled with suggestions of hospitals like MD Anderson, Johns Hopkins, St. Luke's, New York Presbyterian, and UCLA, along with many personal recommendations of doctors from all over the country.

And these treatment suggestions radiated throughout the world. There was cryosurgery in China, Mongolian herbs, Ayurvedic Medicine, bicarbonate of soda in the U.K., biological immunology in Germany, Toad Venom from Asia, which was recommended alongside chemotherapy. It was an impressive list that included everything from snake charmers to modern angiogenesis protocols.

From the start, Patrick and I drew a strong boundary—he was in charge of his own treatment. We took suggestions but made it clear that the final word would be his. Our learning curve

was intense, there was a lot of information out there, and the
emotional stakes were undeniably high. It was important to us to
create an atmosphere of support for those closest to us, not one
of fear. In an email I had sent out to all our friends and family,
I had borrowed a "Helper's Code of Service" that was written
for our dear and beautiful friend Mela, who was facing her own
battle with ovarian cancer:

> *We are here to support Patrick's Healing Journey. This is*
> *the Guiding Spirit of our Service. We are like a chariot with*
> *horses and Patrick is the charioteer. Whether medically, emo-*
> *tionally or spiritually, Patrick makes decisions for his healing:*
> *we help to empower him and support his decisions. We may*
> *have opinions, yet we do not try to "sway" Patrick's decisions.*
> *We bring information and ideas, contacts and resources, offer*
> *physical service and the Power of Prayer. Our agenda is Pat-*
> *rick's healing and we are unified in this quest. We hold space*
> *for Miracles and are guided by Mystery.*
> *Peace & Light*

It was perfect.

I cannot tell you how much everyone's support and encouragement meant to us. I know it was meaningful for Patrick, particularly because he had felt a little forgotten in the last few years,
at least careerwise. It was the old "You're only as good as your last
movie" axiom. He had worked so hard and given so, so much. He
wasn't a perfect individual, and he'd often be the first to admit
it. But he was tirelessly kind to people and went to great lengths
to treat them well. And he had a brilliant spirit. It was like he
had a radiant light that he could shine on people. He had a talent for making everyone who came into his orbit feel special and
important. And often, he had to plug in and recharge that "shin-

ing light" battery, because he ran it down every chance he got. Among the letters he received were those from people letting him know how he had changed their lives, or helped them through a bad time. For many of those people, it was Patrick's taking the time to stop and give them advice or an encouraging word that made all the difference for them. He was—one of the good guys. For him to see the impact that he had in people's lives meant a lot to him.

For me, this outpouring of support restored my faith in the kindness of humankind. For some time I had lived in a world of people who judged success by money and status, people who sometimes couldn't even find it in themselves to have basic human consideration. And that can wear on you. The reaction to Patrick's illness turned that around for me, and quick. It renewed my belief that people are basically good. Given the chance, people *will* do the right thing.

My mother once had mused how some psychiatrists in the 1960s insisted that a human being's true nature is to f*#k and kill and it's only socialization that keeps us from doing this all the time. "Well, then," asked my mom, who was a dedicated nurse, "why is it then that all babies want is to be held and loved? Why is touch so important?" Yeah . . . and I think there are aberrations, the odd "didn't get enough serotonin to the brain" individuals. But mostly, I think it's much like what happens with horses, the beautiful majestic beings that Patrick and I loved so dearly. Horses are basically inherently good-natured, forgiving animals. It's damaged people who mess them up.

And I am still cynical about some people out there. I've learned to be wary and try to protect myself from the ones who don't believe that goodness really exists, the ones who don't even feel it in themselves. And they are out there. Not everyone around us during Patrick's illness always acted in a caring way.

Some greed surfaced, and some people were more concerned about what Patrick's illness was doing for them. But they weren't the majority, and I don't think they are the greater part of what's out there in the rest of the world either. I just think that when they go around destroying things and hurting people they make a loud noise. I think the majority of people are good, decent, caring people. What a gift. To realize you live in a world with these kinds of people . . .

Patrick and I felt empowered by these people who lent their support. And if prayer and intention could bend the universe, they all could. We could. And when we needed it most, their support gave us a kind of . . .

Magic.

And it was what we so needed. We needed magic to happen.

Patrick was about to get his first set of scans since he started treatment. The results meant everything.

Chapter 7

IN GOD WE TRUST, ALL OTHERS BRING DATA

Patrick at age thirteen or fourteen.

O N APRIL 2, 2008, we flew up to Stanford for his first set of PET/CT scans since he started treatment two months before. We were escorted to various places on the Stanford campus, ending up in kind of a trailer arrangement on a circular drive outside one of the hospital doors for the scan. A PET (positron emission tomography) scan is not all that comfortable a procedure. They have to inject a radioactive material into your vein before they scan. That bothers some people more than others. For Patrick it felt awful. It burned. The first time he had one done back at Cedars-Sinai, he told me that he came very close to panicking; he thought he might be dying. Not a very pleasant experience for him. But he was going to do it again now and not complain. Are you kidding? We had spent the last two months in high anticipation of what these scans would tell us.

After the scans were completed, Patrick emerged from the trailer, and Patient Relations escorted us to an out-of-the-way sitting room of theirs off a quiet hall. It was small but very comfortable. There was a TV there. I turned it on, changed one channel . . . turned it off . . .

And we waited . . .

After a long, long while, Dr. Fisher came in. He was nodding. And it was good.

Yes . . .

Dr. Fisher logged into the computer in the room and pulled up the scans. They showed that the lesions, or spots, on his liver had not grown and they were actually less active. The tumor on the head of the pancreas also did not show any new growth. With no more new lesions, no growth of existing lesions, and the PET scan showing an improvement in the liver, this was confirmation that the chemo was actually working well at controlling the disease. *Controlling the disease.* As far as pancreatic cancer is concerned, that spells SUCCESS.

Patrick and I smiled and nodded, albeit briefly, as we received this news and we remained focused as Dr. Fisher showed and explained the scans. But inside we were jumping around with joy! When we were able to privately catch each other's eye, it was hard not to be flooded with sparkling emotion. And in his eyes I could see him distinctly say, as if he had said it out loud, *"Looks like I'm going to be around for a little while longer!"*

I was overflowing with happiness.

This was all we needed to hear. We were still in the game. We just had to deal with the next problem that came up. But that seemed minuscule in comparison to the big picture.

—

DR. FISHER scrolled to another part of the scan. The good news was that the scans around the pancreas and liver were good, and . . .

"Take a look at this," Dr. Fisher maneuvered the image on the screen, "Here's your spine, and *this is your stomach . . .*"

He started scrolling down through the image, and farther down, and farther down. The bad news was that Patrick's stomach was extremely dilated, enlarged. The tumor was obstructing the exit where the stomach empties out into the small intestine, and everything was backing up and stretching out his stomach. Patrick had been complaining for the last couple of months about the terrible indigestion he was experiencing, "I feel like I'm topped off!" he kept saying. This would start at the beginning of the day and get worse as the day wore on. He had started sleeping almost sitting straight up, otherwise he'd feel nauseated.

He'd also burp frequently, which frankly didn't smell all that great. I was flying the plane one trip with him next to me in the copilot's seat and found myself trying to hold my breath. I told Donny later, and he concurred that the smell was not good but said, "I'll take his bad breath any day. I'm just glad he's here." He didn't intend it this way, but I felt pretty small. I mean, if I couldn't take a little bad breath, *how was I going to get through this thing?* A friend of mine whose husband suffered with cancer mentioned how her husband had to endure extreme loss of bowel control, had to rely on diapers. I have a terrible gag reflex when it comes to vomit or warm poop. *What if things got really bad and*

Patrick needed me? Was I going to be one those squeamish people you couldn't rely on? Did I not love him enough? I chastised myself for being such a weenie and worried that I might not have the stomach for some things.

The bad-smelling burps should have been a pretty good indication of the problem—it smelled exactly like the kitchen garbage. Yep, all that food and the protein shakes he was being so brave in forcing down to keep his weight up was just sitting there in his stomach, decomposing as it piled up, and blowing it up like a balloon! Of course *some* food was getting all the way through, but not much, and very, very slowly.

Patrick was mighty pissed off that no one had figured this out before this. It had been terrible for him, "I can't believe it. Why didn't anyone check this earlier? Why?" he complained for days after.

It certainly explained why he had been so uncomfortable. A stomach enlarging like that can push on other organs as it settles into your pelvis. Of course the whole time he was suffering, he complained little to moderately, and only on occasion. Patrick had a high pain threshold and could buck up when he needed to. For all he knew, this could have been pancreatic cancer pain. But now we entertained the thought that maybe he needed to complain a little more when he was hurting that much!

In fairness, none of our immediate circle of doctors at Stanford had *ever* seen this happen in a patient who was responding well to therapy, and who looked as good as Patrick did. Dr. Van Dam called a GI colleague to discuss the situation and the colleague had indeed seen this happen, *once* before, in over *twenty years* of practice.

They felt sorry for Patrick. "Poor guy," Dr. Fisher said, shaking his head in dismay, "When I saw the scan . . . it's no wonder he was so uncomfortable."

—

SO THE bad news was that Patrick's stomach was blocked and enlarged. The good news was, now that we knew what the problem was, we were going to figure out what to do about it. Right now.

Within an hour or so, Dr. Fisher had organized a think tank of sorts in an out-of-the-way room at Stanford. We had Dr. Fisher, Jacques Van Dam, the surgeon Dr. Norton, and Albert Koong the radiologist all in the room at the same time. Patrick's scans were up on the screen, and each was giving his opinion of the situation and what to do given Patrick's current and unusual state. Each made suggestions and played devil's advocate, bringing in new ideas, shooting holes in existing ones. Treating Patrick was not such a straightforward thing with pancreatic cancer involved. Listening to them, I was impressed and fascinated. I had always had something of an old-fashioned view of doctors—that they all knew what they were talking about, that they had the answers. And here I was listening to these highly respected doctors trying to figure out the best course of action. *Trying to figure it out.* It made me see how truly creative medicine is. How it's not a cookie-cutter endeavor. Each person is an individual, different, and treatment has to reflect this.

I also realized how important it is to have good doctors. The good ones know what it takes and are not afraid to think outside the box. They are like scientists with bedside manners. And they are smart, creative, and highly dedicated and responsible. In that room, I also realized that they can be wrong. They may not be remembering one aspect, one piece of the puzzle that could make all the difference. Or, they can be overloaded with work, or . . . they could just be having a bad day. Long-term treatment can get very complicated. It's not a straight line. And you can find yourself getting into a lot of "chicken or the egg" discussions if you don't pay attention.

I realized that day in the room that *I, Lisa,* was a part of the doctors' team. I was the one constant out of everyone. I heard *everything,* I had my big yellow legal pad, and what I knew, saw, and kept track of was invaluable in Patrick's treatment. I saw later on, as I became more savvy about medical treatments and their associated lingo, that I could catch mistakes before they happened and fill in details that made a difference in the next decisions.

At Stanford, in that "think tank" room, I was just getting the idea of how important my role could become. That it could be even more than administering and keeping track of medications and calories. I was being let into the circle. And I was there to be of service to our team and to play as important a part as anyone else.

—

VAN DAM placed a stent to open up the blocked connection between the stomach and the intestine, and we kept our fingers crossed. There was always the possibility of complication, such as the stomach returning to its natural contractions and motility. And in addition to medication to help the process and give Patrick more immediate relief, Dr. Van Dam put in a PEG tube or G-tube, basically punching a hole through the left middle abdomen into the top of the stomach and then placing a tube there. Through this tube Patrick could drain off excess material in the stomach instead of waiting for it to pass through his newly improved, now unblocked exit. The tube coming out is fairly smallish, and you tape it up when you're not using it. Later, you can get it cut down and have a button put on so it's not dangling. It's not as bad as you think. Really. And it's a very simple procedure. That is . . . unless you're Patrick.

"I feel like I've been shot!" Patrick groaned, "Literally shot!"

"He's got a lot of muscle," Van Dam said with wide eyes, "I had to go through a *very* thick layer of muscle." It was like he just discovered that Patrick was maybe superhuman after all. Just like you'd think a movie star would be. Bigger than life with superpowers, not just a normal, fragile person! But I guess superpowers come with a downside. Because Jacques had to punch through this wall of muscle, it made the procedure site *very* painful for Patrick.

It may sound funny, but it was truly miserable for Patrick. I'd never seen him in this much constant pain. Unfortunately we made the mistake of not going home right away. A mistake because if he was hurting this much on the first day, the second was going to be even worse once the anesthesia wore off.

We had to laugh about what it's like when people get shot in the movies. "Yeah," Patrick said, grimacing through his smile, "Someone gets shot in the abdomen in a movie and then, by the next day, they're up and running around. *I don't think so.* If you're shot in the stomach, you ain't going nowhere!"

But we gathered him up and we bravely set off for home. Every little movement, every little jerk of the car driving him back to the airport was agony for him. It was very rare to see him as uncomfortable as this. And it took almost two weeks for it to feel better.

But he loved that PEG tube.

I knew he would. He figured out how to use that thing to its optimum and became a master at it. He'd even adopt a dance pose, an arabesque into an elongated penché, in which you raise one leg behind you and lean your torso over forward as your leg goes higher. He'd do this when he wanted to get every last drop he could out of his stomach.

—

PATRICK HAD the curious ability to look at his body in an objective manner. For instance, if he was going to dive off a cliff into a lake, like he did on our honeymoon as we camped out on Lake Travis in Texas, he'd look at the height, figure out his rotation, gauge his trajectory over the rocks below, review how he wanted to hit the water—and then execute a beautiful swan dive. Of course it was beautiful. He had total confidence in his calculations. He knew his body could do what he asked of it. And of course it was going to work.

Many times he put himself in what looked like peril to other people. He would just scoff when people expressed concern. Many times I begged him to back off of doing something. But it wasn't because I didn't think he could do it, it was because if something did go wrong, or his or someone else's timing was off, the physical ramifications would be severe. But he was never thinking about failing; that notion did not exist for him. Not until many, many years later when he came off his horse when he was filming *Letters From a Killer*. He was galloping on the horse bareback, the horse zigged, he zagged, and there was an oak tree in the way . . . he broke his femur in what could have easily been a fatal accident.

That *Letters From a Killer* injury hurt his confidence for some time. He hated it. He believed as his character Bodhi believed in *Point Break*, "Fear causes hesitation and hesitation causes your worst fears to come true." And suddenly he was feeling fear. He proved that he could overcome it later on by jumping on one of our spirited Arabian horses in an open field in New Mexico and running off on her—no saddle or bridle, nothing. Just free and galloping in the middle of four other running horses. Now, was that showing the best judgment in the world? Probably not. But if there was a flaw in his thinking, it wasn't about his ability, talent, or timing. It's just that sometimes he forgot to use his full wisdom. Ya know? But still . . . still . . . I can't help but admire someone who just wouldn't be squashed. He was going to go "full out" no matter what anyone ever had to say about it. And wouldn't let anything stop him, let alone a little fear.

Also, being a dancer enhanced this ability of his to meet challenges. In so much of dance, if there wasn't some kind of "mind over matter" attitude, there would be no way your body could do some of the things you asked of it. There are things that your body simply was not made to naturally do. And how do you do it? You visualize, you "feel" it, and you jump in and do it. Patrick danced, and he did athletics and stunts his whole life with a high-school football knee injury that plagued him at every turn. But it never stopped him. There are other dancers who do the same. I've seen delicate-looking girls with abscesses on their feet put on pointe shoes and go dance onstage—and smile while they're doing it. You learn to ignore discomfort, even pain. You learn how to let your adrenaline kick in and help you through it, and know that on the other side, eventually, hopefully, it will be better. But you don't let it stop you.

I think my background in dance helped me also because, although I might feel squeamish in some areas, I had a perspective on pain and discomfort similar to Patrick's. I didn't panic. I already had a good idea of his pain tolerance and knew not to baby him, until it was time to baby him. There's a kind of clinical way dancers have of looking at our bodies. We deal with physical problems calmly and professionally. And we think it through.

Patrick brought this calm determination and this "mind over matter" attitude to battling his disease. And he approached his whole treatment and every procedure as if it were an adventure. It was like his body was his, and my, personal science project; it's just that the stakes were very, very high. Higher than they'd ever been before. Which only made us work and concentrate even harder.

—

AS WE were pushing through this new territory, the inexorable drive to keep breaking my own barriers and keep learning continued. I got to redeem myself after the bad breath comment. We had been instructed to keep an eye out for swollen legs and shortness of breath, which may indicate a blood clot forming. Pancreatic cancer loves to make blood clots. And a week later, there it was—swelling in his left leg. A visit to Mark Taper Imaging and one ultrasound later confirmed the existence of a clot, or DVT (deep vein thrombosis). Patrick was put on the blood thinner Lovenox. This is given in a subcutaneous shot (just under the skin, usually in the abdomen) twice a day.

Okay, now . . . I have a real "thing" about needles. Needles freak me out! And suddenly I'm being asked to give Patrick shots twice a day? Our main nurse in LA, Jose, was going to teach me how to do it. Even gave me a little rubber pad and a syringe and needle to practice with. And I practiced over and over and over, along with watching the instructional DVD that came with the Lovenox package. When it came to real human flesh, it was a different story. The first time, I poked Patrick, "Ow!" I immediately pulled the needle out.

Patrick exclaimed, "What are you doing? You pulled it out!" He was looking at me like I was a fool.

Jose shook his head, "Naw, that's not good. You've got to throw it away and start with a fresh one."

"I've got to throw it away?" I asked with dismay.

Jose and others had been filling me in on the fine points of keeping things sanitary, something that's crucial when dealing with someone who was as vulnerable to infection as Patrick was. My mom had been an excellent nurse, and many of her cleanliness habits transferred to the home, so I already had a head start. Jose instructed me that I couldn't set the shot down after I'd unsheathed it, couldn't touch it to anything, and . . . couldn't stick it in and pull it out and stick it back in again. Okay! I threw the shot away, which probably cost fifty dollars, and coming as I did from a family of six kids with two working parents and having starved in New York as a young dancer, throwing away a fifty-dollar syringe . . . hurt. I was determined to do it right the next time.

You know, Patrick, who was very blasé about needles, could have given himself the shot, but for whatever reason, he wanted me to do it. I think he wasn't as blasé as he made himself out to be, or maybe he thought it was good for me. Maybe he just liked me doing it.

I did think that it was a handy skill to have. I mean, what if I ever had to give one of my horses a shot and there was no one else around to do it? Up to that point I would have been too frightened. As it turned out, I became expert. I got lots of practice, and many doctors and nurses marveled at the lack of bruising from my shots. Patrick actually asked me to do it even when there was nurse around because I gave a better shot than many of them. Well, you know what? If I was going to do it, I wanted to be the best. No, that's not true. I just never wanted to hurt him, and I had to be the best so I wouldn't.

—

A WRITER-DIRECTOR friend was visiting one evening. I asked him how his new script was coming along. "Great," he said, "Although I came out with two different versions in one part of the story."

It had obviously put him in a dilemma. "So, what did you do?" I chuckled.

"I finally had to go back to my original notes," he said, "to see what I intended this whole movie to be when I started out."

I had found myself wanting to go back, too. Everything had been turned on its side. I wanted to go back and refer to my notes when I started out on this life. The notes on how I wanted it to be, what I wanted it to mean . . .

And then there was my time with Patrick.

He and I had spent most of our lives together and I felt myself wanting to go back again, but in a different way. I wanted to go back with him. We were now nearing the end of his second cycle of chemotherapy. I had written this two months previously, the day after Patrick started his treatment at Stanford and we had such high hopes:

—

Forever

> *'Cause I wanna go back*
> *To the beginning*
> *I wanna start all over again*
> *I wanna try and fix the places where we went wrong*
> *I wanna go grow wise*
> *And sing a heart that's true*
> *I wanna laugh loud and long*
> *At the terribleness we avoided*
> *I wanna touch you*
> *Forever and ever my love*
> *And know the joy that*
> *That has always brought me*
> *I wanna hear my voice when it caught in my throat, my*
> *   mouth*
> *'Cause I can't say enough*
> *Of how much I love you*
> *I wanna go back and drive that car again*

I wanna pick you up and feel the freshness of together again
I wanna go back and do it all over again
So that I can have more time with you
Double the time with you
Triple the time with you.
Until the end of time.

June 2008, at a roundup in New Mexico.

Chapter 8

RUSSIAN ROULETTE

GOOD-LOOKING PEOPLE TURN Me Off, Myself Included."

"The Idea of a Promiscuous Poke Never Turned Me On."

"All I've Got Is My Integrity 'Cause, to This Day, I Ain't Never Seen a Hearse Pulling a U-Haul."

These are a few of Patrick's quotations that appeared in various magazines. You never knew what Patrick was going to say next sometimes. It could be surprising. I don't know where he was getting these ideas, it was almost like he just opened himself up and channeled them from some alternate universe. "A Promiscuous Poke Never Turned Me On." If he was going to say something that showed his fidelity to me, I might have preferred something like, *"I love Lisa so much I could never, ever, not in a million years imagine being with another woman."* Instead I got "A Promiscuous Poke Never Turned Me On." Okay, I'll take it!

Sometimes he told the press a lot more than he should have because he figured, "If I tell them everything then they can't hold anything against me." Hmmm. I had to think about that one for a while. Here and there, I had to remind him to not share my deepest, darkest secrets with national and international press, as I tend to be a more private person. And he did his best to try to remember that.

93

There was another quotation of Patrick's that was embroidered in a brown, cream, and rust pillow that we kept in our house for many years. TV icon and journalist Barbara Walters had this cushion made and sent to us after her interview with Patrick after *Dirty Dancing* in 1988. The embroidery said: "Our Fights Are Huge But Our Love Is Huge."

Twelve years later, I looked at this pillow, shook my head, and said to Patrick, "We've got to *burn this pillow*." We had come to a place in our relationship where we needed a little cool water poured on our brow and knew how long a way a little tenderness would go. This pillow, with this quotation, celebrated the tempestuous, argumentative parts of our relationship. We had grown older, and wiser, and knew this was not what we were striving for. We were striving for passion and loving actions. Not passion and throwing household items. It was hard to let go of that pillow—but we burned it in a little ceremony and vowed to elevate ourselves to higher level. If there is such a thing.

Does this mean we didn't argue?

—

WE DON'T always get asked to step up to the plate, and we wonder what we would do if faced with a terrible terminal illness. We imagine that our reaction would be like the movies, or at least a TV movie of the week. And of course, if we have a lick of sense, we know that it may not be as pat and perfect as a Hallmark card platitude. Judy Kaufman, a wonderful lady in Patient Services at Stanford Hospital, said to me, "We learn never to judge anyone. Whether it's the patient, or the family, everyone handles illness in a different way. It doesn't mean it's good or bad. It's just . . . different."

Never judge . . .

She was saying this as I tapped my foot, waiting for Patrick to get off our airplane. We had flown into the Palo Alto airport, and he was rustling inside for God knows what. I had long dis-embarked, checked to make sure we had everything, had secured the plane, and had paid the ramp fee. I sighed and turned to her and wanted to say, "But he's *always* done this." And it was true. Patrick was chronically, historically late. I was always waiting for him. But even so, I had to entertain the possibility that this time, yeah, he was probably nervous about going in for chemotherapy treatment and that *could well be* the cause for his procrastination. *Could be*. This time. So, instead of yelling out that he needed to hurry it up, I made a decision that I was happy as long as he got to the center and got his treatment before everyone went home for the evening. Not such an easy thing for me.

In all fairness, though, there were times I did yell at him. Really yelled and berated him to get him out the door, other-wise he *would* have missed his appointment. I'd make an ugly fuss and put on a big unhappy show as I pushed and prodded him. I remember once, when he was out of earshot, turning to our housekeeper, Celinda, who was just trying to mind her own business, to whisper secretly, "I'm not really mad. I just need to get him out of the door." Even so, I always regretted raising my voice. As soon as we were on our way, I'd reached out to hold his hand to let him know that I loved him so fiercely that I wouldn't let even *him* get in the way of his treatment and the possibility of getting better. He would always squeeze my hand back and all harsh words were gone instantly. As if they never existed.

Our journey through this illness was not without bumps, arguments, impatience, sadness, and fear. But never, never in doubt was the love we had for each other. And yes, it could be exhausting, and the stress we experienced gave new meaning to the word. And as much as we were moving through amaz-ing feelings and places together, here and there, tried and true problems would raise their ugly head. For example, I found that cancer could be used to excuse all sorts of things! I have a girl-friend who, at the same time Patrick was being treated for his illness, was taking her longtime boyfriend for treatment for head and neck cancer. A curable disease, but the treatment is awfully brutal. He and she got into a big argument and he threw up the "C" word to her, to which she sneered as best she could, "Thaaat's riiight! I should leave you alone because yooooou have caaaan-cerrrr!" I cracked up laughing when she told me about this. It was so . . .

Classic.

I wrote the below when I was feeling sorry for myself and woefully unappreciated as I struggled with the stress of the re-sponsibilities I had taken on:

> *I got so pissed off yesterday and it's still lingering today. What about? Well . . . Seems, yeah, Buddy's sick, but . . . he's still doing his same old behavior, i.e. staying up late, disappearing in his studio, no help, being late, late, late, unmotivated to be pro-active in his life . . . It's just he has a better excuse for all of this behavior now. Cancer.*
>
> *And here I am, busting my ass. Doing the shopping, giv-ing his medications, fixing him shakes, food, making sure he eats, driving him to his appointments, lifting anything heavy, calling people, making the appointments, waking him up, or-ganizing his life, his career, his press, his world . . . And let's face it, he's well enough to hang out outside, drinking coffee, picking up emails, and smoking cigarettes! Now . . . is this his fault that he hardly lifts a finger to help himself? Or, is it mine? Is this really having to do with his behavior sans sick-ness, or . . . ?*
>
> *Let it go, let it go, let it go.*
>
> *March 29, 2008*

Hah! That last line is set to the tune of the Christmas carol "Let It Snow." *Let it go, let it go, let it go,* instead of, *Let it snow, let it snow, let it snow.* A little in-house joke we used to sing out when someone infuriated us and there was nothing that could be done about it except to just move on.

It wasn't the last time I was going to have a moment when I felt like I was a plowhorse pulling the whole load with little help. But clearly, I had unequivocally chosen that path. And when you came down to it, I was grateful for it and for whatever I could do for him. So I got over feeling underappreciated pretty quickly. Particularly when it was clear that Patrick *did* appreciate everything I did. But often I felt like one of those one-man-band things, you know . . . where the guy is honking on a horn with one hand while the other hand clangs the tympani, and his foot beats the bass drum and his mouth blows on a kazoo.

In my role with Patrick I did a number of things and played a variety of parts. I knew I wanted to empower Patrick to have the best attitude he could about his illness, and this was not always a one-note approach. I tried to be wise about what he needed at any given moment. We had been together so long, I knew where his "buttons" were, when he needed prodding, and when he needed me to hold his hand or just be plain left alone. Some years ago, we took a rafting trip on the Colorado River in the Grand Canyon. One of the guests was the great basketball coach Pat Riley and his wife, Christine. Pat had his book *The Winner Within* coming out, and I was asking him about what it was like to coach, really coach people. Even then I was heading toward directing and learning what I could about getting the best from people.

"Everyone's different," he said. "To get the best out of a player sometimes demands very different approaches. There are some players that do their best when you use encouragement and validation. And then there are the ones that need you to get on them, yell at them and push them."

Sometimes I felt like a coach with Patrick, and I was always changing my game plan. In addition to being a coach, I was also nurse, administrator, wife, friend, and lover! A one-man band.

—

PATRICK CLEARLY knew that we were in this together. Once he complained when someone said, "*We're* going to get treatment next Friday."

Patrick was peeved. "It's not *we*. There's no *we* about it," he said to me in private, "*I'm* the one who's getting treatment!"

I winced, "Then I'm guilty of the same thing," I confessed, "I'm always saying *we* this and *we* that."

"That's different," he said. "You're allowed."

There was only one time when Patrick said in anger . . . like my girlfriend's boyfriend did . . . that *he* was the one who had *cancer*.

To which I replied with upset and anger, "This is happening to *me*, too!"

I'll never forget the look on his face. He can be so stubborn and willful, but his look showed such a deep, empathetic anguish for me. I knew he felt sorry he was pulling me into this, and it pained him that it hurt me. He never, ever, said that again.

—

WE HAD been so lucky thus far in the progress of his disease. And we lived in fear of getting a bad result in any one of his tests.

But what about how hard it is to receive good news when the one you love is so sick? There's an incredible irony to this situation. Nobody told me about that.

Monday, June 9, 2008, I was sitting in the treatment room at Stanford. Patrick was lying on bed after being doted on by the nurses, and was waiting for the results of his next scans to come back. I would smile at him, take inventory of how good he was looking, so, *surely,* I thought, *the scans would come back with a good indication. Surely* . . .

While we waited, we talked about who called us that day, what was on our agenda; turned on the TV in the room to see if anything was on; arranged the furniture so I had a makeshift desk I could put my computer on; picked up emails; filed the flight plan for the trip home; ate lunch . . . talked about whatever, and waited. The scans would show if the treatment was working or not. It would determine whether he continued on the course he was on, or that the well had gone dry and it was already time to try another of the precious few alternatives.

Waiting for the scan results with a deadly cancer like this was like playing Russian roulette. It was like coolly waiting to find out if there's a bullet in the chamber or not. What do you talk about while you're waiting for the trigger to be pulled?

Of course we didn't talk about the what-ifs of the scans. *Wow, what if this time you're really dead?* Didn't try to predict. *Gee, this could go one of two ways!* We ignored it, as if this all-important moment was minuscule in the grand scheme of things. Because if the scans came back bad, part of us was prepared to not take that news as something that would seriously affect his longevity. If they were bad, it meant there would be a bump in the road. Just one more difficulty to deal with. That's what we would bravely think to ourselves. I know that's what he was thinking and he knew it was what I was thinking. We'd chat pleasantly and be upbeat to the nurses as they came in and out. We'd make them laugh . . .

But your soul knows what a bad scan means. And you just can't go there. But what if . . . what if . . . the results are positive? What if that hammer clicks on an empty chamber, no bullet? What if all your hard work and diligence in treating this terrible disease pays off? What if you're just freakin' lucky? The victory is so sweet you savor it like it's the most delectable morsel ever. At the same time, it's still painful . . . because there was the fear, and you know without a doubt just how much, how desperately you hoped for this positive result. You are aware of the consequences. And good news means a reprise. It means that, once again, you will know hope. And hope lays you open and vulnerable, and it's harder to build your courage back up to the next time that the chamber gets spun and you put the gun back to your head for the next set of scans.

Crazy, huh?

Crazier still was going through all that and then having the trash tabloids killing him off every other week. It's hard enough to face a life-and-death situation without having national and international tabloids taunting that you're a dead man. Patrick always said that the worst of what that reporting did was that it destroyed hope. And hope is one of the few precious weapons you have against an illness like this. And hope is not just a wonderful, float-y, smile-y feeling. Hope takes courage beyond courage. This hope is earned in a way few people have to earn it. By going through hell and back again.

But enough of that now. I'd like to go on a tabloid tirade, to tell you all the ways they tried to kill him off. You wouldn't believe it. But not now. Later . . .

Because now, Dr. Fisher walks in and beckons us out into the empty hallway. He wakes up a waiting computer . . . and we look at the results of Patrick's second scans.

And they are good.

They are good . . .

So we start getting ready. We have about forty-five days. We're going to Chicago to shoot a TV series.

Chapter 9

EMBRACING THE ALLIGATOR

Happy day. July 13, 2008—Patrick, me, and Kuhaylan Roh,
with Lucas lying nearby. (Photo by Brian Braff)

IT'S HARD IN a situation like this not to agonize about the future. There were times when fear came and bit me hard. But it wouldn't last too long . . . it separated me from what I loved. I didn't want to waste any time worrying about the future, not when I had the chance to be with Patrick now.

I had a dream several years ago that I've always tried to remember. In that dream, there was a monstrous, prehistoric alligator-type demon that was tearing down Foothill Blvd. in our neighborhood, causing mayhem and brutally eating anyone unfortunate enough to be in his way. Everyone was doing their best to escape the line of death and destruction the big reptile was making. And then I realized, the monster was coming straight toward me! I was quickly looking for whether I should jump off to the left or right to escape when suddenly—my instinct told me to stay . . . and I did. I stayed right there in his path and as he approached fiercely. I opened my arms to him. He slowed as he came upon me . . . and then laid his big, craggy head softly in my arms. He looked at me, his eyes full of hurt and gentleness. And I realized that all the monster wanted was to be understood. And that's what I had just done.

June 7, 2008

I had been learning to "Embrace the Alligator," as I called it. Those thoughts about the future were about hurt and fear. But under that hurt and beyond that fear lay love and gratitude.

—

ON JUNE 12, 2008, we were on our ranch in New Mexico for the thirty-third anniversary of our marriage. Once Patrick was feeling better and his treatment was stable, we started spending as much time at our ranch as we could. Rancho de Dias Alegres had been our longtime dream from when we were first together as teenagers and young adults and is several thousand acres of varied mountain forest, streams, and open rolling terrain in raw New Mexico beauty.

We had been looking at ranches in various states for a number of years when we, by accident, happened to visit an Arabian horse breeder's ranch just a stone's throw from Rancho de Dias

Alegres. I remember driving onto the horse ranch's property in a beat-up old car we had borrowed from the local airport we had flown into, and we worried that the car wouldn't get us back since we had to time the climb up the hills so that we'd be heading downhill when it stalled. Anyway, we pulled into the breeder's drive. And when I got out, and my foot touched the ground . . . tears came into my eyes out of nowhere. *The land had so much soul.* I was so moved, and I knew for myself that this was the place. Patrick loved it, too, and wholeheartedly agreed.

When Patrick got sick, one of the first things he said, and said painfully, was, "I just got all the camping equipment organized at the ranch . . . and now I may not ever get to use it." It was curious that this was one of his first comments when he got sick, but it showed me how much joy the ranch gave him. And he'd spent hours, days, weeks organizing, wrapping, and fixing camping equipment for us and for our friends when they'd visit. He loved it there. So much so that it was hard for him to leave it sometimes.

For our anniversary on that June 12, I fixed a picnic of food that I could heat up over a fire, and we headed out to our favorite camping spot—a lovely sloping meadow with a pond reflecting Hermit's Peak in the distance. We had a fancy lunch (for a cookout anyway) with a red-checked tablecloth set out with champagne for me and Gatorade for him, and enjoyed the afternoon, strolling through the camp talking about what else we'd like to do with the campsite and watching the sun set with the smell of warm pine surrounding us.

In earlier weeks we had tentatively broached the idea of renewing our wedding vows. I say tentatively because neither of us wanted the other to think that this was some kind of last-ditch effort because someone might die in the near future. When we finally said it out loud to each other, we discovered that we had both been thinking the same thing.

"I always thought renewing our vows would be a neat thing to do," Patrick said.

"Really? Me, too!" I replied.

But we put the thought on hold. Mostly because things had been so busy and stressful, and then shortly after, the tabloids reported that we had already renewed our vows in New Mexico and somehow it just kinda spoiled the spontaneity of the idea!

In late June we joined our friends Steve and Marci at what we called the "Burro Pasture" on the south part of the ranch. It was a family round-up, doctoring and branding the new babies near the Tecalote River. We gathered up about thirty mamas and their young calves.

Steve had brought an extra horse that was well trained for cattle work, and entreated Patrick, "Ride him, I think you'll like him." Patrick, dressed in his cowboy gear and chaps, jumped on him to start roping and bringing calves over to be treated.

All the cowboys at the ranch like to do things the old-fashioned way. Keeping the old skills alive. They also believe it's less stressful on the calves than driving them through tight-squeeze chutes and such. I have to say, it's probably more work doing it the old-fashioned way, but more fun for them. I was impressed with how much more organized everyone was than the last time I saw them do this. I say "I saw them" because I don't have much of a desire to tug little calves around and stick something hot and sizzling into their backsides! But I love the cattle, and I enjoy walking alongside them on my horse, and looking at their big beautiful eyes. Everyone had a job—Patrick, Steve, and Steve's ranch manager, Jeff, would sort, rope the rear legs of the calves, and drag them to the fire. Steve and Marci's sons and a couple of friends held the calves down while one did the branding. Marci and Jeff's wife, Phyllis, prepared the shots and administered them quickly before the calves got too rowdy. Me? I took pictures and tried not to get run over by a horse steam-rolling my way. And then it started to rain! One of our freezing afternoon thundershowers. Take all this activity and speed it up two to three times faster! Patrick was soaked to the bone as he rode out the gate. We were wet and cold as we hurried to load horses back in the trailers, grab our overcoats, and get in our cars, wondering about the mud we'd encounter on the way out. What the hell. We were having fun! And I have to say that inside I was laughing. I was laughing happily because Patrick wasn't even supposed to be alive. And here he was. Doing ranch work and fully living his life.

—

DR. FISHER had always said to Patrick that he should give himself the freedom to do what he wants to do during his illness. *Does he want to work? Does he want to go off and spend time on an island somewhere? Travel?*

Patrick would kind of screw up his face in puzzlement at that question. Later he would confide in me, "I don't know what to think about that."

"You have any ideas?" I asked.

He thought a moment, and then said, "Well, I *don't* see myself going on *vacation*." Like it was some kind of preposterous notion.

So that left the second option—to work. I'm glad he didn't dream up the third option—to do nothing and be depressed. It's an option that would be easy to choose when you've been di-agnosed with a fatal disease. How could you not be depressed and just give up? Many people do under the weight of such an oppressive diagnosis. Many just don't have the energy. Patrick's courage and commitment wouldn't allow him to accept his diagnosis. And he never said, *Just leave me alone.* He was going to move forward. And with the reward of a prognosis that definitely indicated a positive trend, he had dared to move ahead with a TV series, *The Beast.*

Returning to work, especially on a project that demanded so much time and commitment, was a bold decision. We had about a month and a half from his last scans before we had to be in Chicago where the series was going to be shot. There was a lot to do. Meetings, phone conversations about what Patrick needed there, prepping the transfer of all his medical stuff, deciding where his scans would be done, figuring out the best shooting versus chemo schedule, finding where we were going to live for five months, talking to lawyers, doctors, and insurers . . . A big hurdle in getting the TV series together was the fact that A&E and Sony were unable to find a company to insure Patrick for less than it cost to shoot the entire series itself! A&E and Sony took a leap of faith and decided to move ahead—if Patrick wasn't insured, at least the rest of the production would be.

I was busy preparing and carefully anticipating everything I possibly could for the series while he continued his treatment at Stanford. And we kept busy just plain living, living as much and as fully as we could every day. That was the easy part.

And it was a week and a half before we were due to be in Chicago that we finally made the last-minute decision—to get married again.

—

IT WAS a Wednesday when we again brought up the subject of renewing our vows. And we agreed that—to hell with being busy, or how this or that might look—we both wanted to do it. Okay, great . . . how to do a wedding ceremony in—we checked the chemo schedule, appointments, travel plans—four days. And that included the Wednesday we were now in. Patrick would have chemo the next day and be pretty much down for the count with fatigue for the following two days. I don't know how I thought I'd organize it all to happen in such a short time, but I knew I could and a little bit of magic would just have to take care of everything else. I figured I'd go for everything—the flowers, the music—and then let go of the things I couldn't get.

Amazingly, I got it all . . .

We decided we would get new wedding rings to add to our original ones. And through the help of our jeweler friend, Kenny G, we were able to get two beautiful, slender, diamond-dotted bands. We got this accomplished with FedEx shipments, so we had the final rings in a Saturday morning delivery.

Wouldn't it be great to have a quartet playing before the wedding?

"I don't know of anyone that could do this. Let's ask Will," my brother Eric and his wife, Mary, said. Will's my wonderfully talented violinist nephew, and with a couple of phone calls, he had a worthy quartet for us.

I luckily was able to contact a singer (the wonderful Suzie Benson-Rose, who sang with Patrick on a song for our film *One Last Dance*) and a pianist (Donnie Demers, who also composes) to play and sing the song "Since You've Asked" by Judy Collins. (Will would accompany on the violin.) Patrick and I had this song performed at our original wedding thirty-three years ago. We still loved it. And it meant so much to us. Even more so thirty-three years later . . .

> *What I'll give you since you asked*
> *Is all my time together*
> *Take the rugged sunny days, the warm and rocky weather*

Take the roads that I have walked along
Looking for tomorrow's time, peace of mind . . .

I bought loads of one of my favorite flowers, blue hydrangeas, from the local nursery to scatter around. Food for a buffet (friends and family could help lay it out). I moved my baby grand piano out onto the flagstone patio, overlooking the pool, where the ceremony would take place. Set out chairs . . .

But who was going to preside over the ceremony? I tried to find Father Welch, who had married us over three decades ago! *Maybe I could fly him out here to do the ceremony.* I was sad to learn that he had passed on several years ago. A woman minister came highly recommended, but she was out of town until Tuesday. I found someone else who ended up not being available but had a wonderful American Indian ritual to suggest. This was getting tough. And then I decided . . . Mary, my sister-in-law, could preside. Mary has always been very spiritual and has beliefs similar to those (or a similar openness to beliefs) that Patrick and I have.

"Yes, I am a minister," said Mary, "and actually *anyone* can be a minister. It's pretty easy to do online," she said. Mary doesn't know how to be anything but completely honest, "So, legally I can do it. But unfortunately, with the organization I work with, we promise not to use our ministry to do things like legally marrying people."

Ah, hah! "So, Mary," I started to reason, "Buddy and I are already married. So, you're not really breaking the rule."

Mary thought and then grinned, nodding in agreement.

Sunday morning, since I had some time, I went over to a designer friend's house to see if I could find a dress. And I did. A long dress with an Empire waist in luxurious, thick, white, Irish linen. And I decided to go barefoot.

Oops. Before I went to Jane's for the dress, I needed to write my personal vows to Patrick. I sat out on a raised part of the patio that has a pergola covered with wisteria vine. It would be the spot where the classical quartet would play before the ceremony later that day. I hoped with my whole being that I could just open my heart and let the words flow. I hoped they would have the same magic that I felt. And as I wrote, I cried.

As we reached that afternoon, people started to show up. We were still running around getting things ready, and everyone was fine. Everyone was happy. It was like there was truly magic in the air. Like a love potion had been emitted into the atmosphere and made everyone unusually happy and giddy. Patrick came up to me, standing and discussing final ceremony notes with Mary. And then said . . .

"I think I want to ride in on Roh."

"Huh, really?" I balked, quickly thinking of all the problems a strong handsome stallion not ridden that often could cause.

"I think it's a fabulous idea!" Mary enthused.

I smiled. And Patrick turned to go off and get the horse.

I was standing at the back door ready to make my entrance, and Patrick was at the side of the house, mounting Roh, who was prancing all about, nervously wondering what the hell was suddenly going on. Once Patrick was aboard, he and Roh, our silvery, blinding-white, brilliant stallion, set off and trotted out and fairly floated around the pool to the "Ooohs" and "Aaaahs" of all our guests. And they were breathtaking indeed. He dismounted near the patio when Roh had settled . . . and held out his hand.

I was smiling ear to ear as I walked forward through the crowd and up to him, taking his hand . . . And I couldn't resist. I turned to our guests and grinned, "After thirty-three years, he *finally* rides up on a white horse!"

They all laughed. And tears sprang into my eyes . . .

Susie, Donnie, and Will performed the song beautifully: *"We have seen a million stones lying by the water . . . You have climbed the hill with me to the mountain shelter . . . Taking off the days one by one, Setting them to breathe in the sun . . ."*

Mary stepped forward to us and beamed as she introduced the Native American Indian hand-washing ceremony we had planned. As she poured water over our hands into a bowl she explained, *"Water is used as a symbol of purification and cleansing as the bride and the groom wash away all past hurts."*

Patrick and I washed our hands with the cool water, and then reached out to hold each other's hands. We smiled at each other as Mary continued.

"You have come into the presence of these loving witnesses to profess that which lies deep in your heart . . ."

It was a beautiful day, warm, crystal and clear as we stood in the soft, sheltering shade of a coral tree, blue hydrangeas surrounding us. Our guests murmured, smiled. But mostly I just looked in my Buddy's eyes. And it seemed that I had never looked so deep, so long into his soul as I was now. And I saw in his eyes that he was treading into that same deep place in me and I saw my own joy reflected back at me. How I could breathe, I don't know, for from the time I stepped out of the house to take his hand, my heart was bursting with a happiness. How it didn't jump out of my chest and my dress and start dancing, swirling, and celebrating in the air, I don't know.

I read my vows to Patrick. Ending with . . .

" . . . And then I knew why writing my vows to you had been so hard. Because I am already so committed to you. And have been always. This love I feel for you seems to transcend time. I loved you even when I was a small child and hadn't met you in flesh and blood yet. And while the future is an unknown, the one thing I do know, is that

I will love you. I'm very lucky to have found you in my life and am grateful that I have had the ability to open my eyes and see just what I have (occasionally!) because what I have—the love, the greatness and enormity of what I feel, informs everything around me. And in cherishing the most there is for me, I cherish you even more."

Tears were rolling down my cheeks throughout reading this and I had to have someone pass me a wad of tissue to stem the flow. At which point Patrick turned to our guests and shared loudly . . .

"This, from the woman who, at our *twentieth* anniversary party, raised her glass for a toast to thank me for *three* of the happiest years of her life!"

The guests chuckled, and as they realized what he had really said, erupted into huge laughter. I laughed, too. And Patrick looked very pleased with himself. We high-fived each other. *Good one, Buddy!*

We pulled ourselves back together, took a breath . . . It was Patrick's turn. And he blew me away with the eloquence and beauty of what he had written for his vows . . .

"How do I tell you how lucky I feel, that you fell into my life? How grateful I am that you chose to love me? I know that because of you, I found my spirit, I saw the man I wanted to be. But most of all, you were my friend.

"Together, we've created journeys that were beyond anything we could imagine. Journeys that dreams are made of. We have ridden into the sunset on a white stallion, countless times. We've tasted the dust in the birthplaces of religions. Yet you still take my breath away. I'm still not complete until I look in your eyes.

"You are my woman, my lover, my mate and my lady. I've loved you forever, I love you now and I will love you forevermore."

We ended the ceremony with the rings . . . As we slipped them on each other's fingers, Mary read . . .

"The ring is used in this ceremony because the circle is the only symbol that has no beginning and no ending. The circle is our oldest symbol for God, or Spirit, that which was in the beginning, is now, and ever shall be, world without end . . .

"You may kiss the bride! And may you live in Light and Love!"

We kissed and embraced, warm and strong. There was applause all around. Everyone hung out, ate, laughed, and talked until one in the morning. It was truly a celebration and I felt high as I saw everyone's smiles and felt the love.

—

YOU KNOW . . . back in 1987, Patrick and I did a movie together in Namibia, Africa—*Steel Dawn*. It was our first time in Africa and I fell in love with Namibia. It turned out to be one of the most special places in the world for me. When we first arrived, we had flown almost thirty hours to get there (with an eight-hour layover in Frankfurt sitting in a hard, molded-plastic seat). When our plane finally landed in Namibia, we went straight to the production office. One of the producers offered to drive me out into the desert to take a quick look. I wasn't expecting much, but said "Sure." *Why not.* The Namib/Kalahari Desert is one the oldest in the world, at one time being beneath the ocean. My tour guide pulled over on the desolate road and I got out and walked a few feet out from the car.

"We call this the moonscape," I heard him say.

But I was stopped. The land in this area was hard, and dark, and it rolled in smooth, undulating waves against the mercilessly open sky. And its startling beauty took my breath away.

I say it took my breath away because . . . it literally took my breath away. I'd always heard that expression and never thought to take it at face value. And to that point, it hadn't truly been taken away. But that day it was.

I'd also always heard the expression, *"One of the happiest days of my life."*

I'm making a long point by telling you all this, because I want you to know, truly know, what I mean when I say that, on Sunday, July 13, 2008, Patrick and I renewed our vows . . . *it was one of the happiest days of my life.*

—

IT WAS on to Chicago.

An ad for The Beast *on the side of a New York City building.*

Chapter 10

THE BEAST

ALWAYS CRY AT weddings, and I cried at both of mine. After our vows renewal, I noted that the second time around is even more special. Why? Because this time *you know* what you're getting into and you are *still* saying "yes." It's a real testament to what you mean to each other.

And I'm trying to be a bit light right now, but I have to say . . .

. . . Remembering the happy stuff can be harder than remembering the bad. And remembering the bad isn't always a walk in the park either. But recalling the good times is very hard in a very particular way because the hurt digs down excruciatingly deep. Remembering has crippled me as far as moving on with my day, and then crippled me for the next one, and then the next. It put me down for an entire week, and then another week. I've slowly had to find my way back up to the surface again.

"Look. You're still healing," a friend says.

When you're grieving, you never know what can knock you flat. And sometimes you can feel like you've gone a little mad. A year after Patrick's death, I arrived at the ranch in New Mexico and had to, was compelled to, pick up all the pictures of him that I had nicely framed and march them to the far end of the house where I couldn't see them. And then I closed the door on them. I know a woman who lost her husband, and she was given a beautiful photo album full of pictures of their wedding together. She threw it down the trash chute! She couldn't bear to look at it, even to have it in the same room with her. I know . . . it just makes you too sad. Funny . . . only a month before, my beautiful framed photos had given me *such comfort.* I can only imagine that at some point they may again. Or maybe they'll mean something entirely different to me.

Ah . . . And here I am thinking about those photos. His beautiful smile, how it looks like he loves me . . . good stuff again . . .

Wait. There . . . I'm coming back now . . . And . . .

. . . I feel better.

Maybe it's emotional exhaustion, and I can let down now that Patrick is gone. When I had to live and battle his illness, I just kept going. The renewal of our wedding vows gave me a completion and positive energy that I carried with me to Chicago. I was a barrel of energy. Unstoppable. But though I still had plenty of energy at that point, well, maybe I didn't have so much energy at that point, you know? I think about Chicago, and I feel tired. And no doubt about it, it was physically and emotionally draining, nerve-wracking also. We were taking a certain amount of risk by his going and shooting a TV series. I knew that Patrick was capable of doing some of the most amazing things, but there are some things that even he didn't have control of. And once we were there, I knew I would have to think even faster on my feet, tap dance three times faster. And . . .

I'm still having trouble moving on to Chicago. Why am I having trouble? All I said is true, but . . .

Maybe my senses were getting inundated in there. Once again, I was faced with the worst of what life could be, and the very, very best of it. I still had my private angst, the tension associated with Patrick's treatment and the feeling that the emotional pressure was beating me with a stick.

At the same time, I looked out on every day, and it glistened. I don't remember a bad day in Chicago.

Chicago was happy. That's what it is. With bad times, you can steel yourself and keep your head down as you plow forward. The happy times lay you open . . . vulnerable.

And Chicago was happy . . .

It was tough and it was challenging, and even as a tornado threatened to come through one evening and stranded me downtown when I was riding my bicycle, even that ferocious wind was like a current of air rushing into me, whipping the sound of aliveness in my being, *you're alive, you're alive, and . . . he's alive with you!* Nothing was too bad. I rode back in the rain that night, the streets shiny and wet, still fairly empty from being evacuated. And it was *magical.*

In case you forgot—Patrick wasn't even supposed to be alive at this point. Every day . . . every day was a living victory and a miracle. And it was like living *inside* a victory, not as a momentary thing but as something you are immersed in. A living, breathing victory. *What an incredible place to be.*

The challenges and hardships associated with shooting the *The Beast* in Chicago were a small price to pay for being able to live so preciously. And yes, it's still hard for me to launch into telling this part of the story. But how do I not? It was an amazing experience, and it was a moment in time that was going to be an inspiration for many.

—

OUR WONDERFUL driver, Gus, was taking me home from the set at about two o'clock in the morning. Patrick was still due to shoot a couple more hours, and I wanted to take the dogs for their final walk before settling in back at our apartment. Lucas (our standard poodle) and Murphy (our border collie mix) rode happily in the back as we bumped along the late-night Chicago streets, content in the knowledge that a walk in one of their favorite dog parks awaited them.

I trusted Gus. He's a good person, with a good sense of humor and lively intelligence. He asked me how I was holding up, if things were getting too much . . . and I remember saying, "In a way, this is one of the happiest times of my life."

Gus kinda glanced sideways at me. "I wouldn't say that to too many people if I were you."

Hah! I hadn't thought about how that would sound. *My husband has pancreatic cancer and I couldn't be happier!* Wow, what a field day the tabloids would have with that quote!

"Yeah, you're probably right about that." I grinned.

The Beast was an ambitious project in what they were trying to accomplish, and the shooting schedule was grueling. An enormous amount of work and passion was going into the series. No shooting day was less than fourteen hours, and more likely sixteen hours, sometimes more. The number of pages of dialogue Patrick had to learn every day was staggering, in addition to trying to read the next episode's script, give notes, make suggestions and changes, and then, he still had to show up and actually shoot the thing. But Patrick had transformed.

Before we went to Chicago, he had been spending the majority of his time in bed. Let's just say that his activity level was very low. *Very . . . low.* To make the transition as smooth as possible, Donny stayed with him while I packed up the plane with our luggage, medical supplies and dogs and flew it to Chicago a day and a half early to set things up. "You better have a very big van, we don't travel light!" I warned our driver before I arrived, and he showed up with a van that I probably could have fit all our stuff *and* a small pony and a couple of square dancers into. I quickly set up our living arrangements and made some calls, and then Patrick was due to arrive.

From the moment his foot touched down in Chicago, he was like a different man. He went from staying in bed all day to hardly *ever* going to bed. His enormous burst of energy floored me. I say that he "was like a different man," but the fact is, he was like his old self, going nonstop, and always the extra mile. I got Patrick back! He was his usual take-charge work self, and even moved into some of the occasional "star" behavior, the stuff that would always drive me crazy, like making last-minute, arbitrary demands and suddenly being the unquestionable authority on . . . just everything in the universe.

Wow, things were almost normal! But being a self-centered star was not Patrick's only mode of being. One of the writers showed up at our hotel for a meeting and was surprised that Patrick was out with me, walking the dogs. Here he was, star of the series, fighting cancer, dodging paparazzi, and he's out walking the dogs and picking up poop.

As usual on set, the crew loved him. Patrick's situation with battling cancer brought an extra effort from all concerned. It was like all the crew, the directors, and the producers upped their game. Let's face it, it's pretty hard to worry about your usual petty grievances when a star like Patrick is battling a tough cancer and still showing up to work and never complaining. The respect level was high. And I know that the crew was aware of the significance of what they were witnessing. There was a sense of being honored to be involved in this endeavor.

Patrick was also adamant that he not be "written down." Meaning, he didn't want the show's writers to make his role not so demanding, put him in fewer scenes, or delete action or chase sequences because he had cancer. And the writers didn't. Actually, by the time they got halfway through the series, they *forgot* he had cancer when they were planning the episodes.

But in the beginning there was a little "getting to know you" time. The producers and director were worried about his doing too much. Not just because of the cancer, but also because he was the star and couldn't get hurt. Patrick came back from the set one day, shaking his head, steam still fizzing out of his ears . . .

"They didn't want me to jump over the wall!" he exclaimed to me with disbelief, "I'm supposed to chase this guy and jump over the wall after him. They wanted the stunt man to do it! 'No, man, *I'm* jumping over the wall!'"

After some polite but heated discussion, he did the stunt. He wasn't about to give up on doing those things. But everyone was learning what I had already long known about Patrick's capabilities. He'd been doing this a long time, and though his illness compromised some of his strength, he knew his limits as always, and that bar was still set very, very high. And I loved it that I still saw that confidence of his shining through.

He also never took any pain medication when he was working. He didn't want it numbing his mind and affecting his performance. His work was important to him, and he wanted to do the best job possible. He wasn't there to "phone it in." He was so adamant about not taking pain medication that once he was home and off work, I had to remind him that he could indulge himself in a little prescriptive relief. "Oh, yeah!" he'd say, like it was a novel idea, one he hadn't thought of until then.

Patrick knew, as only he could, the limits of what he could and couldn't take. Every once in a while I weighed in, taking measure from him on how he was feeling, asking if this was getting too hard for him with the level of pain he might be having. In one such discussion, he nodded at my concern but then shook his head with simple frankness . . .

"I've worked with worse *hangovers* than this," and he leveled me a look.

That statement was so classic Patrick. So often he'd act as if he could do no wrong and was master of all, and in the next moment, thoroughly bust himself with funny and startling honesty.

And though sometimes he wasn't feeling well, he could still find inspiration for a practical joke and a laugh. He could have some intense abdominal pain at times, and along with his treatment came some pretty bad-smelling gas. Patrick labeled them "Chemo-Farts." Late one night on the first episode, he and his costar Travis Fimmel were shooting a scene where Travis, as "Ellis," comes over and jumps into a parked car next to Patrick, as "Barker." Everyone had put in a long day already and was tired, but still going full steam ahead. I was sitting next to Michael Dinner, the director, and in between takes, Patrick came over and whispered to me . . .

"I am having the *worst gas,*" he said. "That's why I keep opening the car door between takes. So I can air it out . . ." And then Patrick went kind of silent . . . And he wandered back to the car when they picked up shooting again.

But as they shot, I noticed that Patrick was no longer opening the car doors. And *he seemed to be concentrating inside the car.* I think he was making good use of his time in the enclosed vehicle . . .

On the next long take, Travis jogged from all the way across the street, looking furtively this way and that, then hopped in the car with Patrick and closed the door.

Immediately, Travis blurted out, "Ooooh!" and tumbled out of the car! Patrick had just seriously blasted him with Chemo-Gas!

Patrick sat in the driver's seat, trying not to laugh and to keep a straight face, but doing very poorly. Travis was recovering outside the car, hooting and shaking his head. And then there was me, trying so hard to stifle my laughter that tears threatened to spill down my cheeks.

Michael, the director, turned to me. "What happened?"

"Uhm, I believe Patrick just doused Travis with a Chemo-Fart."

For the next two takes, Patrick and Travis couldn't keep a straight face, breaking into broad grins and chuckles. It took monumental effort, but they finally pulled it together to get serious again.

—

THERE WERE still the emotional lows during this time. But there were also some positive things happening for me, whether I was hanging out on the set, reading scripts, or whatever. I was happy to "be there" for Patrick during this journey, and be whatever I needed to be for him. Without a doubt, I wouldn't have had it any other way. I had transitioned to directing and writing a few years back and loved it, but all that had been put on hold. Occasionally it was hard being around the set, since I was there merely as the "wife" and not really, officially, involved. But still, it was very positive—being around the shooting was stimulating, and it started me thinking creatively again. A wonderful thing for me.

I was also very touched by how many people befriended me. Roy, the director of photography, first camera Billy, Gino the gaffer, the writers, and many of the directors who came on board . . . all treated me as an equal. I can't tell you what a difference that made. I got to share my passion for this work as we talked about camera, lighting, and scene set-ups, and it would be like a little piece of heaven for me. I put together a steadycam set-up for myself and the camera I already owned, and Billy made a special case for it (along with some great steadycam instruction!). Roy handed me different high-def cameras to play with. Several of the directors leaned over when I was sitting next to them, "So, Lisa, when are you going to direct an episode?" Of course I was delighted they'd asked, and laughed as I shook my head happily.

"Naw, I'm here for Patrick. Maybe next season." Their acknowl-
edgment and support gave me much-needed hope in a situation
where I felt like there was so little for me. Their support was better for me than any Bahamas vacation could ever be.

—

THE LOGISTICS of being in Chicago could be challenging. It was
much harder to avoid the paparazzi than it was in LA simply
because there were portions of the shoot that took place outside and were open to the public. After a couple of weeks at our
hotel, I found us a wonderful, spacious, airy, two-bedroom apartment overlooking the vast, blue Lake Michigan, and the building
had three different ways of getting Patrick in and out without his
being seen. They were happy to let us lease for only five months,
and the building was dog friendly. Up to that point, I'd been
walking the dogs three times a day, and it took me a full ten minutes just to walk to where they could start doing their business! I
seemed to spend most of my day walking the dogs and still trying
to do everything else, and it was wearing me down! At the new
place, I rented furniture and kitchenware and we could take the
dogs right across the street to a fabulous park. It was a beautiful
walk. And during the warm months we had front-row seats for
spectacular fireworks displays right outside our windows twice
a week. The apartment was also a front-row seat for the big air
show Chicago has every year. We threw one of our parties for
this, and of course, as pilots, we enjoyed the scream of jets going
past our windows, so close it almost seemed like you'd felt their
jet blast!

As I said, the shooting schedule was tough. It would have
been tough for a healthy person, let alone someone fighting pancreatic cancer. As we moved into fall, some of the late nights saw
temperatures dip to below freezing. Patrick persevered. There

were times when it was difficult for him to get going because of painful discomfort, whether it was gas, trouble with his digestion or bowel movements, or some other mysterious ailment. And he made sure he was never too far away from a bathroom. But he always found a way to come through.

In the middle of this busy schedule, we managed to arrange a day to fly back to LA to appear on the all-major-network, televised, "Stand Up to Cancer" telethon. This was the first time that Patrick was going to do something like this to raise awareness for cancer. Up to this point he had been very careful not to put himself in that position. He didn't want to be the poster boy for cancer. It wasn't how he wanted to be thought of. But this was a special event, and its impact could be huge.

When we flew in, we were ushered straight to a hotel across the street from the Kodak Theater so he and I could change clothes. His being there was a secret, so we skirted past anywhere that people could see him and into the backstage of the theater. It was a live show, and there was a bit of a time crunch (remember Patrick is *always* late?), and he barely had a few moments to review the words that he was going to say, which I had helped write and shape for him, before we were ushered into the wings and it was time for him to walk out onstage to open the show. He got a standing ovation. The phone lines were instantly flooded, and people had to keep trying back to get through. It was an incredible show, and from Stand Up to Cancer's efforts they raised over $100 million toward fighting cancer. Some of this money went to pancreatic cancer research, which has been woefully, embarrassingly underfunded.

—

FROM THE beginning of the shoot into the first month or two, Patrick actually started to do . . . better. When we were into the month of September, he turned to me one day with hope in his eyes, venturing to say, "I've been feeling so good . . . I almost feel *normal*."

We had managed to carve a niche for ourselves that gave us privacy. What small respite we could provide for ourselves was much needed. We were still fighting a serious illness and behind the public face that we presented to the world, we dealt with it every day. It was kind of funny because I felt like we had a dual identity—the TV series and all that went along with that work, and then our alternate life, chemotherapy and treatment. Like "The Shadow" or Clark Kent, here was the public face, and then, step into the nearest secret hospital and out comes "Chemo-Man!" Or, "CT-Man!" depending on the day. There's something surreal about shooting a TV series where there are dramatic life-and-death situations—people getting shot, beaten to death, or poisoned—and then showing up for a real-life chemo treatment where the stakes *really* are life or death. No doubt about it, it brings you down to earth pretty quickly.

To add to our secret identity vibe . . . We usually had our appointments after hours when the hospital floor was empty. George Fisher had transferred all our medical files to Dr. Mary Mulcahy at Northwestern Hospital. Mary was a team player, smart, dedicated, and caring. Everyone did their best to be flexible, and we were able to schedule Patrick's treatments for Friday evenings or on Saturdays at the very latest. This was not only for privacy, but more important so he would have the couple of days he needed to recover from the enormous fatigue he always experienced before he had to show up for work Monday morning. It was a critical balancing act.

And then, of course, there were the always-sobering scans. In mid-September, a CT scan showed a slight increase in the spots in Patrick's liver.

—

WE WEREN'T going to panic. For now we were going to hold our right to panic in reserve. We were going to keep a close eye on it. And then a week later . . . his CA19-9, the blood work that roughly measures increased protein, thus possible tumor activity, went up again.

These were all little signs that something was awry, but it wasn't enough yet to lead us to abandon his course of treatment. But needless to say, we were *very* concerned.

And then, in early October, Patrick had yet another scan to ascertain the trend of what was now happening inside him. The spots on his liver were stable, and in some cases, decreased! He had amazingly, miraculously, somehow dodged yet another bullet. We didn't know what caused the change in scans—maybe a pocket of infection that suddenly unclogged, or maybe the treatment suddenly worked where it hadn't earlier, and then, who knows, there's always the possibility of magic, that all the prayers and good wishes that were coming his way were paying off. But it was a sobering scare. Man! We were getting pretty tough about taking these ups and downs in stride. We had remained steady and fearless throughout. We just kept collecting ourselves and kept putting one foot in front of the other. But we couldn't help but be shaken.

Another thing that *was* discovered in that CT scan was that he had developed colitis, an inflammation of the large intestine that would account for much of the abdominal pain he was experiencing. Mary suspected the PTK was the culprit in causing the colitis, and had Patrick stop taking it to see if it cleared up. I hated *any* interruption in his treatment, but . . . *Lisa, remain steady, steady* . . . no doubt about it, if the colitis cleared, he would feel better and it would improve his quality of life. And colitis, unchecked, could very possibly result in surgery. I waited on pins and needles until he could get back on treatment, and kept my eye out for any signs of trouble in the meantime.

In addition to the new colitis condition, there were some things that started to happen, things that we had long been warned of that came along with the territory. We considered them to be "housekeeping items": the stent that kept his bile duct open clogged again and had to be replaced, and the chemo started to trash his veins so much, it would take sometimes over seven painful sticks to get an IV needle in, so he had a portacath put in to remedy this. The portacath, while not glamorous, is a wonderful invention (though not without its own set of problems), in which a semipermanent access for intravenous treatment is placed in the upper chest just under the skin and connects to the jugular vein and into the superior vena cava, which is a short, thick vein that carries blood through to the right atrium of the heart. No more having to get stuck with needles for chemo, just stick a Huber needle into the access that is already hooked up to a vein. As luck would have it, the very day after Patrick had the portacath put it, he was scheduled to shoot a fight sequence for the show. And wouldn't you know it? The actor he was fighting with ran into him. It was a direct hit on the new portacath! Needless to say, it hurt like a son-of-a-gun.

—

ONE EVENING, one of the writers asked me how Patrick would feel about an episode being written where his character, Barker, dies. I'm glad he asked me what I thought and not Patrick. This was just about the *worst* idea I'd ever heard. And I couldn't believe I was being asked. I knew he had to ask, that he had to be responsible to the show, and Patrick was indeed a sick man. On the outside, I'm sure I just looked calm and like I was considering it thoughtfully. And then, wanting to make sure I was being perfectly clear I said, "No . . . no . . . he wouldn't like that at all."

Part of me would have loved to have a normal life at that point, you know? As grateful as I was for the life we had, I'd be crazy if there weren't times that I just wanted it all to go away. Depression would sneak in and grab me here and there, as witnessed in a private observation I had written down in October of that year (probably right around the time of the scans). The page was full of anger, self-criticism, and bitterness at how unfair life can be. Let's just say that I talk about how *"worthless"* I am, how *"fat,"* how *"I was wrong about life being fair,"* that I'm a *"wuss."* And now worst of all things, *"I may be losing my husband. And I don't know if I can do this. It's beyond unbearable."*

I'm only giving snippets here. It's just too hideous and unattractively self-pitying to reprint the whole thing.

But, what could I do about all these feelings?

I can't change the choices I've made. And I couldn't make my husband live if he was not meant to. But what I can do is change the way I think about it. I can decide that I will go on. That every day is a new day and I get to choose the person I want to be, make the choices that are before me, and show the love I wish to feel and give to the one I love.

And regardless—sometimes you get the bear, and sometimes the bear gets you. There is no way you can stop feeling. And nobody ever said it was going to be easy.

—

IT'S BEAUTIFUL in Chicago. I ride my bike, walk the dogs, buy food, do Patrick's meds, watch on set, help with scenes, run interference, and watch fireworks. Not bad. And now the air is getting cool and crisp. The sting on my face feels invigorating, and when it rains, I navigate under my umbrella with my dog's leashes and I laugh inside as I dodge the raindrops.

When we get to a weekend in October, I'm in the kitchen

rustling up some food and I mention to Patrick that a director of an upcoming episode has dropped out and there are some people encouraging me to submit myself to direct it instead.

"And . . . ?" he queries. When I shrug, he says, "You should do it."

I shake my head, "Eh, maybe next season." That makes me a little sad. There may not *be* a next season and I don't like to think about that.

"Why wait?"

"That's not why I'm here. I'm here for you." I smile at him.

He rolls his eyes. "I can take care of myself."

Now, did I believe him? Not entirely. Not that he wasn't intelligent or capable enough of taking care of himself (though sometimes he could make you wonder). But his treatment and medication schedule was complicated and involved. Consistency is not Patrick's strong suit. And then there were the food issues, the dog-walking issues . . . and the issue that things were hard enough on him as it was.

But the idea was now out in the light of day, and there was no turning back. Once Patrick established in his mind that I wouldn't pass up a possible opportunity because of him, this was something that was not going to go away. Now his pride was involved in the issue.

And, yes, I still didn't believe him. What—he was going to jump up and start doing all the things I had been doing for him the last eight months? Uhm, naw . . . But I was going to come up with an idea about how I could be covered for the couple of weeks I might be working. But as it was, it was way too early to get excited. I didn't have the job yet. And getting it was going to prove to be one of the biggest hurdles.

On the set of The Beast. *(Photo by Roy H. Wagner, ASC)*

Chapter 11

IF YOU CALL ME CAPTAIN, I'LL CALL YOU DADDY

Y OU NEED MORE time to prepare," "We're only using A-List TV directors," "It's really hard to break into episodic television," "This is a really tough schedule," "It's particularly hard for women to break into episodic television," "It's complicated," "The studio and/or network is not keen on the idea," "It's just too hard to work it out this season." These are some of the things I heard when I first broached the concept of my directing an episode. And then there was . . .

"Next season?" I was talking to the line producer on the phone. I took a breath, "Look . . . I've been around this business long enough to know that that's just another way of saying, 'no.'" He laughed. It was true. But in all these excuses, I didn't hear one that convinced me that I couldn't or shouldn't direct the episode that was now available. I had directed a feature film that I also wrote and produced, had put together several other short pieces for which I shot, edited, engineered sound, and output the final polished version on my own. I had been on film sets for over twenty years and was not without experience or talent. True, most of my experience had been in and around feature films. But in the last four months I had gotten to sit behind every talented A-list director that came on *The Beast*. It was a wonderful experience to get to see them work and how different they were—how they handled scenes, interacted with the crew, the actors, the writers and producers, their perception of the material . . . I felt lucky that I got such a heavy, concentrated dose. It was valuable seeing all of them work on what was essentially the same material. A wonderful opportunity for anyone. I had also started directing some B-roll (additional shots and unscripted scenes) and second-unit shots on the show, and shot a scene with Patrick with minimum crew to help out when the schedule was tight. I also had the advantage of really knowing the characters inside and out, in addition to the actors playing them, the crew, the writers, and producers, and the show's consultant.

So, what was the problem?

But they, whoever *they* were, weren't budging.

Now, probably anyone who wanted to be nice and not rock the boat would have backed off. But I had gotten braver than I used to be in my early twenties when I was so quiet I had trouble saying "hi" to the grocery store cashier. And to tell the truth . . . there's something about facing cancer that makes you not scare off as easily. Facing a deadly illness can make you unafraid about many things. Why? Because most things are *so incredibly insignificant* in comparison. I was facing Death. Do you think a TV executive was going to scare me off? So, did it really matter that they had considerations about my ability to deliver the work? My unafraid answer: No. And what was I going to do about it: Not go away.

I was going to pull out my Sisu for another purpose here . . . I had experiences with being told "no" before. Hollywood loves to say "no." I definitely had faced that when I did my movie a few years back. But I hung in there and simply wore everyone out until they couldn't say "no" anymore and it was easier for them to say "yes!"

And with *The Beast*, I wasn't alone. I had so much support from everyone, most notably Roy Wagner, the director of photography. Roy had clued me in on the open spot in the first place. "That's BS," he shook his head and muttered when he heard they were balking. "There's no doubt you can do this! And listen . . . Patrick is a *star*. He can insist." He went on to tell me how his first directing job was on *CSI*, and he got the job because one of the *stars* insisted that they hire him. A star with far less "pull" than Patrick.

Patrick and I never liked to use the "star card," which is probably why his being one never seemed to help me. I always wanted to be hired on my own merit (a crazy and pure thought!). But Patrick called in to say that he'd really love it if I directed an episode. And still . . . nothing moved. Why would it be so easy for others to insist but not for him? Maybe there *were* some gender issues involved. Or, maybe because I was his *wife*? I don't know. But I had no reason to doubt what Roy said, and Patrick and I decided we would play that card. If it came to that. We hung in there, knowing that the only way you get what you want is to not give up. We had had plenty of opportunities to learn that lesson. It had certainly been the case throughout Patrick's acting career.

—

PATRICK SEEMED to have to work hard to get the films that he really wanted. And when he got them, he worked hard on making them the best possible.

On *Dirty Dancing,* he was up every night working with the writer and director improving the script. Patrick worked tirelessly. And then, after hours and on weekends, he'd take his "time off" to learn choreography and hone his routines despite swelling in a bad left knee that sent him to the hospital to get it drained. A year later, he was at the Golden Globes with a nomination.

On *Ghost,* Jerry Zucker, the director, stood up after viewing *Roadhouse* and said, "Over my dead body will Patrick Swayze do this movie." On that note, Patrick still went in to audition and read practically the whole script for him. People in the room were in tears, and he got the job. And another Golden Globe nomination.

On *City of Joy,* one of his favorite movies of all time, once again he was an unlikely candidate. But he managed to get an interview with the director, Roland Joffe, and he told him with sincerity, "If you give me this job, I will give you my heart." Roland went to his producer and financiers and said, "We have to have him."

On the audition for *To Wong Foo Thanks for Everything, Julie Newmar,* Patrick went in and had full makeup and dress drag put on. And after he was dressed up like a woman, he had the balls to insist that he improvise a scene as Vida Boheme rather than read the appointed scene. Director Beeban Kidron and the casting director took the tape of his audition in to Steven Spielberg and the other producers. They didn't even tell them who Patrick was when they showed them the audition. When the producers were bowled over, Beeban and the casting director revealed who it was, and they were further bowled over. And so was everyone else when they saw the performance that garnered him a third Golden Globe nomination.

We always thought it was odd that the really good projects had to be fought for, and the ones that weren't of such good quality or potential always offered a lot of money. It's like, wait a minute, isn't there something wrong with that picture? Wouldn't it be nice if you could do the really good projects *and* they paid the really good money? We could never figure it out. Not that we were complaining. Patrick was one of few actors who could make a more-than-good living in his chosen profession. Also, yes, he could have chosen to do the movies that paid a lot, but that wasn't the kind of choice either of us was making in our lives. There were things more important than having a ton of money in the bank. We were doing the work we wanted to do. Hah! And if things went south, we had lots of skills to fall back on! We could go back to doing carpentry if we wanted. We could dance, round up cattle, train horses! Fly airplanes! You name it!

—

YOU KNOW . . . back in October of 2007, four months before Patrick was diagnosed with cancer, we went to flight training at Simuflite in Dallas, Texas. It was a requirement every year, and was valuable in keeping our skills sharp. This was the first time we were going to specifically learn our Beechcraft King Air 200. We were going to learn it inside and out during a demanding six-day course in which the first four days are spent in a classroom, and the next two in a full-motion simulator. Patrick and I took all our training very seriously and prided ourselves on our commitment. Patrick loved to say that we "fly as a cockpit team," and that we "operate up to professional standards." But we were going to be presented with a whole new concept in regard to Cockpit Resource Management.

We got to the full-motion simulator and spent time alternating as pilot and copilot, doing engine failures on takeoff, stalls, emergency procedures on approach, you name it. I was in the pilot's seat, executing one such emergency, and Patrick was talking a million miles an hour. I waved my hand for him to just calm down and wait a minute while I finished what I was doing. Suddenly, he grabbed the yoke from me. "If you won't listen, I'll fly it." Needless to say, I was not pleased. But I didn't want to argue in front of the instructor. The instructor of course saw exactly what happened, and in his slow, Texas drawl, told Patrick that grabbing the yoke probably wasn't the best thing to do at that moment. I was doing fine and had the plane under control. A few moments later, he introduced an idea . . .

"I found that this can really work in the cockpit. Whoever is in the copilot's seat should call the pilot in the left seat 'Captain.' It's just a reminder of who's flying the airplane and whose decision it is to respect."

"Hmmm . . ." Patrick and I were considering this.

I was thinking about how hard it might be to remember and how you'd really have to *want* to remember to do that. And I saw that Patrick was having a little trouble with the whole concept himself. The look on his face said that he wasn't buying the idea at all. But for me, what the heck, I try anything if it'll make us better pilots.

"It might be a good idea," I said, and shrugged, "You know . . . it'll just remind us who has command of the aircraft."

Patrick sat thinking for a moment. And then seemed to make up his mind, nodding firmly, "Okay. I'll call you Captain . . ." and then added with an impish grin, "But only if you call me Daddy."

I laughed. How could I not be charmed? I did my best to call him "Daddy" when I was in the left seat thereafter.

But it pointed out something—for all Patrick's generosity and openheartedness, he liked to be first. And in case you haven't noticed, he could be competitive. What else can you say about a man who would take on cancer as if it were some mere mortal enemy that he could defeat by sheer will and intention? My calling him "Daddy" was a cute joke, but it couldn't help but point out the contradictions he embodied. He would be the first to brag about me in every area of my life, how talented, how smart, how beautiful I was, and he included flying, always saying with pride, "I created a monster when I talked Lisa into flying. Now she drops me off when I'm working." And, "Women make better pilots because they don't make decisions from their crotches!" But when push comes to shove, he really liked to be the Captain.

Much of the time it looked like I was the one whose will prevailed. That I got "my way." But on a closer look, I could see that Patrick *always* got his way. The scoreboard gets a little fuzzy here. If you really analyzed it, it would be difficult to figure out where one of us left off and the other began. *Who really is flying this plane?* I guess that tradeoff made us unusual and perfect complements. Balanced us.

Patrick was like the perfect "bad boy." Charming, unpredictable, exciting, and sometimes unreliable. Now, most women I know have devastating experiences when they get involved with bad boys. Bad boys cheat, treat them badly, leave and don't call . . . not Patrick. He could drive me crazy and that's what bad boys do, but he could also be faithful, commit fully, and love fiercely without question for over thirty-four years. He was like a wild bird who let himself be tamed but somehow always remained wild. Or, appropriate for his Leo astrology sign, like a lion, big and dangerous, yet relaxed and cuddly as he lies there, surveying his kingdom. *His* kingdom. *Him* as the center of the world.

And I was his queen. His *"Bad-Ass Goddess,"* as he liked to call me.

—

EVEN THOUGH Patrick wasn't afraid to fight for certain projects, he didn't like to push too hard for someone else. He was down to earth and I'm sure he worried about people thinking he was throwing his weight around and using nepotism. Also, I think he secretly wanted me all to himself, so that I would be watching and paying attention only to him. Actually it wasn't all that much of a secret, as other people noted this. And I don't blame him for that. There were shows I did that I would have given anything for Patrick to be there watching behind camera. It's incredibly valuable to have someone there whose eye and opinion you trust, because not everyone is looking out for you, and in some cases, no one is. It's also great to have that person there to steer you in the right direction when you're going off track. And you know that person is not selling you down the river for some personal gain, that his intentions are pure.

There was a moment when Patrick started to slide back in his conviction in helping me get the job on *The Beast*. It was becoming clear that he might have to use some muscle in the situation and pull out his "star card," and he started to look uncomfortable. Seeing this, I started to back off, too. And then I thought about it . . .

It was late one night, and I walked out into the living room where he was tapping away on his computer. "If you think about every project where there was a possibility that I could be involved," I started, "I don't think it worked out because we never hung in there and went the distance. We *always* backed off. And in each of these projects . . . if you really think about it . . . if I had gotten the job, it would have been at least *as good* a choice, if not *better* in some cases." I was able to name every instance, and in every case, what I was saying made sense. "So . . . *why* did we let *them* decide? As if they knew something we didn't?"

Patrick nodded. He got it. Funny, but . . . the only person I hadn't sold the idea to yet was Patrick.

And a few weeks later, I had the episode.

—

ROY, THE writers, the crew, and I were elated that I was going to direct what would be the last show we would shoot. There was only one person who didn't seem thrilled. Oddly enough, the moment I was actually confirmed to do the episode, Patrick suddenly ceased being so generous! I couldn't believe it! In his eyes it was like I had gone off to the other side, the enemy team. I think he was having one of his "oops, now I really have to call Lisa the Captain and I'm not sure I like it" moments. But it was to prove to be only a momentary reaction. Patrick was a different man now. He abandoned his first little knee-jerk reaction and stepped to my side. And he would show what a stand-up man he was in the weeks to come.

Now it was time to pull out the backup plan I had been holding in my back pocket. I called Donny . . .

"Donny, is there any way you can come to Chicago for the last two weeks of shooting and walk the dogs for me, track Patrick's medications, get him to appointments, and make sure he gets up, and . . ." I went on with the list.

"Uhmm, sure. I'm not doing anything right now. Sure, I'll come," he said. "How soon do you need me there?" Later he confided that it took all he had not to say, "I thought you'd *never* call!" He had been in agony sitting at home in California not really knowing what was going on and not being able to help. He was actually grateful that I called; it was a godsend for him. And his coming to help me out certainly was a godsend for me!

Thank God for Donny and for his being such a good brother to Patrick. Even with Donny's help, Patrick's illness weighed on me, and it was a lot to ask of myself to direct this episode under the stressful and emotional burden I was carrying. There was a moment I worried that I had bitten off more than I could chew. That I might not have that much energy. At some point, everyone hits a wall. But I gauged that mine was still a ways off. And I was already committed. I was going to direct.

After his last scans and in the weeks leading up to the episode, Patrick had started to feel bad, bad enough that it was making it much more difficult to work. And though there were times that everyone had to wait on the set for him, sometimes up to four hours before he felt good enough to shoot, he still got the work done, and he *never missed a day.*

Of course he was tired. Everyone was tired and beat up from the hard schedule they'd been on for almost five months. But the abdominal discomfort had amplified. So much so that it was hard for him to get going in the morning and he never wanted to stray too far from a toilet. He described it as intense cramping, or the feeling of having a crippling kind of gas, sometimes sending him to the bathroom floor until the waves passed. We scrambled to do everything we could to relieve his discomfort. Still he refused to take pain medication unless he was finishing working and he'd have plenty of time to get it out of his system before reporting back to the set the next day. He was going to do this the hard way! I know it was tough on him, and he knew it, too, but not taking pain medication was still the choice he wanted to make. But his increasing pain was concerning.

I felt like I was on hyper alert—I had a full plate with the upcoming episode, and still I wanted to monitor and gauge how he was feeling in case . . . in case of *anything.* I asked him if he still felt up to work these last weeks. And though he wasn't feeling well, he grinned.

"Absolutely."

But I was grateful that there were only a couple of weeks left in the schedule. He only needed to hang in there a little longer, and he would have completed shooting the whole show. A phenomenal feat to have finished shooting an entire series' season.

So, we pushed on to the end. And it was even more special because we were working the last show together.

—

I KISSED the doggies good-bye and left them in Donny's capable hands, and I was launched into the wonderful, thrilling, and extremely challenging experience of directing a TV episode. I had done as much as I could to prepare, I had a wonderfully strong script, I had my locations, etc., etc. But prepare as one might, there are still many unknown factors until you get on the set. Things happen, the schedule can change . . . But I love that. You have to be fluid. You have to think on your feet. And television in particular is like tearing down a mountain in a downhill ski race. You have to come up with creative solutions quickly. I knew the schedule was fast, but I didn't know it was *that* fast. I had worked quickly before when I did a low-budget feature. But this . . . this was faster! And that made it very challenging.

I loved the show and what they were doing with it. Of course I was determined to do the best job possible.

Hard as the show was to shoot, I had additional pressure that none of the other directors had to deal with, and it wasn't just worrying about Patrick—it was people watching me closely. In the South we call it "bird-dogging." When I was sitting behind camera there were at least four people sitting behind me! And then on another day, I had five more people added to that for my behind-camera audience. These were A&E Network folk, who came on set to observe. And then, Barbara Walters's crew showed up to get some footage of Patrick and me working so they'd have it to use in an interview scheduled for next month. It was very difficult to be a pheasant under glass like that, but I wanted the job, and if that was going to make everybody comfortable, then so be it.

The support from the crew, the actors, and everyone was fabulous. It was a great group and there were so many people who really cared that I was doing this. And Michael, the original director and the show's consultant, was there to act as my mentor at any moment I needed him. After I completed shooting my first scene, I could swear I saw him almost get a little teary-eyed and puff up proudly. Little did he know just how much this meant to me.

After a couple of days, the seats behind me became emptier and emptier. I guess everyone figured they had better things to do than to watch me all day. As entertaining as I might be.

We were getting into late November, and the temperatures at night were starting to get very cold. During one long night shooting a fight scene, it was eighteen degrees, and we started having snow flurries. But I had my Canadian Snow Goose down jacket from Manitoba, my super gloves, high-tech long underwear, and LL Bean headwear. I was bundled up, ready to take the cold, and having fun.

I worked hard and loved the whole experience. What surprised me most was how much I loved the "boy" story. *The Beast* was very much a macho kind of show with lots of fights, intrigue, criminal acts, and aggressive male behavior. And I loved it! Where that came from, I don't know. Later, when I mentioned how much I liked shooting this macho action stuff to my choreographer friend, Doug, he ventured, "Uhm, do you think that's because you're a strong woman? And you can pretty much kick ass yourself?" I laughed. I never think of myself that way. I always think people see me as this very feminine, delicate sort of individual. And I feel that way a lot of the time. I guess it's good to have friends who remind me otherwise!

I'd always wanted to do the style of shooting that we did in *The Beast*, that kind of docudrama, fast-cut, urban-grit style. And once I was off and running, I quickly understood how it all worked. Also, shooting the fight scenes was tremendous fun. Patrick was always excited to shoot a fight scene no matter what movie he was doing. He'd always try to get me to come watch, and I'd try to find something else to do because I found them incredibly boring. And now suddenly, I realized that the reason I was bored was that *I wasn't the one doing them.* Because now, shooting them, it was like heaven. I could shoot fight scenes all day long! It's like dance choreography. It's like getting to punch a pillow over and over. And no one gets hurt! It has all these emotions you do your best to avoid in the cold light of day. After my first fight scene I went straight to Patrick. "Now I understand why you love it so much!"

Patrick pulled out his best for me. I know he wasn't feeling well, but he made sure he was there when I needed him. And it took monumental effort for him to do so. He knew the schedule was tough for me, and he walked onto the set to work at times when I knew he would have been better off in the trailer. I know it was hard for him, and I know he was doing it for me. But like I said, he was a different man now, and he was going to be there for me every step of the way. And I needed him to know what he had done for me.

My hopes had been raised in a way they hadn't for so long. The future had looked so bleak for some time now. Working on this project reminded me of what I loved to do. It had been so . . . positive for me.

We were back at the apartment, and when I found the right moment, I turned to him, and it was hard not to be emotional. "I just have to tell you how much this has meant to me. For the first time in a long time, I feel like I have a future, and it's something that I thought I'd never feel again."

Tears had filled my eyes and now brimmed over and rolled down my cheeks.

He stood still and looked at me. He didn't say anything . . . he didn't need to. He just smiled. And I saw that he had concern for me . . . He knew the future that I was afraid of. And he was afraid for me, too. If there was any way, any way at all he could change it, he would. I knew he loved me . . . and for those last two weeks in Chicago, it was his pleasure that I was his Captain.

—

WE HIT our last weekend and were able to catch our breath for a couple of days. I still had one day left to shoot on my episode, one that would be the hardest of all. And not just because of schedule.

On Sunday, November 23, we had an appointment at Northwestern Hospital, and Patrick had another set of scans done. The always-dreaded scans. We sat in the small dark room with Mary Mulcahy, studying the results together. The number of spots on his liver had increased. And the mass on his pancreas had grown. It was very clear now that the treatment he was receiving was no longer working.

—

WITH EVERYTHING we had on our agenda, our brains had been going in what felt like hyperspeed. When we got the news that the cancer was growing, it landed with a dull thud right in the middle of everything. I looked at the scans, and though I saw the spread of the disease, my mind had to peer at the screen, focus closely, to understand what it really meant. I looked at Patrick, and his face was a mirror of everything that I was feeling. Fear crept in, but it was like it was some foreign body that had suddenly insinuated itself into our lives. *Keep thinking, Lisa. Just keep thinking . . .*

Quickly, we made plans to change his treatment, nodding at Mary's suggestion of a new drug. And before I went to the set for my last day of shooting, I picked up Patrick's new medication at the pharmacy—Xeloda. It seemed strange to me that you could just pick up what we hoped to be Patrick's life-saving drug at the local pharmacy. Like you pick up aspirin or ibuprofen. The chemo was in pill form and could be started immediately. When we got back to California, it would be perfect timing for him to start the heavier Oxaliplatin, another intravenous drug that would be taken in conjunction with the Xeloda.

My final shooting day was hard and took a lot of concentration after having just gotten this information the day before. And of course, we didn't share what we had found with anyone, lest some kind of leak happen. Still, there was a wonderful sense of completion when the day was done. The series had officially wrapped, and there were smiles of celebration. The next day was scheduled for additional shots that were needed for various other episodes (and one for my own). That next night, Patrick and I were standing out on the street with two of the writers, Vincent and Bill, talking about the shots that were coming up next. We were just about to launch into deep discussion when Patrick put his hand up.

"Listen . . ." he said and took a deep breath, "before we go any further, I just gotta say. *I can't believe I just made it through this whole thing.*"

Intense emotion filled his eyes, and he started to tear up. And then he laughed. And inhaled the night air with a deep breath.

He had gotten through it. And it had been an amazing thing. Not only for everyone involved with the production, but for people who were grappling with their own tough illnesses. We had started hearing of people who had renewed hope from watching him—*"Patrick Swayze has the same thing as I do and he's still here."* Even Mary Mulcahy at Northwestern Hospital shared with us, "I can't tell you how many people you've inspired. I have patients that are hanging in there more than ever and living their lives, and you know why? They say, 'Well, Patrick's doing it.'"

As if this was all the reason they needed to keep going. What a gift.

—

STRAIGHT FROM directing the show, I spent the next two days packing up the apartment before we moved back to LA. The last few weeks had been exhausting, and still there was so much to do before we had to leave. Packing up a five-room apartment felt like a Herculean effort for me. But I committed myself to doing it. *I'll rest when I'm back in LA.* It had been so busy, still was, and there was hardly any time to think about this change of direction in Patrick's health. But inside I was fully aware. And while I was all alone in the apartment and sitting in the middle of packed and unpacked boxes, I stopped and wrote this:

> *Sometimes I feel like such a little girl*
> *A little girl that is on the verge of being lost*
> *That Buddy will let go of my hand and leave me.*
>
> *I am so strong*
> *I feel the blood in my body*
> *course through me*
> *Like a tidal wave*
> *a force of nature*
>
> *I can bend steel*
> *with my bare hands*
> *& bend spoons with my mind*
>
> *But I do not know how I will survive*
> *Without him*
> *'Cause when you turn on the light*

In a cold dark room
I am just a little girl
a little girl who holds on to herself . . .

And then I begged life not to take him away from me . . .
Then, I finished packing up the apartment.

Early December 2008, at Rancho Bizarro with Barbara Walters.
(© Ron Tom/American Broadcasting Companies, Inc.)

Chapter 12

DANCING AS FAST AS WE CAN

JUST BECAUSE PATRICK and I decided to get along in the cockpit of the airplanes we flew didn't mean we never had any serious "differences of opinion." I remember once as we were heading to our ranch in New Mexico during the summer months, during which, over Arizona, there tended to be a lot of large, potentially dangerous thunderstorms in the afternoon. On one such trip, we were in our Cessna 414 at the border of California and Arizona looking at a monster cloud that was developing right in our path. This thing looked evil. I was in the left seat flying, and I looked left and right . . . to go around it would take us fifty to one hundred miles out of our way, making us have to stop for more fuel. The thunderstorm was still in its early stages . . .

Patrick said. "I think we should go up to twenty-seven thousand. I think that'll put us on top. We'll go over it."

I peered at the building clouds. "Naw, I think we should go under it. That way if things get bad, we can just land and wait it out. It's still early in the afternoon; if we go high, we'll get caught on top."

"No. We. Won't. You're crazy."

"*You're* crazy."

"*Noooo . . .*"

And we were off in heated debate about the best course of action as the clouds loomed closer and closer. I don't remember what we decided to do. I probably used my trump card of flying left seat to take the plane wherever I damn well pleased while letting him, grudgingly, help me pick my way through. Later, to settle our disagreement, though, we got on the phone with Frank Kratzer, our longtime flying instructor and beloved mentor. We made our respective cases for "going under" or "going over" as clearly and convincingly as each of us could.

And then Captain Frank spoke. "You're both wrong."

We looked at each other with surprise.

"You don't go over it and you don't go under it. *You go through it,*" Frank said, "You guys! This is what you train for. This is why you have your instruments and weather equipment! Trust your instruments. And stay on your altitude."

The next flight that we had a monster cloud in front of us, Patrick and I looked at each other and smiled, took a breath . . . and entered the cloud. Relying on our instruments and training, we threaded our way through. Never even hitting a bump. We exited the area of bad weather, and it was as if it was just another day in the airplane and we were focused on the approach into our destination. But we knew what had just happened and had a sense of personal satisfaction, elation, and pride.

Yes. And that's how you get it done. You go through it.

—

SOMETIMES WHEN things got really hard and it was getting too much, I would feel a part of myself go a bit numb. I joked that somehow, somewhere, I lost some brain cells along the way. Areas that I was sharp in before, I now seemed to be fairly hopeless in.

Information that didn't have to do with Patrick's illness (or shooting a TV episode) I had trouble retaining. Since the beginning of his illness, I had been unable to read anything that took too much concentration, like a book. I would start to read a page . . . and then I would have to read the same page again . . . and again. After five tries I'd put it down and quit trying. Honestly. I had labeled this as having some kind of imperfect mind filter. While some of the bad stuff that was happening was getting filtered out, what I had for breakfast and figuring out a dinner tip got filtered out also. I was told later on that these lapses and being dazed is, in fact, a coping mechanism. It's your brain saying *this is too much and I've got to shut this down.* It's a way that your mind protects you, so you *can* be there for the things that are important and meaningful. It's just, you have to endure some temporary stupidity while some of the more unnecessary things get crossed off the daily list.

Of course there are things that snap you back into reality. Things that change everything and jolt you fully awake and sharp as a tack . . .

—

"FORTY THOUSAND dollars! It cost what?"

I was in the treatment room at Stanford asking our wonderful patient relations guy, Michael, to confirm what he had just said as he organized the new paperwork for Patrick's first Oxaliplatin treatment.

"Forty thousand." Michael nodded. "Insurance may cover it, but you have to sign the paper acknowledging that you are responsible in case it doesn't. Sometimes they don't cover it if they consider it experimental."

"It costs . . . *forty thousand dollars?*" I was still flabbergasted. I quickly glanced at Patrick and went back to Michael and homed in. "Is that for *several* treatments, or for a *full cycle,* or . . ."

"It's for one treatment," Michael confirmed.

"Wow," Patrick said, sitting on the bed with his feet up. He was impressed but seemed to be calm. Like it was all going to work out so he wasn't going to worry too much about it.

"*Forty thousand* for *one* treatment?" As you can see, I was still in shock.

Michael explained good-naturedly, "Believe it, or not, there are some treatments that go up to a hundred and fifty, sometimes two hundred thousand dollars a pop. We have some people from other countries who come in carrying up to two hundred thousand in cash. They pay *in cash*. It's pretty wild."

"I had no idea . . ."

Michael looked at me. "I have a friend I can call who would be able to tell me pretty quickly if it's covered under your insurance plan. Would you like me to do that?"

I smiled at him. "Yes. That would be great."

He was gone about ten minutes.

In the time he was gone, my mind was whirling with the possible ramifications if our insurance didn't cover it. It was scary, and it scared me for other people facing the same situation. I saw that this is how people lose their houses, and quickly put themselves into a debt that they, and their families, can never recover from.

I remembered a woman who, soon after Patrick was diagnosed, was using Patrick's name on a website to try to get some drug company in North Carolina to give her their new drug to treat her pancreatic cancer. The site made it look like Patrick was involved and supporting her cause, and if you helped that lady, all Patrick's fans would be helping him as well. It was wrong that she was using his name, but although it was wrong, I was beginning to be less critical of her actions and to understand her predicament. She had wanted to get into this drug company's

clinical study program because it's *free*. She had been refused by
the program because she was not qualified—just like Patrick was
before we discovered his bilirubin levels were right. So there were
two good reasons she wanted to get this experimental drug: because 1) the current drugs out there are just not effective enough
in the fight against pancreatic cancer, 2) the clinical trials are *free
of charge*.

I had been so focused on fighting this cancer with Patrick
that I never thought about the money. That's what we had insurance for, right? And now I remembered Doctor Fisher and Doctor Cabebe intoning when we first signed up at Stanford, "And
because it's a clinical trial, it's free!"

We were so lucky to have insurance. And we were so lucky to
have been in a clinical trial that had helped Patrick survive for the
past ten months. Treatment is phenomenally expensive and so
are hospitals. And we hadn't seen the end of them yet.

Michael came back in after checking on the insurance. I held
my breath. Yes, he confirmed, the Oxi would be covered by our
insurance. I breathed easier and signed the paper of acceptance.

And once again, I was happy we had insurance.

Actually, a month earlier in Chicago, we almost lost our insurance. I got a letter in the mail from the Screen Actors Guild
Health Plan saying that Patrick's insurance would be expiring
within thirty days. It said that he had not met eligibility requirements. This I couldn't believe! Patrick had been a working actor in
the Screen Actors Guild for almost thirty years! And even on past
projects, he still had money coming in that would have qualified
him for the insurance. I called Melissa Gilbert, who had worked
with Patrick two years earlier on a musical project. Melissa was a
former Screen Actors Guild president and all-around great lady.
She put me in touch with someone who might help me at SAG.
But it was true. Patrick's insurance was being canceled. Turns out

that SAG puts a cap on earnings—that is, you can only count up to a certain dollar amount for eligibility and then it no longer counts. How crazy is that? So all the movies he had done no longer counted. Melissa shook her head with sympathetic understanding, "Unfortunately, that's the way it is," she said. "Listen, even Patty Duke is not eligible for the Health Plan." And of course Patty Duke is a legendary actress *and* a former Screen Actors Guild president. I was disgusted. Luckily though, the series *The Beast* was going to qualify Patrick for the AFTRA Health Plan (American Federation of Television and Radio Artists). We just needed to bridge the gap over a month or so until it kicked in. Jeez.

It was a good thing we had an alternative. This was not the time we wanted Patrick to be without health insurance! I was thankful he was covered. And I knew how hard it must be for those that weren't, the hoops that they had to jump through, the limitations on forward-thinking treatments, the long waits and worry. I know I would have given anything for Patrick to be better. I could surely imagine that others felt the same about their loved ones.

—

USUALLY AFTER we finish a job, we have a little time off to recuperate. Unfortunately, though, cancer doesn't go on vacation. And besides, we had some other cookies in the oven. So, three days after we landed back in Los Angeles, Patrick had that first treatment of Oxaliplatin at Stanford, and then three days later we were sitting down for an interview with Barbara Walters at our Rancho Bizarro home in LA.

This was the first interview Patrick would do since he was diagnosed, so it was particularly sensitive for him. He had done the Stand Up to Cancer program, and had shot the television series. Now it was time for him to speak publicly and personally. It was important to us that we focus on the positive things—that he was living his life, and not just that he had a disease that proves fatal so quickly to so many people. Well . . . that's what *I* wanted anyway.

We chose Barbara to do the interview. Not only because she's a consummate pro, but also because there was some history there. Over twenty years ago there was a warmth and connection that started with the interview she did with Patrick after *Dirty Dancing* and the ensuing whirlwind. It was an interview that was remembered for a very long time, mostly because of Patrick's emotional moment when he spoke about his beloved Dad's death. And for Barbara, it would show up on the list of her all-time favorite interviews. Coincidentally, I remember (and I'm probably the only one who does) at the end of that first interview, Barbara looked at Patrick and me and mused, "I'd like to come back in twenty years and see how you guys are doing." At that time I thought, *Wow, she's being pretty optimistic considering that marriages in Hollywood don't last too long!* But here she was going to be—twenty years later with us again, even in the same house as before. Unfortunately, now, it wasn't any Hollywood statistic that threatened to part us.

We trusted Barbara to tell Patrick's current story in a fair manner. At the same time, we knew she could be extremely straightforward and blunt with her questions. But that was okay. It was one thing to pry into personal issues and then sensationalize it to the highest degree, and it's another to take that same information and report it as best you could. 'Cause let's face it, we didn't need to be sensationalized. What was happening in our lives was the stuff that highest drama is made of. But not everyone knows how to tell such a story. Barbara does.

Some weeks before her showing up, I had been asked if I would take part in the interview. I said no. I was afraid it would be way too emotional for me.

"They're asking again. They'd really like you to be a part," our publicist, Annett, told me.

I explained some of my concerns. "Look, this could be a hard thing for me to do. And it could come out one of two ways—I could be totally emotional and embarrass myself on national television. Or, I could keep it together so much that people wonder why I'm so cavalier in a situation like this and it'll look like I don't care."

The way I saw it, it was lose/lose. But . . . as the date loomed closer and they were still asking if I'd sit down for the interview, I capitulated and said I'd do it. I just decided that I would have to trust the situation. And however it came out . . . well, that's just what it'd have to be.

There's always a lot of activity when crews show up at our house to film. And this was no exception. Barbara has been doing this for decades, and the quality she and her crew strive for is very high. I loved it that she and her staff cared so much to make sure everything was done right. Everyone was doing their best, but the day didn't come without its own small mishaps and delays. It was pretty hilarious also how much everyone jumped to attention when something was wrong. Even our housekeeper, Celinda, and Dr. Fisher, who had come down for the day to be interviewed, had to be on their toes.

During George's interview there was a fly circling his head and face. Finally, Barbara stopped the interview and called out, "Can someone please get rid of that fly??" And she complained, frustrated, "Where are these flies coming from anyway?" I had to grin. "It's a warm day today and this *is* a horse ranch. There's gonna be a couple of flies around." I tried to swat the errant fly. Another person was trying to waylay the culprit also, while yet another scrummaged in his truck and came back with a can of bug spray. He quickly stuck it near George's face and sprayed all around his head. George held his breath! It was pretty funny that the doctor got bug spray all over his head. But . . . welcome to show business! Whatever it takes!

As if the fly disrupting shooting wasn't enough, five minutes later, the coffeemaker in the kitchen started to gurgle. I guess Celinda had started a fresh pot of coffee for everyone and the water had just heated up.

"Is someone making coffee?" Barbara stopped again and exclaimed in disbelief.

I wasn't in the kitchen, but I could hear people scurrying around in there, and in a few moments, it was quiet again. Barbara went on to finish her interview with Dr. Fisher without further interruption.

For Patrick and myself, the interview was tough. Before we even started, I had to go into our bedroom and give Patrick some moral support before he came out to meet everyone. And then, he surprised me by being what seemed to me angry and a bit bitter during the interview. He had been so unfailingly positive before and suddenly he was letting some of the "dark side" spew. And of course, the "dark side" is something that exists, but I hated that he was focusing on this to the exclusion of everything else.

There was a lot of pressure on him, since this was his first interview since becoming ill. And it's a difficult story to tell. It's like, okay, this is your chance to tell what it's really like. Do you focus on the bad stuff, or the good? Ideally, you do both, but he tended to focus solely on the bad. I was running through my mind, *why he would be doing this* . . . He *had* felt really *crappy* in the last few weeks. Did he feel so bad that he forgot how great he was feeling just two months before? Am I in denial about how bad he feels? He just had new chemo, maybe it's that? During a break in the interview, I stood off to the side with him and reminded him that he needed to tell the *whole* journey, not just the negative parts. He had been so strong and positive for the last eleven months. I wondered how could he have so soon forgotten. He even said that chemo was "hell on wheels." And while chemotherapy can be tough, he seemed to have forgotten the many good days it had afforded him, in addition to its contribution in keeping him alive for the last eleven months!

Do I sound unnecessarily petty about this? Okay, I was a little mad at him. Under this anger, though, what was happening brought forward an awful question. *Have I been totally wrong about what I've been seeing? How incredibly terrible would that be?* And then I remembered . . .

He just got finished playing a role.

Patrick tended to be one of those actors who had a hard time dropping his roles after work. I had always said, "Please don't let Patrick play an axe murderer, 'cause I don't want that coming home at night!"

Did I mention that he could be complicated?

And I'm not belittling cancer, but . . . He had just gotten through playing "Barker" for the last five months, a character who focused on the negative, was angry, and had a kind of smart, sharp bitterness. If you look at how he talks with Barbara and then look at the film clips they show of him as "Barker," you'll see what I mean! He just hadn't completely dropped "Barker" yet.

And by the way, I thought he was incredible as "Barker." I thought it was some of the best work he'd done. It may have been because of the illness, and it may have been the role, but definitely it was because of his talent. He immersed himself in this part in the best way possible. "Patrick" disappeared, and there was only "Barker." And he was stunning. I was so proud. There are things in his work on *The Beast* that *no one* could have done like he did. No one. He was just dazzling.

So Patrick seemed to be taking the opportunity to say every negative thing he could think of in the interview. Me? I was emotional.

When I saw myself later (I had to force myself to watch), I could tell the emotional stress I was under. My jaw clenched and barely moved along with other parts of my face and body, and I smiled a lot. Smiling is what us Southern girls do. We smile when we're angry and we smile when we don't want to cry. As with many women, it can be pretty much an automatic reaction to any intense feeling. Unfortunately, this happens because many of us are taught that if you express anger you are a bitch, and tears make you ugly or a pain in the ass. I teared up during the interview, but I was ultimately pleased that I didn't break down into uncontrollable sobs, which was one of the things I was afraid of. With the exception of a few occasions, I had kept it pretty well together in the past year. And if I was going to finally *let it all out* . . . let the entire deep, dark crevice of pain out . . . I wasn't going to do it on national television. Of course Barbara was going to ask questions like, "Have you faced the prospect of life without Patrick?" and there were people who thought that was unfair of her to ask. But I knew it was a question that had to be asked and I did my best to answer (and still keep it together), because I *had* thought of it. And what I came to was . . . I didn't know what I was going to do . . . I would just have to figure that out when I got there.

So we wrapped up the interview with filming some of the horses in the barn, and then Patrick swung Barbara in his arms and dipped her just like he had in his interview twenty years ago. And everyone left. I worried how the whole interview would come out once it was cut together. Both Patrick and I were very vulnerable. There was enough footage to do a lot of things. It's difficult to reveal yourself in such a raw and unadorned way, and then leave it in someone else's hands. But it was done now. I just had to trust all would be well. And if we were going to trust in someone, we had picked a good someone.

—

AFTER THE interview, Patrick and I headed back into the house to settle in, talking about how everything had gone with the interview, about the fly that zoomed around Dr. Fisher's head, and what we wanted to do with the rest of the day. I went to the kitchen counter to make a cup of tea, and stopped in puzzlement . . . *Where's the coffeemaker?* I looked around, and there was no coffeemaker to be found. And then I remembered hearing Barbara saying loudly, "Is someone making coffee?" and then hearing some scrambling. Turns out that Celinda, upon hearing this, was so horrified that she rushed into the kitchen, yanked the machine's plug out of the wall and . . . rushed out of the house to silence it. We found our coffee machine the next day in our little guesthouse out back, sitting on a table looking very lonely and left out.

—

SINCE PATRICK was no longer in the clinical trial at Stanford and the drug Oxaliplatin was readily available everywhere, we were able to move his second dose of Oxi down to Dr. Hoffman's in Los Angeles. This would be much more convenient than traveling up to Stanford every week, and you'd think we'd be celebrating. But no change in treatment comes without some hesitation and fear.

We had wrung every drop of good we could out of the PTK study and it had kept him alive for months. But the cancer had finally gotten wise and become resistant, and we were now forced to move on. The new drugs, Oxaliplatin accompanied by Xeloda, were an unknown to us, and there was always the possibility that Patrick would not respond to them. We were starting to tick off the few choices that were available to him, and even the choice to "go" with the Oxi and Xeloda seemed a bit arbitrary and unscientific for my liking. It was like pin the tail on the donkey. The choices were the Oxi and Xeloda, Abraxane, Tarceva, and then FOLFOX. FOLFOX is a combination of folinic acid, 5-FU, the intravenous form of Xeloda, and Oxaliplatin. Beyond that were drugs that, for the most part, hadn't worked very well at treating pancreatic cancer. And the list we did have was questionable as to whether they were aggressive enough to target his disease. We went with the Oxaliplatin and were warned of the side effects— extreme cold sensitivity. On the Oxi, even the cool night air can make you feel like it's freezing your throat and lungs, and you *do not* reach into the refrigerator for something without putting on gloves first. But this was more acceptable than the other drugs, which would cause him to either 1) lose all his hair, or, 2) break out in a severe, acne-type rash. Since he was planning to promote his series next month, we figured the cold sensitivity was the way to go. And that's how we arrived at that decision.

I didn't like moving on to another drug. I wanted Patrick to be around a long time and had no interest in exhausting our options, and moving to step two was a step in that direction.

But we were to take a little detour first . . .

"I'm feeling all this pressure in my stomach," Patrick reported to Dr. Hoffman, "like I'm getting topped off again. And I have to sleep practically sitting straight because I'm so nauseated."

Dr. Hoffman immediately sent him over to Cedars-Sinai to get an upper GI series done. Patrick swallowed some X-ray dye and the radiologist took X-rays of his stomach and small intestine to see how fast the dye was moving through his gut and whether there were obstructions along the way. They found that the stent at the exit of his stomach had narrowed by 80 percent. Of course this was causing a delay in everything emptying out.

The doctors were always amazed that Patrick was so tuned in to his body. And they attributed it to his being a dancer and keenly aware of changes in his body. I, however, was also able to confirm his condition before he got the X-ray, because when he burped it had that "garbage disposal" smell!

It was only two weeks since we had gotten home from Chicago before we were back up at Stanford taking a closer look at this new obstruction. Patrick was increasingly nauseated and vomiting and hadn't eaten in two days. Not good. We knew we were heading into another complication, but stayed calm and focused, like we were gunfighters with steady hands.

There was another CT to help determine where the obstruction was. And in the scan we got an unexpected good piece of news. We found that the disease was stable again. Yes! Even with only one treatment of Oxaliplatin, it showed it *was* having some good effect. It was also determined that Patrick needed a gastrointestinal bypass. He was scheduled for major surgery the next morning.

It's called an exploratory laparotomy with gastrojejunostomy. But gastric bypass is much easier to say. Patrick's pancreatic mass had grown to obstruct the first portion of his small intestine (called the duodenum), and this was not allowing food to exit from his stomach. So, what the surgeon would do during the gastric bypass was take the downstream, *second* portion of the small intestine (the jejunum), and bring it up to the stomach where the surgeon would then create an opening, and attach it to this jejunum so that food could pass directly out of his stomach, thus bypassing the obstructed exit. Basically, it's like having a stuck door, and the solution being to simply cut a hole and put another, new door in. We were checked into the hospital and careful attention was paid to our privacy and security.

And once more, I was sleeping on a rollout cot. On a practical note, I was learning how to pack better, getting the right amount of function and comfort. I also brought movies for us to watch on my laptop. I'd climb into bed with him, and we'd snuggle side by side, feet raised and laptop on the tray table. It was comfy! Dr. Fisher came in one evening and saw us in the dimmed room, perched side by side watching a film, and said, "Ah, drive-in movie!"

Our room was in the cancer wing. It was the first time we were not in the general population. It was a little creepy for me when I ventured outside our room to get something to eat; there were more visitors hanging out in all the patients' rooms, much more so than in the general areas of the hospital. It just had a different vibe, and I found myself unsettled by it. There were emphatic signs in front of a few closed rooms stating that you MUST DISINFECT HANDS BEFORE ENTERING. I was puzzled that it was so important to clean your hands . . . before you could see what was behind the door. Almost like it could be the Man in the Iron Mask, or some spooky version of Hannibal Lecter that was shut away behind the door. When I walked through this hall, I had a strong urge to take Patrick out of there. And then I realized why. Some of the patients there were dying from cancer. That's why the increased number of visitors, the decorations that attempted to make their rooms look friendly and homey. Part of me was perturbed. And I had the nonsensical thought, *Why did they have to put us here? Don't they know that he doesn't belong here?* But the other part of me was aware that this feeling I was having was me not wanting him to have cancer, me wanting to stave off death as long as possible. And when I reached our door, we had our own sign taped up. It said, CHECK IN WITH DESK BEFORE ENTERING. But it was for a different reason: We didn't want everyone knowing who he was and coming in for a quick peep!

The surgeon who would be performing the bypass was Dr. Norton. His reputation had preceded him and we felt we were in good hands; we loved him, in fact. But any surgery was scary in Patrick's case. Most frightening of all was that chemotherapy lowers your immune system and makes you more vulnerable to infection. Also because of this, Patrick would have to be off his treatment for *six to eight weeks* while he healed. Pancreatic cancer is so aggressive, I fretted that it would have a chance to start wreaking havoc in his body in that time. We had been warned that this bypass might happen, and we were just now putting together what the ramifications of this surgery might mean to him. But like Patrick said to Barbara Walters, "It's not the cancer that kills you. It's all the things around the cancer." And he couldn't be left like he was now.

Patrick came back from surgery, and I helped them transfer him into the bed. All had gone very well, and now it was a matter of healing. And it was the first time since he was diagnosed that I'd seen him really stoned on the pain medication. He was saying some pretty funny stuff, like when the nurse was trying to make sure the equipment at the foot of the bed was working properly. Patrick starting talking out the clear blue, telling her, "You're not going to get anything done that way. Everything's got to move. It's totally blocked." The nurse and I looked at each other quizzically. Patrick was more emphatic, "You have to move that truck out of the way first. Just move the truck first. It's blocking everything!"

The last time I'd seen him that stoned was way back in New York City when he was probably around twenty-four years old. He had had oral surgery, and someone needed to pick him up.

"I can get home by myself. I'll take the subway at Columbus Circle," he told me.

"No, I'll pick you up. It's no problem," I said.

I showed up on the curb on our Honda 750 motorcycle we had named "Buford" and waited outside the building. I was glad I was there to get him. In all the hustle and bustle of people walking on the sidewalk, I spotted Patrick, just kind of slowly, aimlessly wandering, looking up at the buildings, at the people, with a silly grin on his face. I waved him over, and he grinned at me and ambled over, taking about five minutes to put his helmet on. I stuck him on the back of the motorcycle and drove off. How he didn't fall off, I don't know. But we made it home safely.

And now in the hospital room at Stanford, he was giving instructions in a perfectly normal voice and talking about all sorts of things, none of which *made any sense at all*. I started to laugh, and it felt so good. And the nurse stifled a chuckle. Patrick looked at us, and our giggling only made him more insistent that we listen to him. He was so funny, but he was starting to get mad, feeling he was being made fun of. So, with great effort, I managed to start nodding and pretending I was listening seriously to what he said. It's all he wanted. But I was still smiling on the inside. He stopped talking and closed his eyes to rest.

After a few days, when all was going according to plan and he was healing well, I packed us up to fly back home. The whole ordeal turned out to be a blessing in disguise. While Dr. Norton was "in there," he confirmed that Patrick had a large abscess attached to the outside of his stomach. He was able to drain it, and Patrick was put on antibiotics. I was curious about this abscess but didn't think much of it until Dr. Fisher told me how lucky we had been to find it.

"If the abscess had gone a few more days, Patrick would have been a very, very sick man. Dangerously so," he told me. "It's really amazing that he wasn't already ill."

Once again Patrick had dodged a bullet. Angels were definitely watching over him. And guiding all of us.

Snowed in at Rancho de Días Alegres in New Mexico.

Chapter 13

DARK NIGHTS, GRACED WITH SNOW

WERE JUST a few days away from Christmas when we got home from surgery at Stanford, and I made impromptu plans to have my family over to our house on Christmas Eve, and Patrick's family on Christmas Day, like we always celebrated it. It was harder to organize because, up to this point, I had been able to run out and do errands, or whatever, for a few hours, leaving Patrick on his own. Donny was initially surprised that I could do anything. I supposed it was imagined that Patrick was something of an invalid. But he was active, completely capable, and thinking clearly. Well enough to shoot an entire TV series! And if something came up, he could always pick up the phone. But that was changing now. Postsurgery he was feeling quite weak, and it was hard for him to get around. He was also managing his pain much more with medication, and it made him cloudy.

We were learning a whole new way of dealing with pain medication. Pretty much his whole life, Patrick didn't like taking any kind of painkillers. I always thought it was a little ironic that he could drink himself into oblivion on occasion, but refuse to take half a Vicodin when his knee swelled up like a Zeppelin. But, like he said in another one of his famous magazine quotations, *"I'm a contradiction, and it's okay!"*

As I mentioned previously, he didn't take any pain medication at all while he was on the set of the series. And when he did, it was on an as-needed basis. That was wrong, we were now told. When managing this kind of pain and discomfort, you need to *stay on the medication.* You don't want the pain to get out of control before trying to bring it back to something more tolerable. It's much more effective to nip it in the bud *before* it gets going. This was completely against how we had approached it in the past, and it was a difficult transition for Patrick because, like I said, he didn't like to feel he was relying on anything. He wanted to be able to take it or leave it, and staying on medication religiously made him feel a little like a victim and nicked his pride a bit. But we listened to this advice, and once Patrick decided he wanted the relief, we adapted to this whole new approach.

Between the meds and his feeling frail, I didn't feel comfortable leaving him now unless someone was nearby to watch him. What if he started feeling bad? Needed something? What if he got dizzy and fell? This amped-up concern made things more difficult and more draining. Not having the freedom to just run out to the grocery store brought an additional pressure. I started having to plan when I could take trips to run errands and take care of other crucial items. And when I had an extra body there to watch Patrick, I made the best use of that time to get things done.

—

AT TIMES, late at night on his own, Patrick couldn't help but have some "dark thoughts," as he called them. Privately, back in LA at Rancho Bizarro, he had pulled Donny aside . . .

"You know I'm not going to beat this thing, don't you?" he whispered in a low and confidential voice.

Donny did his best not to be flustered and to react in a positive but honest manner. But his brother had just acknowledged what was probably the inevitable. And after a few quiet moments, they changed the subject.

"And I could get hit by a car crossing the street tomorrow," I'd say when the subject of dying came up with him (or anyone else). We're all going to die. The problem was—when. My comment about crossing the street was an attempt to lighten the heavy weight of the subject. I knew I wasn't going to get hit by a car tomorrow, I probably wouldn't even be near a street tomorrow . . . but I knew Patrick had pancreatic cancer, and his life was in jeopardy.

Patrick and I called ourselves "optimistic realists." We weren't going to give up hope that he could be the first to turn this thing around and thrive. At the same time, we knew the odds were highly in favor of the disease winning and taking him. "I do have this *tiny* bit of hope that I can really beat this thing," he shared with me. And always when he said it, his face couldn't help but be fill with emotion. This meant *everything*. It meant his life, and he didn't want to lose it.

He rarely talked about his "dark thoughts," though. I wondered if that was because he didn't want to upset me. Then again, we were so busy being positive that maybe we didn't want negative thoughts to get too much of a foothold in our lives and start to tear it down. The tabloids were already negative enough, and they were killing him off every other week. We didn't need more.

I know Patrick fought to stay positive, and he did an amazing job of doing so. Along with pancreatic cancer can come depression. Who wouldn't be depressed with a diagnosis that says your mortality card might be coming up? But pancreatic cancer can cause depression on a physiological level. But if he was suffering from depression, he was putting up a good show. And though it might have hit him in private moments and in some long dark nights, he would never let it get the best of him. But I know it could be challenging for him.

"How do you nurture a positive attitude when all the statistics say you're a dead man?" he asked, as if challenging you for an answer.

It's a good question. And along with that question brought a hope, a fear and uncertainty that's the hardest kind to face. And he navigated through all of those things with a tough realism, tremendous courage, and a fearless wisdom that I had never seen in him before.

On the rare occasions that he did say something about his feelings, what was on his mind was so profound that to stand there and discuss it beyond his initial statement would be . . . anticlimactic. "Where am I going to go if and when I die?" "What's going to happen to me?" When he said those thoughts out loud, it was like they filled the air with a weight that allowed nothing else in.

My heart would just jump out to him as I listened to these uncertainties. But I didn't know the answers either. I wished I did. Part of me felt that I should just go with some of the clichéd, tried and true answers that people give and seem to be very sure of, like, "You'll be in heaven," "Your body can't contain the energy that's you," "It will take another form and you'll be in this world again when you're ready." But I couldn't find myself saying that stuff to him. I'd be, not lying, but making something up. I wanted to comfort him. I knew what I *wanted* to believe, but there was no way I could be one hundred percent sure. And I didn't know how to say something that I didn't believe totally without sounding insincere. I was very much like him in this regard. *I'll know when*

I get there. Otherwise I'm just guessing until then. I had to stay with what I knew was true. And what was true was that I understood his fear.

So his questions would land with a loud thud, one that reverberated and shook the dust in the cracks of the house, and lay heavy in the air.

He pondered if he had made a mark on the world. If that mark had really meant something . . . If he had left a legacy with his work, with his work with horses, the forest on our ranch . . . He also wondered if he had been a good person, what kind of man would he be remembered as? It wasn't often that he voiced these thoughts, but he was pondering them . . .

Much of his life he lived out on the edge, and you can't do that all the time without making some mistakes. The edge can be a dangerous place. And I know he had some regrets about some behavior that had been very difficult for him to admit to and live with. And it was hurting him now. But the truth of him is, he's a very sensitive and goodhearted person. What was so hard for him wasn't so much that he hurt other people by his actions as that he let *himself* down. He had a very clear picture of who he wanted to be. And that was someone who was very kind, strong, and honorable. The hero . . .

One thing that happened with Patrick when he got sick surprised me. He became humble. He'd always acted like he was somewhat invincible. He even joked that being raised with his mother was like being in Pre-God School. She demanded the absolute best from him, and subsequently, he always had high expectations of himself. And sometimes Patrick acted like the world revolved around him. He had some bumps along the way, like when he came off the horse and broke both his legs against an oak tree during the filming of *Letters from a Killer.* But he came back, and he refused to be limited. And then suddenly with his diagnosis . . . he became mortal. Now, for some people to fall so far from their own pedestal might make them angry or bitter, lashing out at the cruel turn life had given them. What happened for Patrick was—he became an *even better person*. There is a beauty I've always seen deep inside him. And he proved to me that I was not wrong about this. It's what he called up into his life to face this cancer. And he had his weak moments. But they were the exception and not the rule. He was humble; there was a kind of fearless wisdom, kindness, love, and beauty that seemed as natural on him as anything. And he was *still* a fearsome fighter and a warrior who could be, and still was, kicking ass. He had just taken a higher road. He walked the talk. And it made him an even bigger man in my eyes as I witnessed what he was capable of doing physically, emotionally, and spiritually in this incredibly tough situation. It all came from an impressive strength within him.

—

WE WERE not going to let Christmas pass without celebrating. So we had the families over to Rancho Bizarro, and Patrick, still recovering, made his appearance for the holiday. But I could tell that his heart wasn't in it. It had only been nine days into his recovery after his gastric bypass. But although he felt weak, woozy, and uncomfortable, he would still manage to smile when called upon and grin when there was a joke being made. He even made some hilarity out of a hat that was bought for him and looked terrible on him. Everyone howled as he made a goofy face and then facetiously thanked his sister-in-law for the gift. She laughed, too. Hah! You had to be tough in the Swayze family. They can get as much mileage out of a bad moment as a fantastic one.

Part of me wished I could skip Christmas and just let him rest. And it probably would have been a helluva lot easier for me, too! But realistically, there was always the possibility that it might be the last Christmas we all had together. And what if it was and there were regrets that we didn't have the opportunity to be together one last time? I was concerned about the family. I knew this meant a lot to them.

Everyone of course noticed that Patrick was not feeling well during the holiday. I looked through their eyes and could see that *Patrick looked like he was sick.* For them, this was a different Patrick from what they were used to. Patrick, or "Buddy," as he's called, was usually one of the rabble-rousers. He was the older brother, and his word was law, or so he liked to think. He always brought energy into the situation, whether he was mixing it up with someone or sitting saying nothing. And here he was now—frail, quiet, and skinny. No one said anything about his weakened state and everyone went ahead and conducted Christmas with the usual raucous noise that attends all our gatherings. Patrick was recovering from major surgery, but I worried that they might think Patrick was going downhill.

In a way, when I was looking through my family's eyes, I was looking through my own at something that was hard for me to see. It was not easy to see him look like this. It hurt. I knew I had to allow time for him to heal, but patience is not my strong suit. My brain was always measuring every moment, taking stock of his every breath . . . In a way, his illness kept forcing me to slow down and not keep getting ahead of myself. *Slow down . . . slow down* . . . And when I did, time opened up for me. And it was a good, grounding place to be.

I knew he would recover. I knew it in my heart. We just needed the cancer to stay at bay during that time, and then we could get back on track. In the meantime, we were going back to our ranch in New Mexico.

—

ON NEW Year's Day, we packed up the dogs and cats and flew to Rancho de Días Alegres. It had been almost twelve months since his diagnosis, and we were going to welcome in a New Year. We held optimism that this year would be as good as or even better than the last. Barring any complications, New Mexico was a great place to heal. It was a moment to settle ourselves, get real again, and nurture the strength in our hearts as we moved ahead. Donny came with us, which was wonderful. I was very tired and hadn't yet gotten a chance to recover from our last weeks on *The Beast*, and December had been a busy month. Donny of course had quickly become an expert at helping out with Patrick's health shakes and oral medications, so he was of great service to me, in addition to being great company.

We loved the ranch and Patrick was always happy there. He liked it so much that in the summer of 2002, when things were rough in our relationship and we had a big argument, he went to the ranch and subtly threatened that he might not come back! And at that particular moment, that was just fine with me, a relief in fact! "No, you stay," I said, "stay as long as you want." When he saw I wasn't going to capitulate, he just got on the plane and came back to LA. Of course this was during one of his bad drinking spells, a really bad one . . . It's kind of ironic that it took this illness for him to put away drinking once and for all. And as much as I wanted him to stop and never go back, it was a terrible reason to have to quit. There were more than a couple of people who suggested that he should just go out and drink, raise hell, and have a good time for the rest of whatever time he might have left. What did it matter anyway at this point, they reasoned. Patrick had a certain appreciation of this line of thinking. He would have loved to have had *some kind of escape* from all this, but he turned to me with that ironic smirking grin of his and said, "I *would* go out and party, but I *can't* drink!" Alcohol was painful for him. Like that glass of champagne on New Year's Eve in 2008, it felt like pouring acid on his insides.

We were more isolated in New Mexico, and I was determined to make it as comfortable as possible for him. I set up an extra television in the bedroom for the times he needed to rest, and I had arrived with six large shopping bags of supplies, equipment, and food that he'd eat. I was getting very good at organizing all his medications nearby where they were easy to access. I knew he liked this organization. It made him feel like all his "bases were covered." Same as the backpack he carried with him at all times. That backpack was famous amongst our close circle of friends. It was loaded with all sorts of stuff: pictures, knives, adapters, address books, writings, lighters, scripts, handyman tools, multi screwdrivers, flashlights, Altoids, compasses, computer, nylon baggies, plastic baggies . . . I teased him every chance I got about carrying all that stuff everywhere. His bag must have weighed fifty pounds! "That's okay, go ahead and make fun," he'd sniff in jest in front of our friends, "but let us be back on the ranch and have the truck break down. I will be the only one that can get us out." And it was true. The one time in twelve years that we broke a tire rod back on the ranch, Patrick had the one tool we were missing to fix it and get us back to the house. So, yes, it was great that he was so prepared. And any little thing I could dream up to ask for—Visine, cough drop, walkie-talkie—he would have.

Patrick's energy was very low, and he was taking it slow. He spent a lot of time in bed, but when he was up, he'd quietly spend much of his time in what we called The Outback Room. This was "his" room, dedicated to all the outdoor equipment: special tents, sleeping bags, flashlights, picnic baskets, batteries, fishing equipment, maps, gun safe, gloves, water purification tablets, and on and on. We still had a large storage room in the Cowboy Bunkhouse next to our tack room for the bulk of the camping equipment, but this was the personal, special equipment that Patrick had put together for us. And even though he was not feeling well, he spent hours down there fiddling and organizing.

He emerged one evening and slowly ambled into the kitchen. "I'd like to think about organizing a camp trip in the spring," he announced, "You know, get some people together."

I was a little shocked . . . For him to say this while he was still coming back from major surgery was . . . amazing. It showed he was still thinking positively. His intention was to be here, and he wanted to use that damn camping equipment!

"Sure, let's plan it. We'll make a list," I nodded.

Now, our camp trips are not simple affairs. We don't grab a sleeping bag and a little one-burner stove and just go. We have tents, foam mattresses, horses and saddles, water to haul, cast-iron cookware . . . One camp I even brought a generator out and strung chili pepper lights and played country music on the boom box for a party. It was pretty amazing for people to drive up in the middle of nowhere, and out of the darkness and silence, see the glow of this beautiful camp all lit up and booming out music! What a treat! If Patrick wanted to go camping, then we'd figure out how we could do that. It'd be even more logistically challenging than usual, considering all the medication and health supplies we'd have to haul into the forest, but we'd done crazier things. If he was up for it, I'd find a way. I just needed a little rest first! But I had until spring to figure it out.

—

A YEAR before Patrick's diagnosis, our marriage had almost disintegrated. We had gone through a long, rough time, and I felt we were beyond the point of no return. I had given up. But then the thing that I thought would never happen—happened. We discarded all the things that were standing in our way and came back together with open hearts, better than ever, and we were living the love we really felt for each other. It was like we were Prince Charming and Snow White—the man and woman of our dreams. But we always had been . . .

I couldn't imagine what the journey through this illness would have been like if we hadn't had that profound healing in our relationship before his diagnosis. It was lucky regardless of whether we were faced with an illness or just continuing to live our lives together in health. And although I couldn't believe the cruel timing of this disease, I was grateful that we were with each other now. Of course, after he was diagnosed, even if we had parted, I would have come back to him no matter what. Like I said, I loved him, and that was something that was never going to change. But he would have thought that I came back out of a sense of responsibility and guilt and not because I cared. Because we had this almost fairy tale–like healing before entering into this dark forest of cancer, he knew without a doubt how much I loved him. We faced the journey together, like we had faced the rest of our lives. And my being there made it easier for him, because he could trust me unequivocally with his mind, heart, and body, and he had my strength and love to lean on. And it made it harder in another way—he knew just how deeply I felt.

And then we had our wish granted for our New Year's visit in New Mexico—it snowed. Heavily. Big white flakes covering the mountains, weighing down the tree branches, covering the ground in pure, velvety white. It was beautiful. And it just kept coming until we were completely snowed in and the generator kicked on. Yeah! What might have seemed like an ordeal to other people was a treat to us. And as always, we enjoyed the time, isolated from the world, until a snowplow made it through a couple of days later.

When the snow had melted enough at our local airport, we packed up the dogs and the supplies and loaded the plane to leave the ranch and fly back to Los Angeles. Patrick was feeling stronger now and was due back in Los Angeles for a press conference to promote the premiere of *The Beast*, which was scheduled to air the following week. We took off late in the day, as always, because Patrick always hates to leave the ranch. He was feeling a little tired and weakish by that time, so instead of flying copilot, he sat in the back with Donny, and I flew up front. The night sky was dark and the stars sparkled ahead as I listened to music on my iPod in the glow of my instrument panel. There was not much conversation, so I figured Patrick was sleeping most of the way. Every once in a while I'd look back and Donny would just nod and smile . . .

It was a nice smooth flight. We landed at Van Nuys airport, and I taxied onto the ramp where we park our plane and shut down the engines, their whirring hum winding down into silence. After the engines had stopped, Donny cleared his voice and said from the back . . .

"Uhm, Lisa? We didn't want to say anything while you were flying and upset you. But Buddy's been coughing up blood for the last two hours."

Chapter 14

GIMME SOMETHING REAL

Lucas poses for Patrick's lens.

IF YOU HAD read Patrick's medical reports, as I did not long ago, you would have wondered why we even bothered. In the reports, it looked incredibly hopeless, *"Oooo, this guy is outta here."* But it's different living it . . . Different when you're looking into his eyes . . . Different when you tell a joke and there's laughter all around. A smile, a touch of a warm hand . . . And when you see that the person doesn't really want to go anywhere, when you see him look on the day and see the gratitude he feels, the privilege to be here . . . *then read the medical reports* . . . They have nothing to do with the mystery of living. They can only point and remind us that we are mortal. But a written word, by itself, cannot make us die.

Even our smart, scientific Dr. Fisher said how important it was to see a patient in person. "There's a lot you can tell by looking at a person that you can't read on a page." We aren't stats on a page, we are not our prognosis, and we don't always obey the laws of medicine.

—

I HAD learned to react as quickly and effectively as I could when things came up. And I wasn't going to take anything lightly, especially when Patrick was coughing up blood. I sat in the back of the plane with him, and he showed me the stuff he was coughing up. Bloody spittle. I took out my cell phone.

"Let's just go home first. We can call someone from there." Patrick wasn't about to be too alarmed.

I was already dialing Dr. Fisher's number. "No, I'm going to call him now, this is too important." I put the phone to my ear.

"We've got the dogs anyway, and our bags . . ." he was reasoning.

Dr. Fisher answered and we talked briefly. I hung up and turned to Patrick. "We're going to the emergency room. It's the best thing," I said before he could protest, "Donny? Could you call Paul and see if he can come pick you and the dogs and our luggage up?"

Within a few minutes, Donny confirmed that my brother Paul was on his way so that Patrick and I could jump into our car to drive directly to Cedars-Sinai's emergency room. I called Dr. Hoffman on the way, and by the time we got there, they were expecting us and ushered us through quickly with hopes that no one would recognize us on the way in. Over the next few hours, he had completed a battery of tests and X-rays. I hadn't taken anything with me except my purse, and I was freezing! I felt guilty about snatching a thin blanket out of a closet to wrap myself in, but I was starting to learn how to work my way around in hospitals, and some things were fair game. It was midnight when the results were final and the verdict came:

Pneumonia.

It was a very large pocket, or infectious mass, that was located at the bottom of his left lung. They checked us into a room and began antibiotics. The doctors assured us that the hospital was the best place for him. This wasn't something to fool around with.

"I had pneumonia once," Patrick told them. "Do you remember when I had pneumonia?" he asked me, " 'Walking pneumonia' was what it was called."

"Yeah, I do," I replied. Twenty or so years before, he was feeling kind of sluggish and finally went to the doctor, who told him he had "walking pneumonia." It was pneumonia, but very slight, so he was still able to function, and it was easily treated with a course of antibiotics. It's funny—from then on, whenever I thought about "walking pneumonia," I always pictured Patrick in his jeans coming out of our dusty horse corral down near the house looking tired but bright, and . . . walking. That infection was easy to treat. There was no reason for us to think that this would be any different. We just had to be careful, that's why we were in the hospital, right?

"How long are we going to be here?" I asked Dr. Fisher and Dr. Hoffman. And I think they were a little surprised I asked that question. Perhaps they thought I was getting a little ahead of myself?

"Uhm, all goes well, maybe a week or two," they said brightly.

I made a list of what I would need from home and set myself up for another extended hospital stay. I was grateful that the cot this time didn't have a bar that hit me in the center of my back.

Over the weekend we once again had a trail of visits from various doctors: Dr. Hoffman; a lung surgeon; and Dr. Geemee Chung, our lovely and smart infectious disease doctor . . . And although Patrick may still have been slow and weak, his attitude was great, he was taking this in stride. But we could see that there was great concern among his doctors that the infection in his lungs would not respond to the antibiotics and get much, much worse. His health *was* in a compromised state, after all. In anticipation of this possibility, alternative, more radical approaches were discussed, the most reasonable being to remove the part of the lung with the infection. Okay, I had been keeping a finger on the pulse of this situation, and now . . . I started to feel a good deal of apprehension.

"Can he function with that much of his lung gone?" I scrunched up my face.

"Yes, it shouldn't be a problem," Dr. Hoffman said. "It's just making sure that . . ."

Of course surgery always carries additional risks, and further infection was always a worry. But the biggest problem I saw was that it would put Patrick off treatment for *another* six to eight weeks. That was a very long time for the disease to run unchecked, and that frightened me more than anything. As far as the surgery was concerned, both Patrick and I were like, *okay, if this is what we've gotta do, then this is what we've gotta do.* I could see that familiar look on Patrick's face—he thought this was all pretty fascinating. And it *is* pretty amazing that you can go and have a quarter of your entire lung removed and walk out within a week. Hell, I was fascinated, too!

Donny came to visit and was confused by our attitude. As I found out later, *no one* was as confident as we were about Patrick's regaining his health. Everyone feared that this might be the thing that killed him. Donny saw how Patrick was looking and worried. On top of that, Patrick casually mentioned . . .

"Oh, yeah. If the infection doesn't show some response to the antibiotics tomorrow morning, I'll probably go into surgery in the afternoon to remove that part of my lung."

Donny smiled gamely, but was flabbergasted. *He just said he might have part of his lung removed! How could he be so calm?* Donny, too, feared that his brother might be looking at the end.

The end. Call us ignorant, but we never thought that way. As far as we were concerned, we were in this for the long haul. I looked at Patrick, and I knew this wasn't "it." Everyone could prophesy doom and gloom until the cows came home, but this horse was staying in the barn.

Monday morning came and another X-ray was ordered . . . And guess what?

The large pocket of infection was diminishing. It was responding to antibiotics.

Patrick was dodging yet another bullet. But this one was like Neo in *The Matrix* bending backward with slow-motion ease to dodge flying pieces of metal. I should point out how coincidental it was that we were already on our way to Los Angeles when he started coughing up blood. Angels seemed to be watching Patrick's every step. It wouldn't be the last time that incredible, impeccable timing like this happened for us.

With the new X-ray results, there were smiles of celebration from everyone. But cautious celebration. Patrick wasn't entirely out of the woods and was still considered to be seriously ill. He was carefully monitored as he continued his antibiotic treatment.

While we were in the hospital, we had quite a few visitors. Annett; our lawyer, Fred; our agent, Nicole; and our manager, Jenny, all worked nearby, and in addition to visits, they sent over cookies for us, cookies for the nursing staff, and a steak dinner for me from the Ivy. Various friends and family members were able to stop in. It was a nice change of pace, and the visits gave me an opportunity not only to run home, change my dirty clothes, and say hi to the dogs, cats, and horses, but also to get out of the hospital for a couple of hours, which helped me keep my attitude fresh. All the visits were great, no one stayed too long, and Patrick still got plenty of rest.

It was during one of these visits that our agent, Nicole, mentioned that she had been approached once again by the William Morris book department to see if Patrick wanted to do an autobiography. This had come up again as a result of the Barbara Walters interview, which had aired while we were in New Mexico. Everyone was greatly moved by the interview. People wanted to hear his story.

"I'm just letting you know about the request," Nicole said. No pressure.

When we were alone, I turned to Patrick and asked him what he thought. He kind of shrugged noncommittally, in a way which said to me, *"Tell me what you think . . ."*

I had been urging him to do a book for a few years. "You have so much to say," I told him. I'd even organized a rough chapter outline for him. But he always kind of balked. I think he resisted because he put so much pressure on himself to be great at whatever he did, and with a book, he wasn't as sure of his ability. Also, in the past, I wasn't as available to help him as I was now. But every few months, I had revisited the idea with him, hoping to engage him. I had some nice little cameras, and when he got sick, I even offered to film him telling his story, thoughts, and ideas, and I would transcribe, edit them, and put them down on paper. But filming was getting to be less and less a good idea to him because he didn't feel like he always looked good.

And now . . . now the idea of a book was on the table again. And he had just shrugged, not "yes" and not "no" . . .

"I think if you're ever going to do it, now's the time," I offered casually, shrugging, "The people involved are great. It's the right team, and we can do this however we want."

He nodded affirmatively, "Sure, why not? Let's do it."

And twelve months after his being diagnosed with a fatal illness, after finishing shooting a television series, sitting in the same hospital where he first got the dreadful news of his cancer and where he was now recovering from a scary bout with pneumonia, we decided we were going to write a book. And we started making plans.

"What if I can't finish it?" he finally posed the sobering question.

I had wondered about that, too. What if? But I couldn't think of that. *Of course he can finish it! He's going to finish it!* But I didn't want to sound hysterical; I gave the "more calm" answer.

"Then we'll just have to figure something out."

That sounded like an acceptable plan to him. And I was happy, happy that he was finally going to do it. And happy that he had something to focus on, I had seen what a big difference that made in his attitude and energy. I also knew that it might be a tricky thing to pull off considering his health issues, but whatever obstacles we might run into, like I said, we'd just deal with them as they came up.

—

IT MIGHT seem strange that we'd launch into doing a book when the future was so uncertain. But in a way, I think that the nature of the work we did made it easier to deal with that kind of pressure. Patrick and I had been involved in the performing arts for most of our lives. And if there's one thing about doing a performance, there is never any guarantee how it is going to come out. It's part of what you leave yourself open to as an artist. You're not looking to copy, imitate, or mimic; you're looking for it to be fresh, real, like it's the first time ever. To do this is like putting yourself out on the flying trapeze. When it's your turn, you let go and twirl and *trust* that you'll catch the bar on the other side. Sometimes you don't! But if you want to do good work, you have to take those kinds of chances. It's thrilling, terrifying, and takes a particular kind of courage. For us to launch into a book with such unknown conditions ahead of us was almost normal for us. If we flew into the air without a net and caught the bar on the other side—fantastic! And if we didn't . . .

—

TRUE TO plan (*ours*, anyway) it was exactly one week after checking into Cedars-Sinai that we checked out and went home, just in time to watch the season premiere of *The Beast*.

Of course, after we landed from New Mexico, we had gone straight to the hospital and not *The Beast*'s press conference that was scheduled the next day. From experience we knew what a big difference press made in a project's success—if they don't know about it, they can't watch it. In this day and age, with so much media being thrown in people's faces, it's hard to get people's attention and hold it! You're getting smacked with all sorts of stuff every time you turn around! And now, after a gastric bypass and battling pneumonia, he was looking pretty thin. Other press requests came in, but he felt uncomfortable, and he shook his head firmly . . .

"Could you imagine me going on Leno or Ellen?" he said, "People will be sitting at home going, '*Look, Martha, he looks skinny! Look how skinny he looks. My Lord! I wonder how long he's got?*'" he used his best midwestern accent. "It wouldn't be about the show," he added, "it'd be about how I looked."

I didn't want it to be true, but he was right.

—

COMING OFF pneumonia, Patrick had been bumped up to a stronger pain medication—Dilaudid, also called Hydromorphone. The fact that he was ready for this stronger medication confirmed for me how much his pain had increased and that he needed relief. Hydromorphone is considered to be five to eight times stronger than morphine, and I would draw it out of a vial and then inject it straight into his port, with a saline flush before and after to keep the line clean. It can make a person pretty stoned-looking! I joked that he was like the mother in Eugene O'Neil's famous play *Long Day's Journey Into Night*. During the course of the play, Mom is addicted to morphine and pretty much floats in and out of the room during the entire production saying who-knows-what. Patrick was pretty float-y himself on this morphine derivative. However, its effects are not long-lasting, and I gave this to him on an as-needed basis on top of his regular pain meds.

The Dilaudid was delivered to us shortly after we arrived home along with other medical supplies. There was a ton of stuff! I was amazed at the amount of supplies that was delivered. I had always been economical and avoided waste. I grew up in a large, struggling family, and besides having to be thrifty, we were environmentally conscious about turning off electrical items and not letting the water run unnecessarily, long before it became politically correct to do so. All these newly delivered supplies looked over the top! But I was soon to find that I would use *all* these items and that I could spend all day trying to figure out how to use this stuff economically. But it was easier to just use what I needed, when I needed it. I had also underordered saline flushes twice and kicked myself for being so idiotic. I had to get over myself and go for the gold, ordering more than I needed. Bring it on! And that seemed to work out just about right.

Jose, our Harley-Davidson-motorcycle-riding nurse at Dr. Hoffman's, bailed us out by coming over to take blood and had given me the instructions on how to give shots. Other than these special trips, I had taken responsibility for all of Patrick's care at home from the time he got ill. To have someone unfamiliar come in would have been more stressful than it was worth. We would have worried about what might be reported to the world outside our sanctuary. We'd already had leaks from inside the medical profession. We were private and intended to continue that way. I had also graduated to more advanced nursing care. In addition to injecting the Dilaudid through his port access and giving his Lovenox shots, I also administered his antibiotics several times a day, hooked up fluids and albumin on occasion (which can be messy and a challenge to get going!). I was getting savvy enough to start suggesting possible solutions to some of his comfort issues, and anticipate his reaction to various medications and procedures. I also graduated to changing his port access, which involved the utmost of sterile procedures and additional bravery in sticking him at the port site with another needle, which I would then secure until the next week when I changed it again. This was all with his regular schedule of medication, food challenges, helping with hygiene . . . It was a lot. And I was starting to wear down.

Bad Day . . .

What a beautiful morning it was. Slept late, o'well. I organized myself and felt positive that I could actually get some things accomplished this day. This day . . . until I went in to give Buddy his first pills. He was sleeping. Sleeping late. Later than usual. And I guess I knew he wasn't feeling well before he ever opened his eyes, or uttered a word. And instantly I felt depressed. And it isn't that it's, "Wow, what a surprise," but I was feeling so good beforehand and was reminded how sad

and heartbreaking life can be at this moment. And I can run,
but I cannot hide from this fact. I just have to find some way
to live through this.

It's depressing. And do I blame him for it? Not for one mo-
ment. God, not at all.

February 2009

I was exhausted after *The Beast* wrapped. And then there was
the gastric bypass at Stanford, Christmas, and then the stress of
another hospital stay for pneumonia and waiting to start his chemotherapy again . . . It was all accumulating, and I was running
out of reserves. For the first time I started to wonder how I was
going to keep going and I felt panic rise in me. *What would hap-*
pen if I couldn't hold up? Who's going to carry the flag if I can't? I
tried to fight for the little moments I could give myself a break,
but they were no longer doing me any good. Oddly enough, it
was almost one year exactly since I had crawled into bed with
Patrick and, weeping, told him that I couldn't bear to deal with
this illness. That first time I was emotionally wrecked, and now I
was physically falling to pieces. I was thinking that maybe there
actually was a limit to my staying power, because I was starting to
hit a wall. But then someone stepped in to rescue me . . . Donny.

He moved into the house and started to help me. And his
incredible support gave me the meaningful breaks I needed at
that time. Suddenly my workload was cut by 30, sometimes 50
percent, and I got some of the rest I needed. And Donny was
wonderful, had a keen sense of humor, and was conscientious
and dedicated. I remember showing him how to give Patrick his
Lovenox shot in his belly, gently explaining how to do it, showing him how he could practice the injection on the rubber pad,
offered the DVD that had instructions. And then, hardly blinking
an eye, he went ahead and gave Patrick the shot without fanfare.

"Is that good?" Donny looked up and asked.

Hah! It'd taken me a couple of months to feel really comfortable with giving a shot, and it was a snap for Donny!

"Yeah," I nodded, "That's good."

—

NOW WE just had to hang in there until we could get him back on treatment. It was just a few weeks away now.

We started working on the book by talking, remembering all the stories we had and figuring how to put it all down. This was something that was going to take a lot of focus and effort, and some days he was up for it, and some days not. But he did his best, and we steadily, sometimes unsteadily, plowed our way forward. And it started to come together . . . In the prologue of the book we eventually titled *The Time of My Life,* I said:

> *You'd think that when someone close to you receives a death sentence it would inspire amazing insights and lessons about life. I know that's what I thought. But after his diagnosis and after I started to recover from feeling I was trapped in a perpetual nightmare, I looked around and couldn't see a damn lesson in sight. Yet slowly, as I've been dealing with getting past the initial grief and fear, living each day that comes and running around preparing for all the things one can't possibly prepare for, the lessons have started to ease out into the open. I couldn't force them out any sooner. They come in their own time when they, and you, are good and ready.*

So true . . . It happens in a way that makes you almost unaware that they are happening. Because they are happening on such a level of truth . . . they feel and happen like they are already an integrated part of you. Does that make sense? How about—

They happen before you know it.

I was amazed by how *accepting* Patrick and I had become of each other. Usually I hate that word "accepting." It sounds so . . . boring. It indicates a state of having "given up" to me. You know—*I can't change it, so I'm going to have to accept it.* But this "accepting" was so much more.

Maybe "accepting" isn't the right word. In its definition, some of the first things listed are *consent to receive, give an affirmative answer to, treat as welcome* . . . What I would add is—*with an open heart.* With an open heart . . . What a thing it is to open your heart and allow someone so deep inside you. And you see that other person feels the same. It's like you're giving each other direct access, short-cutting to your truth.

"Compromise" is another word that doesn't have such great connotations for me. But . . . compromise, commitment, sacrifice . . . aren't those words a big part of marriage? On their own, they sound awful, so conforming and restrictive. But when it's about someone you may not have for long, they describe love that is unconditional and unequivocal. And isn't that the love we dream of? Of course when we dream of this kind of love, we dream of it without the high price.

Buddy's and my relationship was just what it was. I discovered I had a wonderful freedom from the thought that I needed to change our relationship, or change him. There had been so many times that I felt there were aspects of our relationship that I couldn't bear to live with, that there were things I needed and felt were necessary for my happiness. But these things dissolved from my life. Evaporated. I'm sure this came about because of the possibility that I might not have him for long.

But do we really have anything, or anyone, for long? Even our own lives? I've always acted like it's a forever situation, and it's not. And it's gone so fast . . .

During his illness, time seemed to expand for me. It had a different timbre . . . It ticked but didn't tock, and it moved ahead as fast as my thoughts could take me backward. What did a day mean? Nothing. Two days? It's only time, and it doesn't do anything. But . . .

> . . . What does the thought in my head feel like? A kiss on your lips? A stroke of the skin on your arm. The light coming through the window just so? These things mean more than time. And are the only things that make me real.

I was becoming startlingly aware of what *was* real in my life. And it had nothing to do with the future and nothing to do with the past. Also, in the prologue of the book, I wrote that I was always afraid I wouldn't have enough time . . .

> . . . that I'd run out of it. That I wouldn't have time to do all the things I wanted. Now I'm seeing each minute that passes as a victory. As something I'm proud of. It's like I can gather all these minutes into my arms as if they're an enormous mass of jewels. Look what I have—another moment!

How could you not love someone with all your heart if it's only today, or even this moment that you might have that pleasure? Then . . . adding another day on to the joy you already feel with this person just adds more pleasure on top of pleasure.

I try to remember that now. When I look at the sky, my friends, animals . . . It's hard to remember that kind of happiness. No, let me put it this way: sometimes as humans, we find it hard to hold such happiness. But I try.

Chapter 15

ABRAXANE—THE BREAST CANCER DRUG

Tina naps with Patrick.

A MAZINGLY, ALL CONTINUED to go according to plan. After three and a half weeks of checking blood work and two CT scans to track the improvement in his lungs, Patrick was ready to start treatment again. And it was a good thing, too. He was feeling more fatigued, and the results of his CA19-9, the blood test that helps measure the activity of the tumor, had started to rise again, indicating that the disease had started to grow and we needed to stop it. Just in time, Patrick was back in the saddle to ride that

193

"chemo-pony" again. This time he was on the drug Abraxane, in combination with its trusty sidekick, Gemcitabine.

"Abraxane, it's the breast cancer chemo!" Patrick loved to tell anyone who wanted to know. He found this information interesting and just a touch risqué, a fun piece of trivia you might mention over a glass of wine and hors d'oeuvres.

The medical profession had found that this drug also had some favorable effect on pancreatic cancer, and it had always been on our list of our alternative options. Although he had had a pretty good result with the Oxi back in the beginning of December, Patrick had voiced his displeasure with the side effect of intense cold sensitivity. I wanted to stay with the Oxi. I mean, it worked, right? But his doctors reasoned there was no harm in giving Abraxane a try, and it was possible that the side effects would be more tolerable for him.

With every passing week on Abraxane, Patrick's CA19-9 numbers recovered dramatically, and his scans showed immediate improvement. It was what we needed. But it seemed to be taking a long time for him to *feel better*. He had always been phenomenally fatigued for a couple of days after any of the treatments he had, but now it seemed to take longer, if he recovered at all. He also had more nausea and vomiting, in addition to numbness in his fingers. But the CA19-9 numbers and CTs were tantalizingly encouraging, to say the least.

—

BY THIS time in his treatment, we were beginning to feel like old pros. It's amazing how fast we can adapt to difficult situations. I was now taking care of Patrick's treatment in an almost, not routine, but . . . automatic way. I didn't have to think things through so much, I just got up and did them. I had come to expect a certain level of alert activity from myself and I was acquiring some of the calm, cool ease of experience. And I didn't panic when Patrick transitioned to a pain pump that he could carry around while it automatically delivered his Dilaudid dose, and the initial programming was too high, so high that Patrick got overdosed. Leaving nothing to chance, I loaded him up and took him to Dr. Hoffman's to confirm that this was what was wrong and not something else. And once it was confirmed that it *was* the Dilaudid, and there was no need to panic, I took the opportunity to happily chat with Dr. Hoffman about other treatments and tests . . . while Patrick sat glazed-over nearby in his chair, barely ambulatory or even able to sit up straight! *Like nothing was out of the ordinary* . . . Nothing was "routine," of course. But that in itself was routine. You expect the unexpected, and then you start to get an idea when it might be coming around the corner.

Every aspect of Patrick's care was important, and Donny and I were very careful to do *everything* "right." There was his treatment, cleanliness and guarding against infection, balancing medications, and nutrition to keep him strong enough to fight this thing. I did my best to make no errors. One or two small mistakes could compromise him. He had to stay well and strong so that he could get better.

As always, eating was a continuing problem. He needed to consume a thousand to fifteen hundred more calories a day than a normal person since the cancer was eating what felt like the lion's share of Patrick's nourishment. The catch is that pancreatic cancer destroys your appetite. Obliterates your taste buds. Crazy, huh? The cancer makes you not want to eat, while it's consuming all the protein and nourishment in your body! What a recipe for disaster. Patrick was diligent about trying to eat enough to maintain his nutrition and energy. But it was hard and an uphill battle every day.

When Donny moved in, he suggested some alternative protein powders for shakes, since his brother was bemoaning the lack of variety. I walked over to a double door cabinet and swung the doors open . . .

"Let me show you what I've got," I offered.

The supplements practically spilled out of the cupboard, and I started to explain the various packages . . . Donny looked at the piles of different supplements in varying flavors.

"Oh," he said, "I had no idea you'd been through so many. Never mind." He grinned.

"And then I've got some stuff in this basket here . . ." I reached up and took down a big basket I had hung from a beam in the kitchen, "It's all high-quality products, please help yourself to any of this stuff. There's nothing in here he likes."

Part of the problem, and what made my, and now Donny's, job so challenging, was that Patrick would find something to eat that he loved. And he'd love it for about two days before he couldn't stand it anymore, and then we'd have to find something else.

In the last month, he was still feeling weak, and it was getting harder and harder to keep weight on him. In April, we put him on TPN, total parenteral nutrition, basically a big bag of white liquid hooked up intravenously in the morning and the evening that would give Patrick his complete nutrition for the entire day. We celebrated! No more worrying about his starving! Anything he ate during the day was now bonus food. I was so relieved. It took such an enormous pressure off.

The downside of TPN for Patrick was that he was hooked up to this thing for at least two hours in the morning and two hours at night. I know he didn't like it because it made him look like a sick person, and for four hours a day it was difficult to move around. But it wasn't going to stop him. He organized a satchel that he could stuff the TPN in along with its accompany-ing pump, and throw it on his shoulder and go about his day as needed. He'd even be out in our horse corral hanging out with the horses with his TPN setup slung over his shoulder! This stuff was not light either.

As with everything, we had to be very careful about contamination that could result in infection. TPN was particularly tricky. It has to be prepared fresh every time, and its preparation was complicated and opened several opportunities for something to get contaminated. Donny and I were serious about this undertaking and the hygiene. I sometimes felt like we were like mad scientists in our kitchen lab mixing this stuff up. There were large and small syringes, vials and packets we pulled from storage in the refrigerator, our particular "mixing" technique, priming tubing and connecting it, and a pump to hook up and start up, all the while cleaning our hands several times with antibacterial gel during this process. As time went along, I starting getting fancy with my measuring technique, pushing air from the syringe into the vial and then letting it automatically pop back with the right amount of substance into the syringe. Unfortunately, on more than one occasion, this backfired on me, spraying my face with a load of MVI adult liquid vitamin! Ugh.

You can't say my heart wasn't in it.

—

WEIGHT WASN'T the only thing Patrick lost during this period. Up to this point, he hadn't lost his hair. It sure had thinned a lot more than he would have liked, but still he had his hair.

"*Now* you're going to lose your hair," Dr. Hoffman prefaced Patrick's first treatment of Abraxane.

No ifs, ands, or buts. Patrick was going to go bald on this drug. And I wondered how he was going to take that. He'd always been so attached to his hair. Many times, I'd tried to get him to cut it and wear it shorter, and my best efforts were only mildly successful.

"I can't wear my hair that short!" Patrick would be emphatic. Why? "Because I have too many knots on my head! From getting hit, and stuff . . ." He'd brush his hand through his hair and then offer, "Here, *you* feel it . . . See?"

And yes, there were knots. *But not bad.* Still, he would never budge. I think he liked the romantic look of longer hair, and this was how he saw himself. I know that until he was well into adulthood, he had a secret fear of going bald. He confessed this fear to me early in our relationship, listing the one man he knew of in his family who was bald and saying that he worried that he'd be next. Whatever it was about his hair, it was always a big deal. His hair had even been written about. And it was noted that in the eighties, Patrick wore his famous "mullet," a hairdo that's short on the top and long down the back. Patrick read that comment and sneered, "I've *never* had a mullet in my *life!*" And then he saw a photo of himself in the eighties and sheepishly grinned. "O-kaay . . . Looks like a mullet to *me!*" He also always loved to tell the story of how the U2 singer, Bono, told a friend of ours that he read somewhere that Patrick had actually invented the mullet, to which he said, "You tell Patrick that *he* didn't invent the mullet. *I* did!"

Patrick laughed when heard that and replied, "You tell Bono that it's true—*I* invented it."

Of course both of them were making good fun of themselves. I mean, who really wants to take credit for a hairdo that looks pretty hideous now? When Patrick mentioned to the writers on *The Beast* that he might *have to* wear his hair shorter because of thinning, one of them made the unfortunate mistake of exclaiming, "But Patrick, you're *known* for your hair!" Patrick was *not* amused.

Many, many hours had been invested in styling his hair. Maybe I wanted him to cut it shorter just so I wouldn't have to wait so long for the hair dryer to shut off. Anyway, hair had always been a big issue with him and he was sensitive about it. I worried that separating him from his coif would be like Samson losing his locks.

"I always thought you'd look great bald. How could you not?" I enthused when he went on Abraxane.

He just lightly sneered at my comment.

I was protective of his positive attitude. I didn't want a little thing like being bald to interfere with it. Who knows? Maybe he *would* look good.

"At least you're a guy," Donny said at home. "I think it'd be a lot harder for a woman to lose her hair."

He knew that Donny was probably right about that. But again, *no comment . . .*

Anyway, we waited for the right moment to just go ahead and shave the whole thing off. And that moment was pretty clear when his hair had thinned so much that anything would be better than the style it was in. So, I went up to the barn and got a pair of horse clippers with a nice, size-fifteen blade and went to it.

I backed off and looked at him. And I thought he looked great. He was gaunt, you could see the stress of the illness on his face, his belly pouched out from accumulated fluid, and he complained that his ankles were swollen like a little old lady's. But every time I looked at him, I thought he was beautiful . . .

> *I don't care if you have speckles covering your nose*
> *I don't care that you're shiny and funky with a big Buddha*
>   *belly*
> *that I can rub and make a wish on,*
> *And I've been rubbing and rubbing . . . and forgot to ask for*
>   *a thing.*
> *I don't care that your legs are swollen and you look like an*
>   *old lady*

I don't care that you tell me that if you sleep wrong, the
        swelling's going to your hips,
or even up to your cheeks, to your jowls.
And I want to rub your Buddha Belly,
I'd finally find the wish that draws me there . . .
and I'm rubbing & I say that I want you.
My wish is that you want me too.

Spring 2009

I knew he wasn't classic, buffed Patrick, but beauty truly is a curious and mysterious thing. When I looked at him, I still saw . . . him. And how can someone *not* look great when you look at him and you feel so happy?

Unfortunately, the tabloids loved this new bald Patrick, but for an entirely different reason. Even one of our friends confided to me, "It's the first time I saw Patrick and he looked like a cancer victim." And yes, it's true, bald is the classic cancer look. And his baldness made him look skinnier. Some of the most unflattering and ruthless tabloid pictures were taken during this time, pictures that made him look as horribly sick as they possibly could.

But once again, I needn't have worried how Patrick was going to handle all this. When the hair came off, there was no trace of vanity. And when the photos were published on the front page, he didn't even get angry beyond a mere, rueful shake of his head. And he handled all of it the same way he handled his pain and discomfort—with a steady grace, strength, and dignity. And I was curious—was it really insignificant to him? Or, did he have to fight to maintain his dignity? Because the place he kept himself seemed not to be touched by such little sources of meanness.

Chapter 16

JUST YOUR DAILY 911 EMERGENCY

The portacath. I took this picture to remind myself how to put it together.

I T WAS THE last Monday in February, and I had Donny take Patrick to his chemotherapy appointment. It was the first time that I hadn't taken Patrick to chemo. I always liked to take him to his appointment myself. But I made some lame excuse why I couldn't go and amazingly, he bought it. After they drove out the gate, I checked the flight arrivals into Los Angeles, jumped in our pickup truck, and drove to LAX to pick up—

Our new Rhodesian Ridgeback puppy.

I had been working on getting a puppy since July of the previous year and had kept it top secret. I knew Patrick wanted another Ridgeback. We had lost our previous one, our beloved Gabriel, almost three years before, and in the last couple of years Patrick had asked about getting a new puppy. But I always balked because losing Gabriel had hurt so much and it was just too soon for me.

He understood, would wait a few months and then ask again. And in the summer of 2009, after he had gotten sick . . .

"I think I'd like to get another Ridgeback puppy," he mused out loud and looked over at me.

I'd say, "It's still just too soon." And I'd wince. But I was using my acting abilities to fib now.

I was already making calls to look for a new pup. We had gotten Gabriel from a breeder in the U.K., and we loved him so much, I went back to the same breeder. Julie didn't have any pups but helped me to find someone who did. And then I just had to wait for a litter to be born. And *finally* there were puppies born December 13. Julie helped me choose one. "He's an absolutely stunning pup," she remarked, "and he's a *big* boy!" I couldn't wait to see him, but I had to wait yet another twelve weeks until he was old enough to travel. After eight months of plotting and planning, our new boy was loaded onto the plane and due to arrive in Los Angeles.

I excitedly went to the airport to pick him up and schemed how I would surprise Patrick. Luckily, when I drove back through our gate, Patrick was home and in the bedroom. Perfect! I would take the puppy around the house, and have him prance out in front of our windowed bedroom doors so Patrick could discover him!

The puppy set foot out of our pickup truck and instantly made friends with our standard poodle, Lucas. This was going to make it easy!

I threw a ball out in front of the door, Lucas went to retrieve it with the puppy following playfully, and they brought the ball back to me. I waited . . . No Patrick . . . I threw the ball again. And again they pranced out in front of the bedroom doors and came back to me . . . Nothing. I tried a third time, and a third time they pranced back to me . . . It wasn't working! Damn.

I finally walked around the house to investigate, casually checking to see if Patrick was still there. As I discreetly wandered by, he opened the bedroom door and stood in the opening, looking at me suspiciously. He didn't say anything.

"Hey! Did you see the dogs outside in the yard?" I asked innocently.

"Yes. I did," he said.

"Well, did you notice . . . the puppy?" Glancing over, there was the puppy, just off to the side in the grass, romping in circles and tangling in Lucas's legs.

"Yes." He took a breath and said, "And I thought it was a neighbor's dog, and that Paul was bringing him over to show him to us. *And it pissed me off.*"

Hah! He thought somebody else's Ridgeback puppy was being flaunted in his face! I grinned mischievously at him. Patrick began to leave his upset behind, replaced by a growing delight . . .

"And then when I saw you . . ." he started to smile, "I knew something might be up."

"Well . . . come meet your new puppy!"

Patrick scooped him up in his pajamas that first day and held him in his arms like a big, relaxed baby. Kuma stuck out his tongue and gave Patrick a big wet kiss on his cheek. We named him Kuma, which means "Bear" in Japanese. And Kuma *is* a big boy, he's the biggest Ridgeback we've ever seen, and also probably the most adorably loving.

It was a wonderful day, with many more after. And you know . . . between the paperwork, the special crate Kuma had to ship in, and transatlantic flight, I spent a good deal of money getting that pup here. But I knew Julie would find me a good one. And what the hell, it was just money. I would have spent any amount of money to make Patrick happy. Money mattered less and less to me. What am I going to do with it anyway? This life isn't going to last forever.

This journey kept revealing lessons to me about life and living. I looked at the past and was amazed at how serious I had always been. Sincere and *serious*! I dubbed it—all those "wasted moments." But it wasn't that Patrick and I were wasting time. We were busy building a life, careers, and always improving our skills and ourselves. What it was that I was seeing when I looked back was missed opportunities. We were always working so hard that we rarely took time to take *real* pleasure in what we had. In my current situation, I lamented about that. More and more I was realizing that I wasn't enjoying myself and what life brought me enough. Maybe it's my Finnish reserve, the idea that I always have to be "better" or that it's "impolite to reward yourself." It's certainly a dancer's trait that Patrick and I shared—you never settle, you can always learn more, and you always strive to reach past your limits. But I've learned that's not *everything*. Yes, strive, but if you can't celebrate . . . you're missing one of the best parts of life. And I had to marvel at what I *did* have. Such riches, such love, such an incredibly fascinating world around me! How foolish is it to have missed any part of it?

I found there were many moments I should have been celebrating and having the time of my life instead of holding myself together in some kind of responsible way. The thing that was so enlightening to me was that those opportunities for enjoyment, love, and life were always there. Waiting for me. I just had to choose them. So what if things fell apart for a while? I could always pull them back together later.

We have a friend, Sheree, who worked as an assistant for us for over ten years. Sheree is very English, a smart, type-A personality with a high work ethic. And her husband, Randy, had been my aerobatics instructor and was bright and funny and wonderful. And he died in a catastrophic plane crash. I was devastated and so were many other people. But for Sheree . . . he was the love of her life. Randy had a unique and irrepressible spirit, and was one of those people who managed to have fun, any and everywhere he went. I remember Sheree saying how hard he tried to lighten her up when he was alive, to make her laugh and enjoy life.

"He tried . . . he tried." Sheree sighed ironically, and she acknowledged how she *just didn't get it,* not until much later.

I knew what she was talking about now. The good thing was—I had the opportunity to learn that lesson now. Before I lost Patrick. Not after.

—

A COUPLE of months after we got our new puppy, we also bought a new car. I was due for one, since the one I had been driving for twenty years had started to have some problems and was becoming unreliable. We could have gone with a Prius or something similar since we're environmentally conscious. But instead, we decided to go in a different direction. We got a high-performance car—the Nissan GTR. This thing is *wicked* fast. And we'd load the GTR to go to one of his chemo appointments . . . we'd pull on the freeway, put ZZ Top's "Tush" up loud . . . and I'd put the pedal to the metal. This thing took off like a bat out of hell. It could pin you back in your seat! Your cheeks felt like they smushed back into your ears. I'd look over and beam at Patrick, and I'd see him looking ahead at the road—a big, shit-eating grin on his face. And he'd chuckle . . .

"Wow."

—

I RARELY ever cried in front of Patrick. He caught me a couple times, though, once when I broke down in the shower, collapsing to the tiled floor for quite a long time while the water poured over me. A few days later when Patrick and I were alone together, he kinda looked off into the distance and mentioned, "I heard you crying in the shower the other night." I nodded, I couldn't say anything to him. What was I going to say? That my heart was breaking? I knew he knew why I was crying. I think he just needed to let me know that he knew.

It was a lot to handle . . . And then there were always the songs about love, about loss. And I had to note one night . . .

How Do I Live?

. . . without you . . . I'm listening to this song that gives me such heartache it's unbelievable that I actually continue. But I do, 'cause . . . you know why? Because it's like I'm someone outside myself, looking at me. I'm looking at me, and the pain I'm feeling . . . And I'm taking mental notes, like I'm observing some alien. "Look at what that woman's feeling." "Why does that woman crave that man's touch so much?" "What is it with that woman? I don't understand." And I guess it's the "I don't understand" that gets me through the song. This feeling is so immense . . . it downgrades to an alien. And I can listen to a song such as this . . . and have a kind of marvel . . . at the pain it evokes from the woman I watch.

March 1, 2009

We find a way to get through. We find a way to deal.

—

THE GOOD news was that as soon as Patrick went on Abraxane, his blood work and scans showed immediate improvement. But he was still spending more time in bed feeling unwell. His abdominal discomfort had increased and was severe at times. He had frequent nausea and was still struggling with keeping weight on. Despite the definite improvement in his CA19-9 markers and CT scans, his condition was deteriorating. Something was not right about it. The Abraxane was working, but it wasn't working.

We had gone to New Mexico between treatments, and what little time he was up, he moved very slowly and gingerly, as if each step he took was on tender feet. When it was time to go back to LA, we packed up and flew back as usual. And the next day . . . he was running a fever. I took him in to see Dr. Hoffman. He ran a CBC and discovered that Patrick had come down with an infection, a different one from pneumonia this time.

"It's something that sounds like 'Club Med,'" I told my sister-in-law, Maria, on the phone.

"Klebsiella?" she queried.

"Yeah, that's it!" I confirmed. "I remember it by thinking 'Club Med.'"

It was a bacterial infection, and he went on antibiotics. But the first antibiotic wasn't enough, so he was put on another one, Rocephin, hold the Abraxane, please. Again, with infections, we couldn't risk lowering his immune system below what it was.

So, I hooked up the Rocephin twice a day after and before his TPN and just waited patiently for the infection to pass. He was looking pretty poorly, but he had looked poorly before. As far as I was concerned, there was no reason to think that this wouldn't turn around. We just had to be a little patient.

I say that like I'm so sure, like it's no big deal. But after being with Patrick for almost thirty-four years, and being so incredibly close our whole relationship, I could be very empathetic with him. This was great because it made me a better nurse. But it also was another burden I had to bear up under. And it took its toll in wear and tear on my energy and my body. Particularly when he was feeling really punk . . .

> *When he's feeling bad, I feel like I'm sick, too. And it's almost*
> *unendurable. Beneath my day, the things I do, the smiles I put*
> *on my face, and the positive things I tell myself, I am beyond*
> *pain.*
>
> *March 15, 2009*

But also . . . because of this closeness, I knew that this infection was going to resolve. He was going to be all right. Who knows, maybe I was getting "spoiled" by all the little miracles that kept coming and showering down on us. And maybe I could feel positive because I truly felt the support of all those people out there in the world sending their energy and love and prayers. Patrick looked terrible, but I could feel him . . . inside . . . and I felt strength.

But to the doctors, the situation could be dire. They warned us about something called "rolling infections," where in Patrick's compromised state, he could start to get one infection on top of another, and they would just keep *rolling* until his body couldn't take it anymore. Uh-huh. That's one to file in the memory banks. But to me, this was a small infection. We hadn't even given the antibiotics enough of a chance to work yet.

Patrick's weakness and poor health were concerning enough that Dr. Fisher visited us at Rancho Bizarro in LA. I thought it was just a "fun" visit since George was in town, a chance to connect and catch up. But there were other things he wanted to discuss.

Patrick was sitting in bed, propped up with pillows watching a little television when Dr. Fisher arrived. And Dr. Fisher did his usual check of all his vital statistics. We chatted, talked about the old, beat-up, taped-up cars we all had in the past, and Donny came in and sat down with us. And after the chitchat came to an idle, Dr. Fisher segued, introducing the concept of DNR, the abbreviation for the order "Do not resuscitate."

"I'm bringing it up as something to think about," he put out there in the air.

I was like, *Why is he talking about that? Does he think we're there? We're not there yet, are we?* But I paid close attention. Like I did with everything.

"Say you hiccup and your heart stops," Dr. Fisher broached carefully, "Things like that can happen . . ."

I looked at Patrick, and he was listening to Dr. Fisher with calm attention.

"Attempts at resuscitation are not as clean and pretty as it is on TV," Dr. Fisher warned gently, "it can be pretty tough stuff what they have to do to you. The lungs could also fail. And you might find yourself having to make a decision if you're going to call 911 or not."

You know, I could either listen, and absorb the information, or I could dissolve in tears. I chose the former and kept listening.

But this made me see how unprepared I was. I don't know what to do. And it made me wonder even more—how do I survive? How do I not lose my mind?

"I'd just hate to see you," Dr. Fisher nodded at Patrick, "or anyone else, go through that kind of treatment if it's not going to do any long-term good."

We were all nodding kind of slowly. It was quiet for a moment . . .

And then Patrick cocked his head to one side and looked at Dr. Fisher a little skeptically . . .

"Are you saying that this is going to kill me?" he queried.

I furrowed my brow and looked at Patrick, and then Dr. Fisher. But Donny, across the room, snorted back a laugh.

To Donny, this was another perfect "Patrick" moment. We'd been dealing with advanced metastatic pancreatic cancer for over a year now. And here Patrick was, sitting in bed saying, *Is this going to kill me?* Like it was a foreign concept that hadn't occurred to him yet! And Dr. Fisher had to take a step back, regroup, and answer as best he could!

There was disbelief in Patrick's voice, a calm "nobody has proven anything yet" tone. Donny heard it. And I did, too. Or maybe that's what I heard because that's what I truly believed. I mean, yes, we were talking DNR, and it was good information to have, and it was wonderful that Dr. Fisher was brave enough to introduce the concept . . . but I didn't see us going there yet. Nobody was going anywhere right then. But okay, DNR, that's good to remember.

A week after the DNR conversation—Patrick got better.

—

DURING HIS infection, his CA19-9 rose from around 2,000 to 4,000. But things were improving. He beat the infection and was on his way back. He also started to look good again and finally regain some of his strength. We were still going to have some more tap dancing to do before the end of the month, though.

In the meantime, enough of that damn Abraxane! It wasn't working for him and was sending him downhill faster than anything. And another week later, we moved on to Tarceva and FOLFOX. FOLFOX is a combination of three different drugs, one of which is called 5-FU. Of course, we couldn't help but have a bit of fun with the "F U" part. The Tarceva . . . well, the Tarceva had the unfortunate side effect of rashes, terrible acne-type rashes that could break out on your face. And this was particularly true when the drug was actually effective. With Patrick, this rash happened only on his head, and only *after* he stopped taking the drug. As is often the case, the chemo's effects could be fairly long-lasting. With us, it sometimes lasted up to a month after being off of the drug. This was a gift when he continued to show improvement even when he wasn't actually getting treatment, and a bummer when the side effects were stubborn about going away.

When talking about chemotherapy to treat pancreatic cancer, Patrick always liked to remind people that it was like treating cancer with caveman tools. And though I hated to agree with him about that, he was right. At this moment, everyone is fighting to find better ways of treating various cancers. We knew going into this that the options available for treating pancreatic cancer were extremely limited, and the survival statistics for this disease were bleak. It's why we wanted to get into an experimental drug study program. Nothing out there was aggressive enough to treat this disease. We always had to be looking outside the box for ideas, because none existed within the regular protocols. But I disliked Patrick's "caveman tools" statement, and politely pointed out that the PTK and Gemcitabine treatments were the reason he was *alive* ten months and counting after his diagnosis. Not only alive, but shooting a TV series, and now, fifteen months later, once more starting to thrive. For me, that was success. Every month, every day I had with him, I cherished as a victory, and I was ready to thank and defend anything that helped him do that. Chemo was helping him to be here. But no, chemotherapy wasn't going to cure him. The best we were hoping for was that he'd live long enough for a newer, better treatment to come out. But as we moved further into the year 2009, we were not seeing one on the horizon.

—

THERE'S SUCH a burden of responsibility in knowing when to give medication, how much to give, when to hold back, and when to change it. Dr. Fisher joked that I'd probably gotten my full M.D. training by now. But like I said before, it was important that I was doing it. No one could watch out as closely as I did, and I was getting pretty savvy at troubleshooting complicated situations. But I had learned, and was still learning a lot.

Even now that Patrick had a pain pump to automatically administer his Dilaudid doses, we still had to watch for when he needed more or less on the dose, and do our best to interpret the situation on both a medical and a personal level. Donny and I were *very* grateful for this labor-saving device. And before we got this pump, Donny had a bit of a funny mishap. Now that Patrick was better, I took the opportunity to quickly update my flight training in Dallas. It was the first time I had been away from him in more than a year. But I had Donny, so I turned Patrick's care over to him, including the individual Dilaudid doses that I was giving manually to Patrick. And when I got home, from Dallas, Donny looked worried and started to complain to me . . .

"I'd just given him a Dilaudid and five minutes later, he'd ask me for another one! So, 'okay' I think to myself . . . this must be what Lisa and he were doing, so I'd give him another Dilaudid." He said, frustrated, "And then ten minutes later, he's saying 'Donny, do me another Dilaudid'!"

"Oh, wow," I winced, "You should have called me."

Patrick was totally stoned on the synthetic morphine. I felt sorry for Donny being put in that position, but I knew what Patrick did. He did it with me! He'd get an injection of Dilaudid in his port, then it worked so well that he'd forget he just had one and ask for another one! I eventually ended up hiding the vials so he couldn't give himself doses at will and possibly overdo it.

This happened when I woke up one night in New Mexico and found him sleeping sitting straight up on the side of the bed with a bare syringe in his hand! And in some ways, maybe the Dilaudid worked too well. Maybe he finally got a little bit of the party he'd been hoping for, if you get my drift. But I was not about to deprive him of any kind of relief. That is . . . as long as it was safe.

So I told Donny, "Just say, 'I just gave you one. Let's wait ten minutes and if you want another, I'll give it to you.'" Fair enough, huh? Usually Patrick would forget about it, and if he didn't, he really needed it.

But when we finally got the pain pump put on, it was the first programming on it that dosed Patrick way too heavily. We had to pull it back and reprogram. But it freed up Donny's and my time—before the pump, we barely had a moment to do anything else because of the labor-intensive endeavor of giving him a Dilaudid injection every thirty minutes. By the way . . . Patrick didn't want the pump. He didn't like the thought that he had to be attached to pain medication and look like a cancer victim. And I know there was the scary, troubling thought that couldn't help but come up—*Will I ever be able to live again without this pump? Or is this what it's going to be from here on out?* It was going further down the road of giving up his life to being sick. And there was the fear that it would be hard, if not impossible, to reverse it.

But something had to give. Though Patrick had mixed feelings about it, the pump was a great relief to Donny and me. And . . . I didn't ask for much, and he knew it.

—

ONE MORE bump . . . In late April, Patrick's WBC, his white blood cell count, went up, indicating another infection. So he continued more antibiotics and went on *another* antibiotic, flagyl po, to treat the *other* infections that can happen when you do antibiotics . . . Okay, that's fine, as long as it works.

And it *was* working . . .

The infection was resolving, he was "coming off" his Dilaudid moment caused by his new pump, and Donny had taken him to Cedars to have the excess fluid in his belly drained off, which had started to accumulate for various reasons that are too frustrating to mention. The fluid was drained on a Friday. On Saturday we loaded up the car with all his supplies, our laptops, sweat pants, and flip-flops, to drive out what we now called our "Bat Cave Exit" off our property in Los Angeles.

But before we got in our GTR (the high-performance car that we had nicknamed "The Beast"), Patrick pulled at the tubing that stuck out of the pain pump pack and snaked its way up and into his port.

"What am I going to do with this?" he said in an unhappy "I told you so" voice. "I'm not going to walk around with *this*."

"Look!" I said brightly and started to wrap and coil the tube around him, like I was dressing a little boy for school, "You put it in the fanny pack . . . and . . . and then the hose can go up through your shirt . . ."

It didn't tuck as easily as I thought it would, but I remained positive, "See? You can hardly see it." That wasn't going to stop us from going. No way. We plopped ourselves into the car, Paul pushed open the gate, and we got on the freeway and headed south.

We were on our way to treat ourselves to a luxurious week at a spa nestled in the hills just north of San Diego where we would recuperate, indulge in being treated, and spend quality time working on Patrick's book.

Chapter 17

OUTRUNNING THE AMBULANCE CHASERS

Standing beside the GTR, aka The Beast,
holding three-month-old Kuma.

WHAT WE CALLED the "Bat Cave Exit" off our five-acre property in Los Angeles came about as a way to thwart the paparazzi. We had our main gate that everyone pretty much knew about. When Patrick drove out this gate with Donny, I'd always tell him in a sugary-sweet voice, "Just remember to smile, honey!" because photographers were lying in wait outside. But we eventually found another way of exiting, at the far, opposite end of our property. It was kind of a hassle, and involved driving over a bit of lawn, but it worked, and as far as I was concerned, *I was damned if the paparazzi were going to follow us all the time!*

Even when we used the Bat Cave Exit, I remained extra-vigilant, made Patrick duck down out of sight in his seat, and flung my dark hoodie over the top of him. Trust me, he didn't like doing this. I mean, he doesn't "run" from anybody. But I was very insistent, and I think it was easier for him to oblige than to refuse me.

Sure, photographers could take Patrick's picture, I mean, what's the big deal? Well, it was a big deal. He was sick, and he was in a life-and-death struggle, and I didn't want anyone *making money off his illness.* You know these magazines say it's "the public's right to know." Well, Patrick is not a public servant, and this information is not in the public interest. He's a movie star. And the "the public's right to know" defense is just an excuse to use his hardship and deeply personal struggle as crass entertainment. I wasn't about to make it easy for them to rake in the cash over this horrible and taxing disease.

People were surprised that we didn't jump up and counter all the false reports about Patrick during his illness. What they don't understand is that, if you do that, you're playing their game. It puts you in the position of always fielding the balls they throw. *You might as well be one of them,* since you'd be participating in *making them more money.* They're calling the shots, getting you to respond to whatever comes into their heads, and gaining critical access that they wouldn't have otherwise. We were not going to let a tabloid decide for us what we were going to say and not say. Ya know?

There are so many reasons why it is better not to respond, not the least of which is your dignity. There was one erroneous report in particular that incensed Donny. He couldn't believe that we weren't going to do anything about this hurtful article. I had to assure him of what I already knew after being in the public eye so often for so many years, "Trust me, it doesn't feel good now, but we're going to take the high road. You'll see, it may be years from now, but you'll see that it was the right choice." And making the right choice for you as a human being *doesn't always give you instant gratification.* But in the long run, it matters, to you.

But does it hurt? Yes, it does. Hey, look, women are devastated when photos of them looking *fat* are printed . . . Need I say more?

We always had to be very careful what we *did* say in the press about Patrick's illness. I tended to be too open and "tell it like it is." And our team always pulled me back. And very early in this situation, I saw that the people guiding us were absolutely right. If we gave too much information, it would backfire on us. It gave the media a foot in the door, it led to further questions, further speculation, further demands for answers. And after you gave *all* of that information, it *still* could be interpreted however that press entity chose to do so. Which would lead to further questions . . .

There were also leaks from within our trusted circle. Friends of friends, friends of family who were "just checking in" with his mom or brother, or God knows who else. It's terrible, but unfortunately we aren't the first ones to have been betrayed in this way. We had to warn family members not to share any information with anyone they wouldn't trust with their life, and sometimes it worked and sometimes it didn't. And in a funny way, this was particularly hard for my mother-in-law, Patsy, who is very open and can be very talkative. We'd have to remind her and remind her, "Don't give any interviews to these people on the phone. Just say 'no comment' and *hang up.*" "I do! I do, do that!" she retorted. We'd roll our eyes when we'd read another report quoting her, but couldn't help but chuckle. I mean, although I'd get ticked off at her, I couldn't help but be charmed. "Patsy," I'd say, "when you say, 'Leave him alone; this is heartbreaking; he doesn't deserve this; I know he's going to fight; I just don't want him to suffer,' you are *giving an interview.*" She'd sigh a little helplessly, "Oh . . . I just don't know how to get them off the phone!" That Texas-bred lady was just too polite to hang up on them.

There also appeared to be leaks back on the set of *The Beast.* And when one person asked me what was the matter with spreading some of Patrick's "good news" to counter all the negative things printed, I had to say, as kindly as I could, "It would be nice to make that choice for ourselves. It's his life, and my life. We'd like to decide our destiny, not someone else. No matter how well-intentioned."

Wow, I sound like I'm already in my tabloid tirade. I was saving it for later, but I guess the time has come now. Hah!

—

AS THEY say, a picture is worth a thousand words. And there were photographers gunning for Patrick. Donny and I got pretty good at spotting them on the streets outside our gate. They were pretty clever at where they'd position themselves, sometimes in several places. Donny in particular became good at drawing them out and making them miserable. If you haven't figured it out, the Swayzes are not pushovers. They don't take things lying down, and though Donny has a heart of gold, he's no exception to the Swayze rule.

It's impossible to talk about dealing with the paparazzi without focusing on Donny. He was the star of the show!

Some of the things he did were . . . He got all of them to follow him on a wild goose chase into a park where he then revealed himself, busting all the paparazzi following him, at which point they got back into their cars, disgusted, and drove off. He drove his van onto Foothill Boulevard and spontaneously pulled right in front of a paparazzo's car, totally blocking his view of our street, and sat staring at him, like, "Tell me to move. I dare you." He'd run interference by driving out ahead of us, sometimes propping up a blanket with a hat in the passenger seat as a Patrick decoy. An avid cyclist, Donny would scope out where they were parked on his rides, peering into one vehicle and coming back to describe how it was outfitted with a camera on a tripod, and so on. We were also told how these vehicles have generators that will keep the air-conditioning going on those long, hot summer days . . . I was wondering how they managed that.

In one of the last confrontations, Donny spotted a car with very dark windows parked on Foothill, close to the entrance to the freeway. He pulled his bike over to stare into the windows, but they were so dark, he couldn't see anything. So he rode back to the house, got our mega-bright Coleman Powermate flashlight, and rode back over and shone the beam right into the interior of the front seat. There he saw a man sitting. And the man was staring at Donny with . . . hatred. Slowly, grimly, the man turned the key and drove off.

With a kind of secret glee Donny confided to Patrick and me that he hoped one of them would come over to confront him. He had one sentence prepared, and he would use all his amazing acting talent and his expertise at playing lots of tough guys to say, "Just to let you know, you're messing with my family, and *I'm not afraid to go to prison.*" When he told us that, we laughed and laughed, and the thought of it kept me chuckling for weeks.

Of course this whole situation was emotionally tough on him also, as well as the rest of the family. And when he went into his usual, local grocery store and saw his brother on the front of a tabloid magazine that was saying something awful about him once again, Donny went to each checkout line, picked up all the magazines, and turned them all backward in their slots. He didn't say a word, just went and did it, then he just checked out his items and left. What's pretty damn incredible is that when he went into the store again, the magazines were gone. Donny could only surmise that they took them down out of respect for him and his brother. It was either that, or they saw him coming and started running around saying, "There's that crazy Swayze again. Quick! Take all the magazines out before he sees them!"

Donny's my hero! So many people would just let themselves be pushed around. I know that my solutions were to make Patrick duck down in the passenger seat and weave in and out of the back streets and try to be clever about parking spaces. It was so "girlie" of me . . . Donny faced it head on. And I loved him for that. He's someone you'd want on your side, damn it! He set an example for me in life. And I learned a good lesson from him.

—

MAY 2009 was one of those months that Patrick was being killed off more than usual by the press. Starting early on May 8, they reported that he had a lung removed and felt he had "done all he could"!

> *LUNG REMOVAL SURGERY . . . in a heartbreaking decision Patrick Swayze turned down a last-ditch effort to prolong his life by removing a lung . . . after months of painful treatments and fighting so hard just to get up in the mornings, he felt he had done all he could.*

And then on the ninth:

> *GOODBYE PATRICK SWAYZE . . . started to say goodbye to family and friends as he prepares for death following the spreading of his pancreatic cancer.*

And on May seventeenth:

> *PATRICK SWAYZE PANCREATIC CANCER UP-*
> *DATE . . . refused potentially life-saving operation . . . lung*
> *infection didn't respond to treatment . . . a long, painful re-*
> *covery was not how he wanted to spend his last days.*

May nineteenth:

> *PATRICK'S LOVING GOODBYE . . . unable to speak*
> *because of sores in his mouth and throat caused by his che-*
> *motherapy treatments. Patrick communicates with his wife*
> *of more than 30 years, Lisa Niemi, and brother Donny by*
> *pointing or writing notes . . . note to him (Donny) to please*
> *look after Lisa.*

WOW. AND you have to figure that if these reports showed up in one place, they were copied by five to thirty-five other tabloid entities around the entire world. That's a lot of wrong press. And then . . . May 20 and 22:

> *SWAYZE'S STILL ALIVE . . . ! Patrick Swayze did not*
> *die yesterday, despite a Florida radio station reporting other-*
> *wise . . . Twitter tries, fails to kill Patrick Swayze on Wednes-*
> *day!*

It was after the reports that Patrick had actually died that we decided to release a response. It was too much! This time we would put out a photo. We were in New Mexico having a nice time with a few friends, one of them a wonderful photographer. Patrick asked him if he would take some photos of us.

"I would love to," Brian responded with enthusiasm.

So, Patrick put on his cowboy hat and we went outside with the dogs pushing their way in front of the lens to get in on the action. We picked a couple of photos and sent them out. We figured a picture of him alive would be all that was needed at this point. The only thing that was missing was, we should have had Patrick holding up a newspaper like a kidnap victim with the day's date on it: May 23, 2009. Proof of life!

—

WE WERE always focused first on Patrick's getting better. The photographers, the less than honorable people, the false and negative tabloid reports seemed like something that was always scratching at our door, hovering in the unsafe world that lay outside our gate. It was as though the tabloids appointed themselves to take up the gauntlet and represent us out in the world. Without any true information. Of course, they didn't care what *we* thought about that. You know . . . Patrick and I were, and are, pretty hardy folks. But reading that your husband is "saying his last farewell" and "final good-byes" as he "comes to the end" . . . Even if it's not true, it can't help but affect you. I tried so hard to be positive, but then there would be a report splashed in my face saying *your husband is going to DIE!* Even if he wasn't sick, if someone was saying to me several times a month that the one I love best in the entire world is going to die . . . don't you think that after a while, it would turn into a kind of insidious torture? To all appearances, I handled it pretty well. I even convinced *myself* that I wasn't affected by all these false, negative reports. But then . . . I'd be having a pretty good day, and by the afternoon, I'd suddenly find myself getting mad, depressed, argumentative, and ending up dissolved in tears. Seemingly for no reason! I looked back at the day to see if something had triggered it all and what would I find? A terrible, negative tabloid report. They affected me far more than I ever imagined. I hate to admit that. I *really* hate to admit that, and reserve the right to take back what I just said. It's a matter of my own personal pride that they not "get to me." But okay, yeah *they did.*

But whatcha gonna do? You can't fight 'em. Not unless you want to spend a lot of money. And again, do you want to spend that much more time letting them rule your life?

If I was feeling this hurt, sadness, and angst, what was happening to the one who had the most to lose? He seemed to take it in stride, but I know it made it harder for him. At one point after reading a negative report that he was once again on his last legs, Patrick closed the article and mused sardonically . . .

"I guess they figure that one of these days they're gonna get it right."

Donny and I imagined that these reporters were sitting in their rooms, at their desks, doing just enough research on pancreatic cancer to make a halfway educated guess about what *might* be happening in Patrick's life. We joked how it seemed like some of these reporters showed up for work, put their feet up on the desk with their first cup of coffee in their hands, and said to themselves, *"What kind of sh*t can I make up today?"* But how terrible is it that a press entity's reports that are picked up all over the world are saying that you are dying, going to die, or are dead already?

"It's emotional cruelty." We finally put that in a statement we released. And when I saw it in black and white print, I thought it looked a tad dramatic. "Emotional cruelty . . ." But the awful truth is, tabloid reports eat through your soul like a worm. And even though I was walking around, functioning, and laughing, I felt it eating its way through, mottling my heart, eating the coating around my veins and killing me.

So, yes, "emotional cruelty" is a fairly accurate way of describing it.

There's a wonderful saying used in twelve-step programs, "God grant me the serenity to accept the things I cannot change, the courage to change the things I can, and the wisdom to know the difference."

We were unable to change how the tabloids reported things. Our calling them on their emotionally cruel reporting wouldn't have changed anything then. And my calling them on it probably won't change anything now. But maybe . . . just maybe . . . people who read this will see them for who they are and understand the lack of integrity in their reporting. And they will remember.

I saw a man from the *National Enquirer* (just one of the tabloids I had a problem with) on *The View.* This was when they had submitted themselves for a Pulitzer Prize for their breaking the news of Senator John Edwards's illicit affair. This guy sat in front of Whoopi, Barbara, Sherri, and Elizabeth and bragged about the stellar reporting at the *Enquirer.* How thorough they are and how much they check their facts. Okay. If I made a list of all the headlines from this and other tabloids, along with the gist of the article written, you would see *just how inaccurate* the reporting is. And I'd probably take great delight in going on a rant and busting a few of these papers. But I'm not going to. Because the truth is, in the long run it won't matter. And certainly by the time we get to the end of this story, it won't matter at all.

So, back to the high road!

—

BUT WAIT, we *are* on a higher road. We are winding our way into the mountains north of San Diego, having ejected ourselves from our Bat Cave Exit and successfully thwarted the paparazzi. We turn on to a quiet private road, rumble over an old wood bridge, and pull up to our destination spa.

Chapter 18

RALLIES AGAIN

On our trail ride with friends.

M OMENTS ARE LIKE jewels to me. I gather them into my arms . . .

And each of those jewels gives me the confidence to stand up and look death straight in the face and say, "No one is going anywhere today." Now, at the moment I say that and celebrate this victory, I back down in humility. Because I know how fragile this life is. How I ultimately can't control the outcome.

But you know what? Still, all those moments, all those jewels,
are just as special. And that makes me a very rich lady.

July 7, 2009

We spent an entire week at the health spa, Cal-a-Vie. Patrick
loved it. Heck, *I* loved it! And it felt like stolen time. I don't think
I'd seen Patrick smile so much in a long time. Of course, you can
really use it to get in shape. The spa offers up to thirty-five exercise classes a day—from cardio, weight training, Pilates, to ses-
sions in their Olympic-length pool, to Zumba, and I was gung-ho
to take advantage and, I hoped, quick-start my routine into exer-
cising more. Maybe even start losing the weight I'd gained from
eating all those hospital cheeseburgers and fries. What a concept!
So I was up early to work hard and happily in several classes before collapsing back at our bungalow for lunch. We'd then spend
the afternoon and evenings working on his autobiography—that
is, unless we had a spa treatment . . .

Patrick always did like to be treated luxuriously. And it
wasn't that he was some snobby connoisseur. If anything, he
seemed like he was a kid being secretly treated to an ice cream
cone or something special like that. He looked to have the same
delight with his clothes. Most of the time he wore faded, torn-up
jeans and T-shirts (long before it ever became fashionable to do
so). And he was one of the few men who could look hunky in a
sleeveless, cut-off T-shirt that read, "In case of nuclear disaster,
put your head between your legs and kiss your A** good-bye."
But he appreciated the finer suits he had to wear on occasion,
straightening a jacket in the mirror before we went out, noting
the material, the cut of the garment, saying, "God, this suit is
beautiful!" It would make me smile. "Yes, it really is." And while
I like his beat-up wardrobe, I loved how beautiful he looked in
the finer stuff.

Patrick's attitude really improved at the spa, and even his skin started to have a bit of glow again. The staff went out of their way for him, tailoring his massages and spa treatments, coming up with ideas that might help relieve the swelling that had been happening in his legs and other things that had been plaguing him. And the chef whipped up his own fresh, delicious protein shakes whenever Patrick wanted.

Of course, everyone's face lit up when they saw him. *And they didn't treat him like he was sick.* I think that's what made the biggest difference to Patrick—for the first time in a long time, he was being treated like a human being rather than a patient. A pampered human being at that. And it was revitalizing to him.

And when we went back to Rancho Bizarro, it was with a fresh attitude, and lots of pages for his book.

—

IN BETWEEN his next treatments of FOLFOX, we were back at the ranch in New Mexico with friends and saddling up for a trail ride. Since he came off Abraxane, his hair was growing back and the short, tight hair looked good on him.

Our friend and neighbor to the south, Steve, also had some friends visiting, and we all decided to ride from his roping pens to our camp meadow through the forest. Steve had plenty of horses, just "come on down and get on," he said. I had been working hard and was happy not to groom and saddle four horses! We were all packing our saddle horn bags with water and lip balm when Patrick announced that he was taking his horse Nation to ride, a handsome, big gray Arabian gelding. My heart sank. Taking Tamnation was not a good idea, not at all, and this was why: First, although Nation can be the perfect gentleman, he is one of those horses who doesn't behave well if he hasn't been worked in a while, and I hadn't worked him in a long, long while. Second,

Nation is a freakin' idiot when it comes to trailers. Nation doesn't even like to be tied next to a trailer, let alone to a fence by himself. And today was no exception.

When Patrick and our ranch hand went to put the saddle on him, Nation squirreled around and the saddle shimmied to the ground, further spooking him and getting him prancing about. I yelped as I watched him step all over one of our favorite saddles. But it was so typical of Patrick to do this. He was always pushing the envelope. What's one more wild horse to deal with? It's not the first time he loaded a too-fresh horse up and launched into an adrenaline junkie trail ride. In earlier days I would go along with his ideas, whether it'd be taking a horse up a mountain, grabbing the yoke of a strange airplane, or jumping off a cliff into a strange lake all the while cringing at what was happening and could happen, but not wanting to be a scaredy cat. If I balked, Patrick would sigh in exasperation, as if I was being thoroughly unreasonable. And sometimes I was being unreasonable, and sometimes I wasn't. As I got older, I learned how to say no to the things I didn't want to do, and it surprised Patrick every time.

"Lisa, why? Come on! What are you worried about??" he'd shoot at me and impatiently throw up his hands.

"Naw. You go do it," I'd say brightly, like it was not complicated, "I'm staying here."

And sometimes he would, but nine times out of ten, he'd turn around and stay with me. I think he much preferred the company. I didn't feel bad . . . he had years of coercing me into doing things.

And today, here in the beautiful New Mexico air, I could have, but I wasn't going to help Patrick with this horse. I kept my mouth shut and held my breath, hoping he wouldn't get hurt handling the silly-acting Nation.

I held my breath. Because of his illness, and although he was looking better lately, he was not moving fast and his strength had dwindled substantially. All his resources had been going to fight the cancer, and it was a tough battle. But I thankfully let my breath out when Patrick walked over to the car. "I'm leaving him here," he said and shook his head with disgust.

Yippee! We drove down to the pens. Of course, we were two hours late and the other party was long gone. (See Chapter 6, Patrick is always late!) No matter, it won't stop us from riding. And we cinched up and untied our horses.

But when we pulled them around to mount them, Patrick heaved his weight up the saddle and promptly settled back to earth after moving only a few inches. He looked at me, a little distressed, and whispered, "I'm so weak! I can't get up on the horse!"

The cancer had substantially reduced his muscle mass. And though the status of his health had drastically improved from the bumps earlier in the year, his weight was still down.

"What can I say?" he shrugged with a wry smile, "I'm a skinny guy."

And though he was pretty bony now, he was still a large man *and his presence was still big.* But strength was an issue, and more than once he'd remark how weak he was with a puzzled kind of amazement. I was tempted to ask him to arm wrestle, but I was afraid I might win this time, and that would not be such a happy victory.

The last time we arm wrestled was when I was flying aerobatics. The plane I flew was a Pitts S-2b, a beautiful, cherry-red biplane. It's a very sturdy and nimble aircraft, but heavy, meaning that the forces on the stick took some muscle to handle. My right arm and forearm had become like steel. I stood in the kitchen one night, showing my arm off to Patrick, trying to convince him of my new physical strength.

"Look! Look how buff I am! Hey, let's arm wrestle!" I proposed excitedly, "Then you can see how strong I am!"

Patrick dropped his head and kinda chuckled a little, "Naw, naw, Lisa . . ."

"Come on! I bet you! I bet I can beat you," I enthused. I mean, I was working my arm on this heavy plane several times a week, and he was pretty much sitting around doing nothing at that point. "Really, just try!" I entreated . . .

He kinda sighed, like he was indulging silly old me, and stuck his arm out. Within about one and a half seconds, he beat me, so easily that I took a step back and looked at him.

"What am I doing moving furniture and loading all the luggage?" I said. "From now on you're the one who's moving all that stuff."

So, the moral of the story is—even though the cancer had made him lose so much strength, I was not about to underestimate him.

And holding on to the horse now in New Mexico, he confessed that he didn't have the strength to pull himself up onto the saddle. I looked at him with concern, trying to figure out how I could support him in this moment, "Can I help some way?" He grimaced and looked around. Our friends were already on the other side of the trailers, out of sight . . . Patrick nodded over at a large wooden spool sitting cocked to one side, "Let's go over there . . ."

I nodded, and we led the horse over to the spool. I knew what he was thinking.

"Let me get up here, and I'll swing my leg over the horse," he said, and he concentrated as he climbed carefully up onto the spool. Of course the horse wondered what was going on and spooked away from him and the spool.

"You're going to have to stand on the other side of the horse and keep him still," he said.

I was already nodding . . . and I moved the horse back into position. I wasn't crazy about my foot possibly getting stepped

on by a twelve-hundred-pound horse. But I so wanted this to
work for Patrick, and the horse seemed reasonable. What's a little
foot getting stepped on anyway? I stayed close to the horse's side
to make sure he didn't move away. And Patrick leaned in and
swung his leg over. He grimaced uncomfortably and then settled
himself in.

He was on!

I ran over and jumped on my horse, and we called out to our
friends as they rounded the corner of the trailer on their mounts.
And they called back, "Whooo-hooo!"

It was a two-hour ride to the campsite, through pine forest and up and down mountains. I hadn't been riding much in
the last year, and during the last thirty minutes of the ride I was
getting unpleasantly sore. This ride was ceasing to be fun and
getting exhausting! I looked back at Patrick to see if he, too, was
getting tired, and he was riding along pleasantly. *Whaat?* We got
to the campsite and *my a** was kicked!* There was no food, we
had no extra water, and I rued the thought of riding two hours
back on my sore bum. And then eureka! I had cell reception!
Quick . . . "Uhm. I can't take any more riding. Do you guys mind
if I call and see if someone can come get us?" This was not exactly a pioneer-woman move on my part.

I looked around for any other sore co-commiserates, and
there were none. Not our friends, and not Patrick, who had
parked himself on a log bench and was enjoying the scenery. My
eyes narrowed. *He must be lying.* But *I* was the one whining. He
hadn't uttered any complaint, not now, and not during the ride.

Our friends did end up rapidly capitulating, and Patrick—
Patrick just shrugged, like, "Whatever blows your skirt up." Happily, I maintained enough reception to call Steve. He and Jeff
showed up with a trailer for the horses and a cooler with beers
and a bottle of vodka. After a quick cocktail (except for Patrick),

we jumped into the truck and headed back to the roping pens. There, Steve's friends had already been knocking on a bottle of Jack Daniels, chatting, and just not hurrying off anywhere. I was sure that Patrick was not feeling well and wanted to get home, but of course not, he stood chatting for an hour or so . . .

"Hey!" Steve had an idea, "Why don't we go to my house and light up the fire and hang out there?"

"Sure," Patrick shrugged and turned to us thoughtfully, "What do you guys think?"

"Ahhh . . . No," I replied, and said that we all were pretty pooped and wanted to get home. I wasn't going to underestimate Patrick's energy a second time. If we went, chances were we were not going to get home until two in the morning.

In New Mexico, we had gotten a beautiful blanket of snow that winter, and spring is always gorgeous with the river gushing and the new green leaves and newborn ducklings, turkey, and fawns. And then summer brings the tall, warm grass and moody afternoon thundershowers. Patrick and I strolled down to the tack room together to visit the horses lazing under their shelter and to look at the camp storage room and the new shelves that were now up and getting organized. The air was breezy, the grass lolled in the wind, and the horses' manes drifted on their necks as they grazed. The sky was just moody enough to cast a mysterious light across the fragile earth. Patrick's gaze took him across our lively flowing river, the pasture, the forest beyond, the setting sun, and the horses with their hooves scuffing the earth . . . he turned to me and his eyes were earnest and misty . . .

"*I want to live,*" he said.

—

ON JULY 6, 2009, Patrick had another set of scans. The scans showed the disease was stable.

Stable!

We were beyond grateful.

—

BACK AT Rancho Bizarro in Los Angeles, at 4:50 P.M. I ran out of the barn as hard as I could and steered down to the house, legs and heart pumping. I was amazed that I could still move that fast when I wanted to.

I burst through the door of our house and yelled out, "Assirah's foaling! Assirah's foaling!"

"Are you sure?" Patrick asked.

"Yes, I'm sure! It's going to happen *now*! You better hurry or you're gonna miss it." And I turned and hiked it back up to the barn, slowing as I approached her stall so I wouldn't upset her. Her water broke and gushed out. At the same time, I felt a rush inside me. *Oh, my God, this is really happening!* A small foot appeared, and then another . . . I crouched in the stall's doorway and waited for more. Assirah paced in her stall, these two little stick feet sticking out of her. *Why won't she lie down? If the baby comes out while she's standing, I'm gonna have to play catch!*

Within a minute, Patrick was there and my brother, niece and others were starting to congregate. I clumsily started to text people to let them know it was happening and to tune in to the webcam site!

We had a webcam set up because I was determined that we were not going to miss this foal's being born. Up to this point, somehow Patrick and I had managed to miss every baby's birth. So I had gotten a foal predictor kit and started milking and testing the mare every day for almost two weeks before her due date. My sister-in-law, Jessica, set up a webcam. It was fabulous. We could be in the house and still monitor the mare. We left it on all night beside our bed. I also gave the site to many of our friends so they could help be on "foal alert." "Please call us immediately if you notice her pacing, or lying down, anything that looks like she's gonna foal," I asked. I even had friends in Europe tuning it (hey, they were up when we were asleep!). Everybody loved it and many left the site on all day, even at work. It was great for them when people came by their office desk (in Beverly Hills no less!), and when asked about it, they'd casually say, "Oh, just keeping an eye on a mare that's about to give birth."

As it turned out, I was checking Assirah's progress on the monitor when I noticed her pacing with a little more agitation than usual, which sent me up to the barn for my discovery.

Assirah finally decided she'd lie down to begin the laborious process of pushing the foal out, and Patrick stood behind me in the stall doorway. When the baby's nose was fully out, I reached over and broke the thick, pliable sac covering his delicate nostrils. He was wet and slick and lay still as Assirah kept pushing and resting, pushing and resting . . . I felt like a basket case. I felt like *I* was the one having this baby! I could hardly stand it! I glanced back at Patrick and he glanced at me, the same wonderment and excitement in his eyes.

The foal kept coming, down to his hips now. I held on to his front feet very gently to give Assirah a little traction. Oh, my God, to see a small horse come out of a mare's uterus is like seeing her delivering a kitchen chair out her vagina. *How does she manage to do this!*

By the time the body was out, I could see the foal breathing. *Thank God.* He lifted his head and wobbled around and then sank back to the straw. Assirah lifted her head, barely, and wearily let it fall back down again. She was totally spent. Beyond exhausted! It took great restraint from all of us to not rush into the stall and to let mother and baby rest for whatever moments they needed.

The baby was the first to move. And instantly Patrick was in the stall!

He tied up Assirah's placenta, which was hanging out the back, so she didn't step on it when she got up. And he moved to assist the baby in standing. It's an amazing fact that foals generally stand within the first hour of life, a necessity out in the wild, where the baby not only needs to stand to nurse, but also needs to run from predators!

I was pretty excitable at that point, happily stressed, my heart bursting with pleasure as the foal started trying to figure out how he was going to get up. "Get out of the stall!" I said urgently to Patrick. "Leave him alone! Let him get up on his own! Please, please!" Partly because I didn't want Patrick to be too invasive with the foal, and partly because Patrick was standing on a webcam that anyone in the entire world could tune in to, and he was not only hooked up and carrying his medication pump, but he was doing so in his cowboy pajamas, the ones I bought him in beige flannel with little red campfires and cowboys cooking breakfast on them.

"You're on camera!" I called out at him.

He grudgingly moved out of the stall, but was instantly happy again and easily forgave me my excitable antics. It was a joyful time, and everyone was pretty excited. When the foal finally stood up, he tumbled back to the earth, clunking into the sides of the stall on the way down. The next attempt had him crumpling with his legs twisting uncomfortably. After one more time of this, I was giving Patrick instructions again, this time for him to "just *get back in the stall!* Hurry! Just keep him away from the wall! Please!" And Patrick helped to protect the baby in his falls. And it was thrilling when the foal finally stood on his own, a monumental feat that never ceases to amaze. He wobbled and within a few minutes he scampered across the stall like an awkward spider. We burst into delighted and charmed laughter, proud of this first flight on his feet.

5:30 A.M. Shirin Jewel gives birth to a filly.

Chapter 19

AND ANOTHER THING

WE HAD ONE new, beautiful foal. Our good fortune wasn't over yet . . .

Three days later, my beautiful mare, my princess Bint Bint Subhaya, foaled. We had another baby! Again, we were present for the birth. Bint Bint had worked so hard during the delivery that several times she emitted a long, high-pitched whine, a sound I'd never heard a horse make. I looked at her afterward and said, "Okay, I'm not going to make you do this again." This beautiful foal was weak, and we stayed with him for hours before he was stable enough to nurse on his own. In the meantime I'd milk the mare and feed the foal, and Patrick and I took turns trying to guide him to his mother's teat once he was on his feet. But fortunately the colt was healthy. As the vet said, "Just like people, some are born a little weaker than others. Won't mean anything in the long run." And it didn't. He was healthy, and, like his mother, he was exquisitely beautiful, and every bit as sweet.

The previous year, we had bred three of our best mares, and now, we had witnessed two births. What luck! Two down, one more to go. And this little filly was due in four weeks.

—

WE SAT in the treatment room at Dr. Hoffman's in Los Angeles. As well as Patrick was doing, it was a battle to manage things like his intense abdominal discomfort, painful bowel movements, and gas. The fluid buildup in his belly had to be drained once, and now twice a week, along with the continuing weight management. We were talking to our favorite Harley-riding nurse, Jose, asking the same questions about these issues. We never seemed to tire of repeating the same questions over and over. Maybe because we never got the answers that would really make a difference. So we just kept *picking* at it.

Patrick finally sighed with exasperation, "Well . . . what do the *other* patients do about this?"

Jose looked a little surprised and then said simply, "Patrick . . . We don't *have* any pancreatic patients that are doing as well as you."

We fell silent. What a thing to be reminded of. And we had to absorb that information. It was quite sobering.

A couple of weeks later that July, Patrick was grappling with his symptoms and fatigue when he told me he didn't feel good enough to make his chemo appointment that day. This wasn't the first time that he hadn't felt well enough to go, but it was the first time that I conceded to let him stay home and rest. Sometimes I felt like a Nazi drill sergeant, ordering him to do the impossible, dragging him to appointments when he didn't feel up to it . . . It seemed to be part of my being his caregiver and coach; knowing when to push him, when to be back off, when to get pissed off, when to hold his hand, when to praise. I knew him pretty well, and we wanted the same thing here, so we put all our efforts toward that. But up to this point, I had never, ever let him miss an appointment, because I was afraid that if he missed it, something would happen and it would be a long time before he was able to get treatment again. The thought of that terrified me for him. It'd be like being in a war and deciding to take a day off. But I decided not to be the drill sergeant for one day and rescheduled the appointment.

"A week from tomorrow? You've got to be kidding!" I protested when I got the scheduler on the phone. She explained it was the very earliest she could get him in. "Ah!" I sighed, "Okay, okay, we'll do it a week from Tuesday."

I told Patrick his appointment was rescheduled for the next week. He crinkled his brow, "Really?" But then nodded, still electing to stay home.

The next Tuesday came, and we sat in the treatment room at Dr. Hoffman's drawing blood to run labs before treatment. The results came back. Patrick's hemoglobin reading was low. "I'm going to give you a transfusion," Dr. Hoffman said. "Have you been feeling tired lately? More than usual?"

I looked curiously at Patrick, who shrugged and said, "Probably." He was fatigued much of the time. If it was more so than usual, I couldn't tell.

"We'll give you a transfusion," Dr. Hoffman said, and nodded. "It should make you feel better. And then you can come in on Thursday for treatment."

Ugh. Two more days.

We knew that some patients got to the point where they needed transfusions to keep their HMG up, but Patrick had yet to need one. This would be his first.

Our other regular nurse, Pia, was there, and another male nurse whom we liked very much. They gave Patrick a "talk through" about the transfusion and what to watch for. We nodded and settled in for the two hours it would take for the blood to trickle in. Just like they said—piece of cake.

When it was finished, they unhooked Patrick and were wrapping things up to send us on our way when, all of a sudden . . .

Patrick started to shiver.

We all looked suspiciously at him.

He took a breath and stopped for about three seconds and then started to shake harder than before. Patrick just looked a little helpless, like *I don't know what's going on but I can't stop it.* He'd seem to calm down momentarily and stop shaking, but then started shaking again, looking worse every time until he was shaking continuously. We were now, officially, extremely worried. The nurses were running around. "Looks like it might be a bad reaction," Pia said. She took his temperature—it was elevated. The male nurse looked into Patrick's eyes, and they were rapidly becoming unresponsive, disoriented-looking. I held Patrick's hand tightly, putting my trust and confidence totally in the highly skilled nurses who were attending to him. They called Cedars-Sinai to alert them of a possible incoming. We were moments from rushing him to the hospital when his symptoms calmed . . . he stopped shaking . . . his temperature went down . . . I breathed a sigh of relief, but the nurses were not thoroughly convinced.

Patrick sat for a minute or two, then nodded tiredly. "I think I feel all right now. Let's go home."

We let a few more moments pass by . . .

"Do you want to check him into the hospital?" the male nurse asked me.

"Uhm, I don't know . . . He *seems* fine now," I said uncertainly.

"You're just around the corner from the hospital now." Pia shrugged.

"I feel fine, let's go home," Patrick said. But he still looked a little worse for wear.

"Uhm, uhm . . ." I stalled. I couldn't make up my mind. It was a big deal to take him to the hospital. We'd have to take him to the emergency room first, and we probably wouldn't get home until the next day, if we were lucky. But if I took him home and something happened, it was a long fifty-minute drive back.

I took out my cell phone. "Hold on a second, let me make a call," and I excused myself and walked out of the room. Outside the door, I walked down the hall and called Maria, my sister-in-law, and told her what was going on.

"Lisa, I would take him to the hospital," Maria advised, "You're right there. You just don't want to take any chances."

I nodded. That's all I needed to hear. I went back into the room. "Let's head to Cedars."

Pia nodded happily, and the male nurse almost sighed audibly in relief. "I really think that's the best thing to do. Look . . ." and he shone a little light in Patrick's eye, "This is what really worries me . . ."

Even though Patrick seemed completely stable, his eyes still looked a little spacey. I nodded at the nurse.

"Pull your car around and we'll meet you," he said. "You can follow us over there. I used to work at the ER, so I can usher you in the back." He winked at me.

It sure helps to know somebody!

Driving the short twelve blocks to Cedars-Sinai's ER, Patrick tiredly questioned whether this was what we *really* wanted to do. I was totally committed now and told him, "I'd rather be safe than sorry." He didn't offer any further argument. And again I realized that I never packed an overnight bag to leave in the car like I said I would. About the time I was thinking this, Patrick started to shake again. He swooned against the side of the passenger door, and rapidly got worse than he had been before. Going to the ER was really looking like a good idea now. We only had four more blocks to go.

By the time we wheeled him into a room in the ER, his temp had skyrocketed past 104, which is as high as that paper thermometer goes. His pulse was elevated, and though his eyes were open and blinking, he was not cognizant. At all. He couldn't even say his name, and I doubted that he knew where he was. It was unbelievable how fast all of this happened. And I was thanking Maria, the nurses, and the gods above for putting us just around the corner from Cedars when all this started happening.

In addition to other things, the ER nurse immediately started breaking and putting ice packs under his armpits and around his neck and legs to try to bring down his dangerously high temperature. I attended to keeping these ice packs fresh as I picked up my cell and called, I don't know . . . Maria, Dr. Hoffman, Dr. Fisher, or all three! I needed information and guidance about what was happening.

I was terrified. Helpless and struggling not to be helpless. Panicked. But again, I had learned to keep all those emotions in check. I knew that people could die from things like this, and that knowledge made me feel like I was being beaten up with a rock tied in a sack. Bruised and aching. But I persevered. I was going to hang in there no matter what. And to anyone walking in, I looked concerned, but calm and present.

After two, maybe three hours, Patrick's temp had come down to 102; he'd stopped shaking, though he still was not fully aware.

The staff was apologetic—the room they managed to get for him was on a different floor than we had had before. Was that all right?

"That's fine!" I readily agreed. "Is the staff good on that floor?"

"*Very* good," the nurse said.

"Let's go."

As he lay on the gurney, I fixed the blankets and his baseball hat over his face to disguise him as they rolled him through the halls to his new room. The two Asian nurses that looked like adorable sisters and would be attending him on this floor greeted us. They set him up in the bed, hooked up his fluids, and we organized the room.

"His temp is at 102 now. It needs to be checked every twenty minutes," I told them. "Are there ice packs available? Make sure they are nearby. If his temp goes over 104 again, we need to get ice on him immediately. He may have had a bad reaction to a blood transfusion, so no blood transfusions. If it becomes necessary, we need to order blood that has been washed, and we should allow for some extra lead time for that. I know that you have a doctor on the floor here. There is also a doctor on call, his name is Dr. Decker, if you have any questions . . ."

I let loose this litany of instructions and information. I'd come a long way since we started this journey. And at this point, I certainly wasn't afraid of stepping on any toes. It would be thirty minutes to an hour before we saw a doctor, and I wasn't going to wait until then to make sure Patrick was okay.

One thing I knew for sure. I was grateful to be out of that freeeezing ER! I had elected to wear a cute little flippy skirt that day. Never, never go to a doctor's appointment in a cute little summer skirt!

The sun went down. And everything seemed to be settling in for the evening. Patrick was awake and he had been stable for several hours. He didn't remember the emergency room or what had happened. But all seemed fine now. It could be a rare, bad reaction to the transfusion, or it could be an infection. We'd know more in the morning. I set up my cot in a cramped corner of the room and told the nurses to please wake me if there was any problem during the night. And after watching a little TV together, I kissed him goodnight and climbed beneath the sheets in my little summer skirt to slumber.

—

IN THE middle of the night, I heard vague stirrings in the room. I opened my eyes. In the darkened room, I could see the nurses fiddling with something on the other side of Patrick's bed, like they were trying to figure out how to hook some machine up. I could see their body language—it said "urgent." I tossed off the covers and hopped up from the cot.

"What's going on?" I asked.

One of the nurses turned to me, an apologetic but worried look on her face. "We hooking up this monitor. His heart rate is very elevated."

"What's his temp?" I asked.

"Temp is 102.5."

I nodded. I was still trying to get my bearings and clear my brain. I looked at Patrick to see if he was sweating, how hot he felt, his pulse . . .

His heart rate was very rapid indeed. Just how much, we would all find out soon. The nurses stepped away from the monitor. In iridescent green at the top, it read—

160.

A normal, resting heartbeat should be between 60 and 100 beats per minute. The monitor started counting up . . .

165 . . .

The glowing green numerals would settle, then tick upward again . . .

170 . . . I was panicking about 160, and now it was . . .

175 . . . But we weren't done yet . . .

185.

197 . . .

And it hovered between 197 and 188 and wouldn't budge. I was fearful. *Could someone survive with their heart beating that fast?* This was not a bad reaction to the infusion, this was an infection, and Patrick's heart was going into hyperdrive trying to fight it in an attempt to deliver more blood to his body and vital organs. The nurses were doing whatever they could, and I was asking questions. I can see why doctors and nurses sometimes ignore the patient when they're dealing with things like this—I was doing the same thing. This was turning into an emergency, and all I cared about were the numbers, his symptoms, and what we were going to do about it. I don't remember if Patrick was conscious, semiconscious, or neither. The doctor on call came in and hovered over Patrick and the monitor, talked to the nurses . . . he was a young man and appeared to be very capable and experienced. The electrocardiogram spit out its reading. Not only was Patrick's heart rate high, the beat was irregular, tachycardia arrhythmia. This didn't make me feel any better. I remembered that arrhythmia was the first sign that our beloved Ridgeback, Gabriel, was in mortal trouble.

I asked how dangerous Patrick's heart rate was, and the doctor assured me that his heart could beat that fast for two or more hours and he was not in immediate danger. He nodded toward me to step outside the door with him. Once outside . . .

"This looks like an infection. I need to talk to you about his Health Directive." He asked seriously, "Does he have a DNR on him?"

My brain froze . . . *DNR* . . . *Do Not Resuscitate* . . . I kept talking, "There has been some talk about DNR, but . . ." I stammered, "I don't . . . I don't know if this qualifies." *Does this qualify? Is this a DNR situation? It couldn't be possible that Patrick would be on a DNR now!* "I mean, yes," I tried to sort it out loud, "there's been some talk, uhm . . ."

I was confused. And this was too important. I took out my cell and punched in Maria's number. She answered sleepily but she was alert.

"This sounds treatable, Lisa," Maria said. "I wouldn't put him on a DNR. This is a reversible situation . . . and Lisa, make sure they are very clear about this. No gray areas."

"I understand," I said. "Thanks. Thanks so much."

I hung up the phone and turned to the doctor, "Since this is a treatable situation I want you to do everything possible to get him well. No DNR."

He nodded, "I think we should move him into ICU."

—

IN THE intensive care unit, the bright young lady checking us in asked the same question about the DNR. She looked concerned. Let's face it, Patrick's file did say "Advanced Pancreatic Cancer," and unless you lived under a rock, you already knew this. He was famous. There were the dire tabloid headlines at the local grocery store . . .

"No DNR." I shook my head. "Of course if his heart fails or he stops breathing, I may need to change that. But you'll ask me first, right?"

"Of course." She nodded affirmatively.

I repeated, "Since this is a treatable and reversible situation I want you to do everything in your power for him." She seemed to be a little unsure. I remembered Maria saying, *Make sure they are very clear.* And then I found the magic words.

"He's . . . he's doing well. He's responding to his treatment. And his disease is under control and stable," I said. "Do whatever you need to do for him."

She smiled, like they were the best words she'd heard all day.

Thinking through this DNR issue felt like walking through thick mud. It was as if it were a physically arduous task for the muscles of my brain, a task it had never been trained to do. Of course I wanted them to do everything possible for him to live.

But what if he did have a heart attack or stopped breathing? I had to follow that line of thought if I wanted to be prepared! If he had a heart attack, they would have to take great measures to get it started again. If that failed they would rush his weak body to surgery, where his compromised immune system was prone to infection, already had an infection, and even if he survived the operation and painful recovery, he could not go back on treatment for two months while the disease took the opportunity to wreak havoc on him. His last days would be full of unnecessary suffering. It can be very difficult to know when to fight with everything you have, and when it would only be cruel to do so.

The way things were now, we were still in the fight! We were in uncharted territory once again, but there was hope in supply.

Patrick was given various drugs, and his heart rate came down to 164, but no lower. His doctors were frustrated. But it's a careful balancing act between not enough of these particular drugs and too much of them. For me, 164 was not a comfortable number, but it was a s#*tload better than 197! With his heart rate at 164 beats a minute, Patrick was more alert, and patiently going with the flow.

"How do you feel?" the nurse asked him.

"Okay. I've got stomach pain, constipated, but what else is new," he said. Then, "What's going on?"

I stepped forward. "Your heart rate has been very high." *Obviously he hadn't been aware last night when we moved him to ICU.* "*Really* high. We moved you here last night."

"Oh." He nodded, taking in the information.

"Do you feel anything now? Any tightness in your chest? Discomfort with your heartbeat?" asked the nurse.

Patrick looked calm and maybe a little puzzled, "No . . ."

It was strange to me that his heart could be thumping at 164 to 167 beats per minute, and he didn't know it and didn't feel a thing.

Several doctors came in to talk to us. The type of bacteria causing the infection and the fact that Patrick's left arm had some swelling in it pointed to his portacath, the access that had been put in his chest, as the culprit of the infection. They felt this was very likely, so likely that it was suggested that they take him into surgery as soon as possible and have it removed. *Damn, Donny and I had been* so *careful dealing with his access, and it had lasted months and months!* But we had been warned that the port site was vulnerable.

"What about his heart rate?" I asked with concern, "Won't that compromise his safety?" This just seemed dangerous to me.

One of the doctors nodded. "It would be better if his heart rate was normal. But we're afraid that if we *don't* get that portacath out he won't improve. We'd be trying to treat the infection, and the portacath would just keep reinfecting him."

"And we'd be chasing our tail." I frowned.

The doctor nodded.

Oh, this is one of those "gotta do something" situations. I didn't like it. It made me fearful, but . . . I nodded in understanding. And when the nurses hooked Patrick up to a monitor before they transported him, we could audibly hear his heartbeat.

Rat-tat-tat-tat-tat-tat-tat-tat-tat-tat-tat-tat-tat-tat-tat-tat-tat-tat -tat-ta . . . So fast. So fast . . .

Patrick looked up in disbelief, "Is that *me*?"

"Yes," the nurse nodded.

"Wow," he said, thoroughly impressed. And he finally understood why such a fuss was being made.

—

DURING THE portacath removal, I took the opportunity to sleep, keeping one ear out.

The doctors walked back into the ICU ahead of Patrick, all smiles. All smiles are good! I hopped off my recliner chair.

They had successfully removed the portacath. However, during the procedure his heart rate zinged up. The female anesthesiologist had the presence of mind and nerve to try one drug no one had tried yet—and it worked! Patrick's heart was now beating normally. I wanted to hug her and give her a medal. Hell, I wanted to give them *all* medals!

"What was the name of that drug again?" I wanted to remember it. Who knows, we might run into this situation again.

After a week of more poking, and prodding, and reining in the rest of the infection, we were back home.

That next Sunday at five thirty in the morning, our third, beautiful mare, Shirin Jewel, foaled a beautiful, long and lanky-legged filly. Again, we were present for the birth, which, thankfully, went easily. Patrick gazed at the little filly through the bars of the stall, and I saw him kinda half smile at her. He was tired. And after a while, he walked back down to the house. He just wasn't as interested this time.

Five-year-old Patrick shows off his muscles,
with his dad and a friend smiling in the background.

Chapter 20

MY SECRET WEAPON

O N AUGUST 10, we showed up at Dr. Hoffman's office for Patrick's chemo appointment. He had been out of the hospital for a full week now and had finished the rest of his antibiotics at home. Finally we would get back on treatment.

It was not to be . . .

Although Patrick was feeling much better, his blood work showed that his WBC, white blood cell count, was still high, indicating that he still had some other underlying infection. Under the circumstances, we needed to hold chemo treatment, and Dr. Hoffman put him on yet another antibiotic. We were learning all these antibiotics and their functions: There was the one that was like a massive all-over spray, the pinpointed-zap-you one, the big mother of antibiotics, and then the chaser antibiotic that you use to treat the stuff that sneaks in because of all the other antibiotics. We never ceased to be amazed at how the antibiotic was administered when we were at home. It was premixed into a small- to softball-size frosty plastic ball. You hooked this up to his port (clean, of course) and released the clip and over a predetermined time period, the ball would collapse, pushing the antibiotic through the line and into the port.

Amazing! Patrick could just stick the little ball in his pocket and walk around anywhere.

Needless to say, the news that Patrick had to hold off on treatment was extremely stressful yet again. We had been through this scenario several times this year, and he had come out the other side with flying colors. But I knew not to take anything for granted. This was a killer disease, and he'd already been off treatment for three weeks again. And now it would be yet another week. At a minimum, it was going to be a full month with no chemo! The very thing I feared was now happening. It was *exactly* what I was afraid of happening when he missed that chemo appointment. I didn't want to say, "I told you so," especially since I had no one to point a finger at, but *I told you so.* I couldn't believe it . . . the *one time* I let him miss an appointment, this happens! And I'm sure it was coincidence, but it was a little strange. Man, this disease just doesn't give you a break. I felt like there had been an error, *my error,* and there was no room for such things in Patrick's life.

—

THE COMPLICATIONS that had arisen made taking care of him even tougher and more exacting. Certainly the previous infection that landed him in the hospital had tested the strength of my nerve. And now, once again, I felt alarm at the delay in Patrick's treatment. And overloaded with responsibility . . .

> *I'm feeling a little bit panicked. Like drowning, gurgling in this mire in all the requirements of things I need to do. I get afraid that I can't take it anymore. That I've reached my limit and will fold into a tiny painful ball, not even good for myself let alone anyone else. I keep searching for strength and find the reserves empty. And then . . . I keep searching again.*

Sometimes I feel like I'm living for Buddy. He can't get up, so I do. He doesn't take care of business, so I do. I even help him up at times to go to the toilet, 'cause as of yet, I cannot defecate or pee for him. I keep positive, I find a way to get through another day. I feel how he's feeling so I know what medications to give him. I feed him 'cause I intuit that his body needs it at one time or another. I open his eyes to the day.

August 11, 2009

I can only imagine that this is how many people feel when they are taking care of someone in such a difficult situation. You start to feel like you actually breathe for the other person. You are so tuned in that you know how he's going to feel even before he wakes up; by how he moves, rolls over, by his breath, his expression, and the position he might hold his hands in . . . And from that moment, it's through your sheer will that he lives through the day, that he smiles, that he feels good, or at least, feels better than he would have.

And maybe it was not so much that I was finding myself exhausted again as that I didn't know where I left off and *Patrick* began. It's living out there in a different place, in a kind of altered state. On top of all this, in your spare time, you take care of everything else in your world—work, bills, legal stuff, groceries, cooking, answering the phone, talking to doctors, ordering medical supplies, cleaning . . .

It tested my Sisu, the limits of my physical and emotional stamina. And I was grateful for every moment of it. There was no place on earth I'd rather be.

—

THAT SUMMER, we received a package in the mail. I hefted it in my hands. Hmm, heavy . . . Upon opening it, we discovered that someone we didn't know had sent us a large, very elaborate book about medicine, its history and art. *Hmm, where did this book come from?* A note directed us to one of the very first pages, it had a picture of a head and brain, and "For the mind and for the heart," and then under it, a quotation from Oscar Wilde: "Life is too important to be taken seriously." And then, a quotation of Johnny Castle's from Patrick's movie *Dirty Dancing*, "The steps aren't enough—feel the music." What this had to do with the book we didn't know, and we opened it to skim through to find out!

Inside we found text and illustrations of different medical treatments throughout the ages. And on first look, they all looked like something out of a horror movie! There were photos of syphilis sufferers, descriptions of eye procedures that were downright barbaric . . . Antiquated, horrible surgery procedures for broken bones and other more serious maladies . . . It was unsettling. Patrick and I looked at each other, and we didn't know whether to laugh or be disturbed!

"*Why* would someone send us something like this?" I said.

"It's really, really strange." He nodded.

Given Patrick's health struggles, did the author think that this book with its gruesome photos and descriptions was going to cheer us up? *People are strange,* I thought. But it mystified me enough to thumb back through it, searching for an answer . . . And then I found it. I excitedly carried the book back to Patrick.

"I know why this was sent this to us! It's not horrible. It's actually . . . quite beautiful," I said, and then read him the quotation from Harvard professor Oliver Wendell Holmes, Sr., that was tucked in before the book's introduction:

> *There is nothing men will not do, there is nothing they have not done, to recover their health, and save their lives. They have submitted to be half drowned in water, and half choked*

with gases, to be buried up to their chins in earth, to be seared with hot irons like galley slaves, to be crimped with knives like codfish, to have needles thrust into their flesh, and bonfires kindled on their skin, to swallow all sorts of abominations, and to pay for all of this as if to be singed and scalded were a costly privilege, as if blisters were a blessing and leeches a luxury. What more can be asked to prove their honesty and sincerity?

We want to live. And this book demonstrated the lengths to which people will go to survive and to improve the quality of their lives. Life is precious, and worth fighting for! "See how much," the book was saying. The significance of that quotation was not lost on me in regard to Patrick. I mean, look what Patrick and I had done for the last twenty months! What we had gone through!

Patrick just sorta nodded like, eh, he wasn't convinced. But I think he was in the midst of what he called a "Dilaudid Moment." So he nodded at my discovery and went off to do something else.

Then again, maybe he wasn't going to get too excited over what I was talking about because it was something that he was living every day. *Life is precious.* Clearly, his life was precious to me. And to him.

I would have gone to any lengths to keep him here with me, short of taking him to voodoo doctors or indulging way-out-there alternative therapies. I emphatically believe in the power of positive thought and intention. And Patrick and I were always open to prayers and healings, and also supercharged waters and supplements, as long as they were okayed by his doctors and didn't interfere with his treatment. But there was no way I was going to entrust my husband's *life* to a treatment that was entirely unproven and based only on testimony. Not unless *he* requested it. There are so many stories of people chasing cures, people like the great actor Steve McQueen who pursued treatment in Mexico, only to be taken for loads of money and suffer because of it. We were doing everything we could for Patrick to live. And every ounce of Patrick's strength was being called upon when he went through treatment. But he wasn't going to panic. As he said, "I want to live. But I'm not going to chase living." His attitude was that of an intractable winner. He was going to be brave enough to do this on his own terms.

By saying this, I believe he was more alive.

—

HE STAYED on antibiotics throughout the week, and we took that opportunity to start recording the audio book for the autobiography that we had just finished. Amazingly, we were finally done with the book. It had been very intensive, hard work, and we were very happy with it. Then there are all the peripheral things to accomplish, such as choosing and getting permissions on all the photos, approving press releases, book cover and lettering to design, proofing the final . . . And now, with no time to waste, the audio book! We planned to record it with the audio book's producer and an engineer in Patrick's recording studio right here at the ranch. It was fantastic that Patrick would be reading it, but I worried about his energy.

This past infection had really taken a toll on him, and he still was struggling to fully recover. I suggested that if he felt like he wasn't up to recording the book, then maybe Donny should read it. Time was running out before the book was to be released, and the recording had to be done. Certainly Donny was talented, had a wonderful "Swayze" voice, and it'd be keeping it in the family.

Patrick scowled, "I think that's a really *bad* idea."

Donny heard him say this, and when he found a moment, he took me aside and confided that his feelings were hurt . . .

"Does he think I'd be *that* terrible?" he asked.

Hah! "No!" I told him, "He just doesn't like to think that there's something he can't do."

You don't tell Patrick what he can't do, only he makes that decision. And nobody but Patrick was going to do this audio book. But come the first day of recording, he was feeling awful. Elisa, the producer, and our engineer sat out on the grass enjoying the day. They were great. "No hurry! Whenever . . . don't worry," they said.

A couple of hours later, I went into the bedroom to check on Patrick, and I gently suggested, "Why don't you just give it a shot. I'll walk down to the studio with you."

"I really feel terrible." He grimaced.

"Okay." I nodded, "Then this is what I think . . . Since they're here, go down to the studio, just for twenty minutes, and if you're still feeling bad, we'll send them home for the day."

It was a deal.

I felt for him as I helped him down to the studio. But we were going to give it a shot. He was unsteady on his feet, and I let him lean on my arm for support and balance. He was feeling pretty rough. After introducing everyone, I excused myself and went back upstairs, since I don't need to be a babysitter! Twenty minutes later, I called the studio on our intercom phone system to check in . . .

"How's it going? Do you guys need anything?" I asked. And I could hear Patrick ask the others if they wanted something to drink. He came back to me on the phone . . .

"No, everyone's fine," he said.

"How are you?"

"I'm okay . . ."

"You want me to make you a shake? That you can sip on?" I offered. "Sipping" was a sneaky term I adopted to not put pressure on his appetite, but always to have food in front of him if case he wanted it.

"Yeah," he agreed, "that'd be good."

I made the shake and took it down and dropped it off. "Call me if you need anything . . ."

And time passed . . .

And then more time passed . . . And I figured no news was good news. But . . .

What were they doing down there? I finally called on the intercom to check in and was greeted by . . .

An energetic, cheerful-sounding Patrick, who was in mid-conversation with the engineer. "Hey, look! I know! I collected all those guitars, and then I had this banjo here. Wait a minute," and he turned his attention to me, "Hey, Lis. Uh, what's goin' on?"

It took me a second. I was flabbergasted. "I'm just calling to check in. See how things were going . . ."

"Uhm, well. We finished the second chapter and were just getting ready to start the third," he said. He sounded strong, and obviously had been chatting away. He shouted out to another part of the room, "How long do you think we'll go?" I heard mumbling in the background, and then Patrick came back, "Maybe we'll do chapter four. We'll see how far we get." He sounded . . . like himself . . .

Incredible! He'd barely been able to move a few hours ago, and now he was operating with the same energy I saw on *The Beast*. You know, I could find the best doctors, the best treatments, food, medicines, prayers . . . but my best weapon against pancreatic cancer had always been Patrick himself. The strength he could find, both inner and outer, amazed me.

He worked in his studio for six hours with them before he finally stopped so we could administer our evening ritual of medications and hook up his TPN. It was well after midnight when he propped up his pillows so he could rest comfortably.

Our cushy mattress had been getting increasingly difficult for him to get in and out of. I had asked him if he wanted an electric medical bed. He didn't waver a second before answering.

"No." He shook his head.

"Why not?" I asked. "I think it'd probably be much more comfortable for you. You could raise the head without all those pillows and put your feet up, too . . ." I was doing a sales job because I thought that maybe he was balking because he didn't want to look like a patient in his own home. But that wasn't the issue.

"I want us to sleep together," he said.

I was touched. And I nodded.

—

AT FOUR-THIRTY that morning, Patrick nudged me awake. He was sitting more upright than usual. I saw him shiver.

"Hey, Lisa," he said softly, "I started shaking . . ." and a shiver cut short the rest of his words.

I immediately jumped out of bed and stuck a thermometer in his mouth. Within seconds it beeped—102.7. I looked at the clock, *four-thirty. Great.* I knew from personal experience in the hospital that Dr. Hoffman was already up and starting to make his rounds. I picked up the phone and called him.

"Hi, Dr. Hoffman, Patrick needs to check into the hospital. He's got rigors and his temp is 102.7."

"We'd better get him in," he said, "I'll get on it."

By early afternoon, Patrick was in Cedars-Sinai's ICU. His heart rate zinged up to 164. Nurses and doctors were alarmed and rushing around trying to figure out how to bring his heart rate down. I was unusually calm in comparison to the hospital staff, having been through this with Patrick only a few weeks ago. They were worried about his bpm being 164? Try 197! Then let's see how everyone can panic! But I was ready and gave them the name of the drug that worked the last time, and I waited for his symptoms to turn around. But I was not about to treat this casually.

Patrick was very sick, and there was a very good reason why he was in ICU. I'd learned to be cool-headed, and I had faith that this infection would turn around like it had before. But I tell you . . . We had been warned from the beginning about how dangerous an infection could be to Patrick, and unlike how unimpressed I was last year, I'd come to respect infection as a formidable enemy. *We did not want to mess around with these!*

One evening, a couple of days later, I stepped outside his ICU room into the bright, empty hall to call and check in with Dr. Fisher at Stanford. It was hard to find a place to have a private phone conversation. I didn't want to do it in the room with Patrick and stress him when he should be resting, the waiting areas tended to have sad-eyed people waiting for God knows what, and it was a long way out of the ICU building to the outside, and even harder to get back in because of front desk security. I liked that security, though. It gave me confidence that no one was going to sneak in to find Patrick. So, the options for a phone call left me pacing the empty, booming hallway, trying to talk in a voice soft enough so as not to echo down the corridor.

I asked Dr. Fisher what the future might hold, reviewing Patrick's options, not only if he had a hard time shaking this bug he had right now, but if he did and became stable enough to resume treatment. I just wanted to be prepared. I wanted to be thinking ahead. And I think that, in a way, it was important to me that I was visualizing a future rather than being carried along into some unknown darkness.

George restated the importance of not giving chemotherapy until all of the infection was gone. To resume chemo too early could, and would, fatally compromise his immune system. "It'd be like putting the nail into the coffin," Dr. Fisher said. I assured him that I understood. (I was bold, but I was not trigger-happy.) And as we were wrapping up our update, he encouraged me to hang in there through this tough spot, and then he paused, before saying, "You know I really regret ever suggesting that Patrick might not make it when we first met," he said sincerely.

"You were being realistic," I said, "and you're not the only doctor that was being very blunt and honest about the situation."

"Well, I wish I never said it, I truly do," he said.

"It's amazing how Patrick has really hung in there." I nodded. "Amazing."

"Well." Dr. Fisher's tone started to brighten, "All I can say is . . . if I'd bet a six-pack of beer every time I thought Patrick was not going to make it, I'd be a very poor man by now," and he added, "I just wish we had met at another time, we could have been really good 'White Trash Buddies.'"

It was funny, and I laughed. He said this because he shared a story with Patrick about a car he had that flooded when it rained, so he drilled big holes in the floorboard to let the water drain out. To which Patrick shared his story of how he had a DeLorean on blocks sitting in his driveway for two years, and that made us "Uptown White Trash."

And then Dr. Fisher said something that I'll always remember. And I don't believe I get this much credit, but . . . but it meant a lot to me . . .

"And I just have to tell you, Patrick wouldn't be alive if it weren't for you. He would have never survived this long," he said.

—

I REALLY appreciated hearing that. And if it really was true, I don't think it would have been wholly because of the attention I gave

him and his medical treatment. Partly, it would have been because he didn't want to leave me. And I'm not saying that he
couldn't possibly bear to be away from me, and then again, that,
too, may be true. What I mean is—sometimes I thought he might
be staying for *me*. That he was fighting so hard so that he could
do his best to "take care" of me . . . He knew that I crazy-beyond-
anything didn't want him to leave me, and I tried not to think
about this too much—because I felt guilty that he might feel pressure, or feel emotionally blackmailed that he *had* to hang in there
because it would hurt me too much for him to go. I didn't want to
see him suffer. But I still had that guilt card in my back pocket as
part of my bag of tricks. And although we rarely spoke of it, both
of us subtly knew it was there. I hoped I would always be reasonable about how I played that card. But I wasn't going to throw
it away. Because the truth of the matter was—I selfishly wanted
him here with me.

—

OUR FOUR days at the hospital were not without some bumps and
hardship. While there, we took the opportunity for some housekeeping items. He swallowed a tiny camera that filmed his insides
while it passed through his stomach and intestines so we could
figure out why he was having some bleeding in his intestines and
stool. We attempted to fix the new portacath, which I hated because it wasn't working *nearly* as well as the last one. And we in-
stalled an IV filter to prevent a blood clot from traveling upstream
into his lungs, which was another thing that could prove fatal.
And when he came back from the IV procedure and transferred
from the gurney to the hospital bed, bright red blood gushed out
from under his hospital gown, and my eyes went wide! Luckily,
the experienced nurse hardly blinked, telling me this sometimes
happens after an IV filter placement, and she went to get some-

thing to clean up. I was so glad she was there! Seeing that much blood gush out can be disturbing, to say the least. I felt like Patrick's line in *To Wong Foo, Thanks for Everything! Julie Newmar* when Vida exclaims tiredly, *"What fresh hell is this?"*

Five days at the hospital, and Patrick, once again . . . once again . . . beat the infection. We went home on August 18, Patrick's birthday!

On the way, I pulled over our pickup truck and jumped out to run into one of my favorite bakeries on Melrose Avenue and pick up a delicious chocolate cake to take home for a private celebration. Earlier in the month I had planned something nifty, deciding to find a Latin dinner club with salsa music and dancing. I even had a dress to wear from one of my shopping excursions. But as the days of the month wore on, it became clear to me that I might not be able to rely on Patrick's feeling well enough to have a celebration. It was the first time that thought had come into my mind. And I didn't like it. He had always been able to rise to any occasion . . . But I had to go with my instinct and cancel the big get-together. As it turned out, it was the wiser choice; our plans *would* have been canceled anyway by his hospital visit. Instead, Donny and I got to pick at the chocolate cake that of course Patrick didn't want to eat any of. (It's the thought that counts, right?) But all of us were rewarded by his being well and returning home victorious over another tough infection. And that's a pretty nice birthday present when you look at it. A hard-earned present.

Sheer stubbornness. It was hard not to take these victories personally. I felt like Patrick and I "willed" them into existence. And we'd wake up and celebrate each day. *He's still here!*

Each one of these infections had weakened him, though. I kept waiting to see him bounce back as strong as he had in the past. Just that summer, he had started to look and feel so good that we had even discussed the possibility of doing a second season of *The Beast*! And now, he was once again trying to "come back." Only weaker and more fragile than before . . . I kept focused on his getting well enough—to give his body a chance—just another week or so—then we can bring out the big guns again and blow this disease away. Just another week . . .

—

ALSO, WHEN we got home from the hospital, a medical bed stood waiting for him in our bedroom. I had to finally order it—he was in serious need of it for his comfort, and it was going to make his life much easier. I also had come up with a solution to his problem with having the bed: I found a second-hand medical bed for myself. And I had it set up and nudged right next to Patrick's, so when we climbed into bed we were in dueling electric beds, still sleeping next to each other. And like always, some part of us was touching the other.

—

PATRICK WAS back recording the audio book for *The Time of My Life,* which had been so rudely interrupted because of the last infection. When he had got back from the hospital, I wondered how he'd ever find the energy to do more recording. And sometimes it would take half a day for him to get in there, but once he did, his performer's adrenaline kicked in, and it almost took a crowbar to get him out of there. Which is pretty much the way he always did things, sick or well! But again, what was stunning was the transformation of his energy. Unless you'd seen it, you wouldn't have believed it.

"It's Robert Johnson's blues slide guitar," Patrick enthused to the audio engineer, "It's beautiful, huh? Here, play it, it's got an incredible sound!"

"Hello? Hello . . . ?" I was on the intercom upstairs in the house trying to cut into the conversation.

"Hey Lis, what's up!" Patrick said brightly.

"Are you guys playing music?" I asked, dumbfounded.

"Yeah! Matt plays and composes. We just finished two chapters, and I was showing him my Robert Johnson," he said, "No pun intended." He chuckled a little.

I had sections to record also, and spent some time just sitting down there with them. It felt like we were a world away. Cancer was still there, and for the hours we were in the studio, it didn't go away, but it sat outside the recording room door. And while we did the audio book, we'd take breaks and have some fun playing music together with Matt. Patrick and I shared a recording of Luke Reed singing "Spanish Rose," one of Patrick's recent favorites, Matt would play one of his upbeat songs on the guitar, and then, we'd break out into a loud, rabble-rousing live version of "Up Against the Wall Red-Neck Mother," before getting serious enough again to actually record the audio book. It was hilarious! And we were all having fun. One night, Patrick didn't stop recording until three in the morning! Matt later confided, "We were worried about pushing Patrick too hard." He shook his head in amazement. "And here he is, and he's going strong and it's passing two in the morning. He's putting *me* under the table. And I'm not the one who's sick!"

It was true "Patrick" style.

Even more amazing, the days he spent recording the audio book, he did so with another infection brewing.

One of our last photos taken together, August 2009.
(Photo by Greg Gorman)

Chapter 21

THE LAST INFECTION

THIS NEW GERM was fairly minor, but Patrick couldn't have been feeling very well. Stenotrophomonas maltophilia, a type of bacteria. Dr. Hoffman put Patrick on the appropriate antibiotic. The fact that his health was undermined and he still put the hours in to record the audio book (over the course of three more long days) points not only to what a truly tough guy he was, but also to how he could downright transcend what was going on with him physically.

As soon as the recording was done, Patrick retreated into the state he was in previously as his body fought the infection. He was very weak and put his hand out to steady himself against something when he walked. He was often uncomfortable, and his energy was very low, and Donny and I had begun to worry about his getting up and wandering around in the middle of the night, as he did often while we were both asleep. It was a big concern . . . there was the definite possibility he could fall and seriously hurt himself, or run into some other problems. He had already taken a spill, catching his foot on a step and hitting the ground pretty hard. Between the compromised strength and the medication, his reflexes were not up to par. I was trying to figure out how I could have someone watch him at night, but that was a tough one—whoever it was would have to sit outside our door and then follow him if he got up. It was kind of a creepy thought to have some unknown person sitting outside your bedroom door all night, and Patrick wasn't going for it. Donny and I briefly discussed one of us taking the "night shift," but then that would leave that person sleeping in the day when all the real work and our lives were happening. I just crossed my fingers and decided to go with the flow. If I *really* had to get some nighttime nursing care, I figured I'd know when it was imperative to do so.

Frail as he was, I still held hope that he could stay well long enough to get back on treatment and turn his process to an upswing again. Miracles had happened before. And he had looked poorly earlier in the past year and bounced back amazingly. Angels were on our side. I wasn't going to underestimate the possibilities. Every day could be, and was, like a new discovery. And I certainly wasn't going to underestimate Patrick.

We had been warned about those "rolling infections"—the infections that start to happen one on top of another and don't stop—and I knew that Dr. Hoffman, Dr. Fisher, and our infectious disease specialist, Dr. Chung, highly suspected that this was what was happening with Patrick.

Sure, he'd had quite a few infections in the last month or so, but he had recovered from them, right?

Although these last ones . . . he'd recovered, barely. But that didn't mean we were giving up. We were hanging in there.

We duly noted the doctors' concerns.

—

IT WAS right at this time that the worst wildfire in Los Angeles County history broke out. It was called the Station Fire, and was described as an *angry* fire. It started at 45,000 acres and within hours, grew to 100,000 acres as it headed toward a 160,000 total. Our ranch is backed right up to the Angeles National Forest, at the fire's back door. People were evacuated less than a mile away, and large animal evacuation shelters were set up at Antelope Valley Fair in Lancaster, Pierce College in Woodland Hills, and then later, right down the street from us near Hansen Dam. With all the firefighters, roadblocks and equipment, it looked like an army had moved into our neighborhood, and we were living under martial law.

In the last twenty years, our property had been threatened by fire a few times, but never by a fire this hazardous and large.

We were in the middle of holding tight to Patrick's health after this last infection. As positive an attitude as we had, the recent downturn in his health worked its nerve-racking concern on our insides. We were all fighting firmly to get him well and back on track. And Patrick was steady and unflinching. And along with these recent infections, other problems had been popping up along the way. Problems with his growing fluid retention, more blood clots, intestinal problems, the persnickety new port that was still not working properly . . . and more and more he was cloudy on his Dilaudid doses. It was challenging for me *and* Patrick *and* Donny. *Very challenging.* And with a dangerous fire nearby, I prayed that I wouldn't have to evacuate the horses, especially because I had three small foals, one of them only two weeks old. Moving them in these circumstances could be very traumatic for them.

Less than half a mile away now, several large horse facilities had mandatory evacuation. My brother Paul and I checked the fire's progress several times a day to try to predict its immediate path . . . And to me at that moment, it just seemed beyond all comprehension that *so much* would be happening. My brain felt

bruised, and I was living in a constant state of alarm and apprehension . . .

> *Looks like there are fires coming from all directions. I just*
> *want to sit down on my haunches, cover my ears, and rock*
> *like a little child. Seems I have this idea in my head that as*
> *long as I can stand, as long as I can breathe, I can still carry*
> *on . . . I'm standing, I'm breathing. And yet . . . and yet . . .*
> *You give me focus. Don't let me think about too many fires*
> *coming my way. And I can rally. I can do it again.*
>
> *September 2, 2009*

Luckily, I had friends step in to let me know I had their help
if I needed it. There was Ame, whose friend had a trailer and had
already been moving horses. Arabella, who was horse savvy and
ready to run over and help at a moment's notice, and Paul, who
had the number of another horse mover . . . The fire raged to the
second ridge of mountains behind our house, less than half a mile
away from our backs. Firefighters parked at the end of the street
outside our gate in case the fire spread down our hill, because if
they didn't catch it soon enough, it would be too late.

Soot and ash covered everything . . .

The metaphorical significance of devastating fires coming
from all directions was not lost on me, although I've come to
believe that not everything has significance, that sometimes sh*t
just happens. I had grown up always believing that this life somehow reflects back at you. That how you feel, what you are, is in
the people, the things, the situations you see around you. It's like
Patrick used to say when he was practicing Buddhist chanting
and when his life was awry, his altar was covered with dust, the
greenery dead, and the water in the cup all but evaporated . . .
"Well," he'd say brightly, "if you want to know what my life looks

like right now, all you have to do is look at my altar!" And now, I was looking around at my life, and it was on fire.

Destruction was heading our way . . .

I had also noticed that inexplicably in the last three months, trees on our property had begun to die. Trees that had been there since before we moved in over twenty years ago and had always been healthy. When I saw the first one start to go, I thought, *Oh, she's an old apricot tree. Apricot trees must die when they get older.* But it wasn't just the fruit trees. Three other trees started to die. And then more . . . until there were nine trees that had suddenly, mysteriously turned to dead wood . . .

Was this reflecting mirror an image of my, or Patrick's and my, life? It was not something I wanted to waste much time thinking about, but every time I looked out the kitchen window, *there were those damn trees staring at me.* If this was sending a message . . . between the fires and the dead and dying trees, it was giving a pretty good indication that my world was tumbling down. But I kept putting one foot in front of the other, and was still tireless. I had to take care of my Honey. And if I had to evacuate the mares and babies, I'd probably shed some self-pitying tears before I picked myself up and just got it done. My world was rocking, swaying under the pressure, but now was not the time to sob. I had come this far, and I'd be damned if I was going to let life break me.

And Patrick was still going to deal with life on his own terms.

—

THE STATION Fire was in its eighth day, and two firefighters had lost their lives. The blaze was only 20 percent contained, and we were far from being out of the woods yet.

Patrick had an appointment at Cedars-Sinai to help drain off the fluid that had built up and was putting pressure on his abdomen and making it hard for him to lie down and breathe easily. This fluid stuff is so crazy—it's a vicious cycle where your body thinks it's dehydrated, so it produces more fluid, but veins start to weep, and you try to trick your kidneys into thinking you're hydrated so it stops producing fluid, and we find out that all along it was never going to get better because of Patrick's disease compromising the function of his organs. There. Aren't you glad you didn't ask? Anyway, Donny usually took Patrick to these paracentesis appointments, or "Tummy Taps," as I called them, but recently I had started not feeling comfortable being away from Patrick's side for too long. The health situation was delicate, and I worried what might happen when I was gone. I didn't want to take any chances. Every time I left the room, I stopped to tell him that I loved him, and kissed him or squeezed his hand. But today was not the day to take him, the fires were too close, and Paul and I needed to stand guard in case we had to start moving horses with only a moment's notice. I was grateful that Donny would drive Patrick in to his appointment like he had before. I trusted his excellent care unquestioningly.

They had gone, and I was keeping track of the news on the fire and catching up on little things. It was only an hour or so later when Donny called . . .

"Lisa?" he began, "We're here at the procedure center and Buddy started having rigors."

I jumped up instantly, "Really?"

"Yeah," he continued, "he's shaking pretty badly. And he doesn't look too good."

"Stay right there," I said firmly, "I'll call the doctor and get him checked in right now. I'll call you right back, okay?"

"Okay," and he hung up.

I called Dr. Hoffman, told him what was going on, then called Patient Relations at Cedars to alert them to the fact that

Patrick was going to check in immediately. I called Donny back . . .

"Arrangements are being made to get him a room now. So, just hold on there," I assured Donny.

"Okay, we'll do that," he said tensely.

I couldn't believe the timing of this infection blowing out like this, and marveled out loud to Donny, "God, what are the chances that he'd already be *at the hospital* when this starts happening?" I had a rush of sweet relief, it was great luck that he was already there. And I took that as a good sign.

"How's he doing?"

"He's feeling bad, and he's shaking a lot. I've got him in a wheelchair, and we're off to the side here. With lots of blankets on him."

"Okay, keep an eye on his temperature. Don't let him get too hot."

I quickly threw together my overnight bag (yes, I *still* hadn't packed a ready-to-go bag to leave in the car) and headed to the hospital. Before I left, I made sure my brother Paul had all the phone numbers of people who could help him move the horses if needed.

Back at the hospital, nice as Donny is, he was getting irate. It'd been an *hour* and he was *still* standing in the small room at the back of the Procedure Center with a disoriented, hurting Patrick next to him in a wheelchair. He finally lost it and stepped out into the pathway of everyone, "HEY! ONE HOUR AGO I WAS TOLD MY BROTHER NEEDS TO BE IN INTENSIVE CARE. THAT MEANS HE NEEDS TO BE *IN INTENSIVE CARE NOW!*"

That got their attention, and Patrick and Donny were personally escorted to ICU within minutes.

I drove out of the gate of Rancho Bizarro and past the encampment of firefighters, tents, trucks, and evacuation horse shelters in Orcas Park, and jumped on the 210 freeway headed west. I looked back at the flames licking Tujunga Canyon near us and the ridiculously large clouds of threatening smoke that billowed up to twenty thousand feet in some places. I was leaving it all far, far behind. If the horses had to be evacuated, it was out of my hands now. And I trusted those who would take care of it.

—

THE RAGING infection, the alarming heart rate . . . Ditto . . . He goes through it all again. And like before, a couple of days later, he's stable enough to move into a regular room. Except the infection isn't resolving. The cardiologist changes his medication, trying to calm his still erratic heart. The portacath that was so fickle is pulled out, since it was a possible source of infection again, which puts Patrick on a regular IV in his arm, which will be much more of a problem to maintain than his last picky port was. An appointment is set up to install a Plurex, a kind of semi-permanent opening via a tube so that we can drain off the fluid build-up, which is getting constant. I pay close attention to instructions on how to do the draining, what to do with the fluid, and I'm worrying that this is one more possible source of future infection. I'm thinking of the future . . . but another part of me is worried about something else . . .

"You know," I was sitting with Patrick in his room, "we had just gotten out of the hospital and I never got you a birthday present. Can you think of something that you would want?"

I could see Patrick thinking. His energy was minimal, but he was giving my question dedicated attention. After a moment, he spoke in a soft and slow voice: "A GPS."

I wasn't quite expecting this.

"A GPS?" I confirmed.

"Yeah . . . one that we can put in the car," he said.

I nodded. But, *where were we going to go, what were we going to be doing that we needed a global positioning system?* I didn't want to be negative, but I had big doubts that we'd be taking off to parts unknown.

I did open my laptop to take a cursory look for where I could buy one . . . but didn't go any further with it.

It was a first sign for me.

—

I WAS afraid. Afraid I was at that "point" now. He wasn't improving and appeared to be declining more than ever. He was so weak it was difficult for him to get out of bed at all.

And I started to think a terrible thought . . . *maybe he's not getting better.* For the first time, I questioned if I was being optimistic . . . *realistically* optimistic about his getting better, or if I was in denial. I was carefully trying to take the pulse of the situation . . . I had always promised myself that when and if the time came, I would let him go and not make him suffer. The situation had to be beyond hope and there had to be no way back. Patrick and I have had many animals, beautiful and loved animals that we had to nurse through sickness. It took us a while, but we learned that to keep them going long after it was their time to go was cruel. As heartbreaking as it was, we knew we were thinking of the animal when we let him or her go, rather than thinking of ourselves. As painful as it was, it was an act of extreme kindness and love.

Was I at that point? Things were not looking good. But I wasn't sure. I wasn't convinced . . . so I hovered silently in that difficult place of questioning the situation, and myself.

On that Friday, Dr. Geemee Chung talked to me about his blood work and the unresolved infection. It was not an upbeat conversation. There was yet *another* bacteria under the current one, she informed me.

It looked like indeed this was the "rolling infection" they had talked about. The evidence was beginning to be undeniable.

"I'm afraid it doesn't look good." She was somber.

I nodded. And I was feeling desperation creeping in. "Give him something to treat the new infection also?" I asked. "Why not just give him everything you can. What's it going to hurt?" I think I knew that this was our last shot.

Geemee nodded in agreement, and together, we resolved to wait until Monday to see what transpired.

Give it one more chance.

—

THE WEEKEND was hard and mind-numbing. Every time he moved to get out of the bed, we scurried to make sure he was supported. When we first moved out of ICU into the regular room, they had asked me if Patrick was a "fall risk." If so, they would put a yellow band on his wrist that alerted the nurses. I had always said "no" on every previous hospital visit. But this time I had to say yes. And when Patrick woke up in his new room, he lifted his arm, saw the yellow band on it, and turned to me and whispered at me painfully, like I was some kind of traitor . . .

"What are you trying to do to me?"

I knew that he felt as if I had taken away some of his power. That I had just made him into someone who was a victim and helpless.

I could only reply, "I had to . . ." And I felt helpless.

I hadn't wanted to, but I didn't feel I had a choice. I had to be honest. And honestly, at that point I was more afraid of his falling and seriously injuring himself than I was afraid of hurting his dignity.

What could he say? We were on the same team, and he let it go. And softly dozed back off.

—

SINCE THE last hospital visit, he had become less and less lucid. I attributed this to the wrong doses of Dilaudid, and was always jumping up and bossing the nurses around about what dose amounts he needed programmed in his hospital medication pump. But this was different. He was not always coherent, even when his doses were right. Instinctively I knew it must be connected to the disease, but it wasn't until much later that I learned that the disease's effect on the liver builds up toxins in the body, and these toxins were affecting his brain and causing confusion.

So, sometimes he was lucid, and sometimes you didn't know *what* was going to come out of his mouth, and sometimes he was unresponsive. Donny and I figured Patrick knew something was up, though, as we went into that weekend . . . He looked at the pumps and antibiotics hanging high above him, following their tubes down and into his arm, and said in a low, distrustful voice, "There's some *bullshit* going on here . . ."

And while I was helping him into the restroom with all his medications and tubings, he had been frustrated with me for the last couple of hours: *"Why haven't you gotten President Barack Obama on the phone yet? It's a matter of national security!"* He was getting very upset, *"You have to understand, I have important information, it's the only thing that will help divert a national disaster! I need to talk to him immediately!"*

I was panicking. I didn't want to agitate him further by saying, "Hey, Buddy, you're talking crazy stuff. So shut up." I found the answer. I said, "I know. And we've put a call in to him. We're just waiting for him to call back."

He nodded and was able to relax after that.

—

THROUGHOUT THE weekend I hoped against hope that the antibiotics would kick in and somehow start booting these infections out of his body and off the map. Come Monday morning, there was no visible change in Patrick's condition when blood was taken from his IV and sent off to the lab.

It was awfully quiet . . . Or was that my imagination? The TV was going, meals were being served . . . but it was quiet. No one was rushing back with the lab tests. And I was not on pins and needles waiting to find out the results of his blood test like before. I already had the sinking feeling that it would show what the doctors were afraid of.

And that afternoon, Dr. Hoffman and Dr. Chung came into the room. I didn't want to discuss anything in front of Patrick, so we stepped out into the hallway, and Geemee and Hoffman sent the nurses away from the little ministation outside our door. They spoke in as discreet and private voices as they could, since we were standing in a small alcove, open to the rest of the big hospital hallway. Out of habit, my eyes darted around to make sure that there was no one near to overhear or watch us.

And I knew what they were going to say . . .

"I'm afraid we're at that point now," they said gravely and with compassion.

I confirmed with them that, absolutely, without a shadow of a doubt, there was nothing more we could do. I asked about the blood results. I asked about his CA19-9. I felt hot, hot tears well up into my eyes, and I pushed them back. I didn't want to start crying and not be able to stop. And I had to agree . . .

I had to agree . . .

I had to agree that this was the end.

—

THERE IS nothing more horrible than letting go. That day had come. The day that I promised myself I would do if we came to it. But what was terrible to bear was that the decision to "let go" was mine.

Realistically, I didn't have a choice. Had to let go or it would have shredded my heart. As it was, my heart was shredded anyway. Except I was left with the nagging, disturbing thought that my timing was wrong, that I should have found a loophole. That I should *never* have let him go. Never given up.

"Pull the plug," you hear on the television programs when all hope is gone and the decision is made to take the patient off life support. In real life, families and loved ones have to say this all the time. And it doesn't matter whether there's a Health Directive, a piece of paper, stating the patient's last wishes clearly, you feel like you are the one giving up. Like God deciding who will live and who will die. The one who pushes "the Button" that sets off mass destruction. And there is guilt. Even though you are acknowledging the situation and doing your best to act with compassion and wisdom, you feel guilty.

We are taught that as long as there is life, there is hope. And dying is about breaking the rules. We don't prepare for this. It goes against our nature. Letting go is about experiencing harsh, harsh loss, before the harshest loss of all comes. When you think about it, what greater loss is there? Death is the ultimate failure. And letting him go, knowing he was moving into Death's arms, I felt like I had failed. The only way I could possibly bear it was to keep reminding myself that this was the act of love I had promised. This wasn't about me . . . this was about love. My love, that stood outside as its own entity, its own body, its own city. And I had to let go, and I had to surrender to my love.

(I never wanted him to go . . . Did I mention that?)

And as we wrapped up our conversation in the hallway, they had to ask me. And I nodded . . .

"Yes . . . *yes* . . . Put a DNR on him."

Within a few, very short moments, the purple Do Not Resuscitate band was on his wrist.

And we were now not getting better. We were dying.

Chapter 22

ONE MORE DECISION

*A self-portrait taken in our first New York apartment,
four months before we got married.*

CALLED DONNY TO let him know what was going on. I guess I
hoped he'd make me change my mind, like, "Don't give up yet!
Did we think about . . ." But he didn't.

I called Maria. I was still making sure . . . making sure . . .
Also I now had another decision to make. "I need to decide if I'm
taking him home or not. The infection is not resolving," I told
her, keeping my voice steady.

"Oh, dear," she said, "What's his CA19-9? Did they say?"

The CA19-9 is the blood test that roughly measures how active the tumor is. When Patrick first started, his number was 1,240. Just five months ago it was 2,000. And now, "156,000," I reported.

I heard a momentary but meaningful silence on the other end of the line. Then she murmured, "That's awfully high . . ." The cancer was taking over.

Patient Relations came by and hung big signs on Patrick's door warning that no one was to enter without authorization. I had let them know that a couple of days ago, some staff from another part of the hospital came by to visit Patrick. I loved these two people, and they had been good to us during our visits, but as they were standing at the foot of the bed, I knew that word was getting around the hospital about how bad Patrick was looking. As they talked, I was smiling, but I was thinking to myself, *"They're here because they think Patrick is going to die and they want to see him one last time!"*

And now I was protecting Patrick in a different way. I knew that information was spreading. I was vigilant at his door. I started to worry and think that maybe I should push my cot up against the door to sleep at night lest someone sneak into the room and take a photo of Patrick.

I got private security to stand outside the door. This was something we generally didn't like to do, because it usually drew *more* attention to the area, but I couldn't take any chances. No chances at all. Patrick had fought this battle so valiantly and with such dignity, I wasn't about to risk his being degraded to a deathbed photo or description. *That would happen over* my *dead body!*

Back on that Monday, when the DNR was put on Patrick's wrist, Dr. Hoffman had asked me if I wanted to take Patrick home or stay in the hospital.

I had never been faced with a question like that and my mind felt paralyzed. "I don't know," I said. "Uhm, what do you think? I don't know . . ."

"It depends on your wishes . . ." Dr. Hoffman was being sensitive.

I don't know . . .

"Some people want to go home and some don't," he continued. "Much of the time we recommend staying in the hospital. Not so much for the patient, but it's easier on the family . . . it helps to distance them a bit from the process. And they're not burdened with a lot of the care . . ."

I don't know . . .

"I need to think about it," I managed to say out loud.

You know, there's the "die at home with your boots on" mentality, and that's very romantic. But this is the real world . . . and the real world is not so romantic and pasteurized . . . I needed to *think about it.*

Back in the room, I asked Patrick if he wanted to go home. But he didn't understand. I leaned over, put my arms around him, and smiled. "I love you," I said.

It was the one thing he *always* understood.

"I love you," he looked into my eyes and half-mouthed, half-whispered back.

I sat down and opened up my laptop. And I ordered the GPS he wanted. I didn't know what he was going to do with it. But maybe both of us were headed into unknown territory after all. And we were going to be in need of some serious guidance.

—

"I'M GONNA take him home," I announced Tuesday morning.

I think I knew in my heart that this was what I wanted to do, but it's my nature to think things through, look at all the angles when I'm dealing with something unfamiliar. Having never been in this situation before, I didn't know what to expect. And there was much that was still unknown. Once I had decided we were going home, things started to move quickly. I met with the aftercare people, and they arranged for a delivery of supplies that would be waiting when we got home, and they asked me, "Do you want the hospice nurse to be there to meet you when you get home?"

I had provided Patrick's home care for the last twenty-two months, so I calmly said, "No, that won't be necessary. Tomorrow around noon would be fine."

It turned out to be a happy choice that I decided to take him home. On September 9, the very day we were to leave the hospital, we found that a leak had been made to the tabloids:

SEPT 9, 09 Patrick Swayze GOES HOME TO DIE . . .
sometimes needs oxygen to breathe . . . "I refuse to die in a
hospital room. I'll go on my own terms—in our home and in
my own bed."

We are soooo outta here.

Bill Mancini, our security man who had so generously provided security for Patrick another time he was at Cedars-Sinai, provided a way to get out of the hospital safely, which involved exiting our current building and skirting through another that was under construction. Patient Relations freaked when they heard that we had an alternative plan that they weren't informed of. But Bill was prepared and confident, and was not about to be deterred from his master plan.

Bill would be taking him through the north end of the hospital to a waiting SUV. I was going to exit the hospital from the general parking area by myself, thus, we hoped, offering confusion to any paparazzi who might spot me.

At five o'clock, we loaded all our bits and pieces into plastic hospital bags and hung them on Patrick's wheelchair like we usually did. And then, Patrick was helped onto the chair, moving slowly, his cowboy hat perched low on his head. I kissed him. We were all set to move, and Bill stopped.

"Wait a minute," and he took me aside, fidgeting slightly, "What if . . . what if . . . something happens on the way home?"

I squinted, trying to make sure I understood what he was saying.

"What I'm saying is . . . *What if he dies?*" he asked.

I could tell it was painful for him to broach such a sensitive question. I shook my head with certainty.

"He's not going to die on the way home."

Bill looked hesitant.

But I knew beyond the shadow of a doubt. I shook my head again, "He's not going to die on the way home." Then I added, "Look . . . I'm following you and won't be far behind. If something happens, you can call my cell, and I'll be there. But he's going to make it home."

Bill nodded. And we were on the move.

—

AS I drove north, back to Rancho Bizarro, I don't remember looking toward the plumes of smoke that still blanketed the sky behind our ranch. But I'm sure I saw them there. The Station Fire was going to burn for more than another month before it was finally extinguished in mid-October. Our ranch was out of immediate danger, though. And for me, if there was a fire still burning, covering everything outside with a layer of fine gray soot, it was of little concern.

But I do remember turning into our gate and driving down to the house. It was just starting to turn to dusk, and Bill was helping Patrick out of the car. We were home.

At Rancho de Días Alegres, New Mexico.

Chapter 23

HOME AT LAST

I never thought I'd see death coming a mile away.
I thought it'd always sneak up on me, find me unprepared.
　　With my pants down.
But no, in this case I see its specter looming in the
　　distance,
positioning itself, waiting, waiting with confidence
for the one.
And I suit up in my karate gi.
I take a stance of defense and combat as I move into death
　　standing there before
me. Examining its MO, Trying to find its weak parts,
its mercy,
any shred of negotiation.
And death is looking at my puny little form as I pace back
　　and forth with all the
courage and menace I can muster. Is looking at the outline of
　　my body as if in an
X-ray, seeing only black and white.
And for all my courage and menace, it only sees where it's
　　going to bruise me as

I resist it. The side of my rib cage. The back of my neck. My
    fatty thigh . . .
And then, if I really try to hurt it, if I don't back off,
it sees where a blow that swipes (and indents) straight down
    from my throat thru
my sternum down to my diaphragm that might just break
    my heart.
He's tried it before, maybe this time, maybe this time . . .

I call to it
It doesn't answer.
I plead to it.
It doesn't answer.
I never thought I'd see death coming a mile away. But time
    is carrying me and the
one I love to it. And that's why it waits so confidently.
It doesn't care about me.
It doesn't care about my losing the love of my life.
I'm merely a curiosity of feelings it will never understand.
    Me, the nuisance.
Like a fly that won't go away.
And its silence says, "Get out of the way. Or, get hurt."
It's as simple as that.

                                                            Fall 2009

I FIND myself wanting to talk about Christmas 2010. Over a year
after Patrick had died . . . How Lucio, my longtime groom and
horse caregiver for the past twenty-two years was about to retire
and how it was like I was losing a piece of my, of our, family. It
was going to be a tough adjustment without him . . .

    But seriously . . .

It's very hard to talk about the last days in Patrick's life.

I find myself avoiding it. Finding reasons to justify putting off telling this part of the story until next month, like I've found reasons to justify putting it off for the last several weeks.

Why?

Because it's so hard to describe what is . . . a state of grace.

A time that was so horrible. And so loving at the same time.

A time that changed my life . . . forever.

I know there are no words to describe what really went on . . . In the same way that, no matter how many times I said "I love you" to him (and there were many, many, many, many times I did), it would never be enough. Words are incredibly poor substitutes for enormous feelings. Feelings of despair, and of love.

I really don't feel like I can do those emotions justice. And I have to take the onus off telling this part of the story by telling you that.

And as I prepare to talk about these last few days, I already feel an emotion of massive grief. A grief that would rule my life for the next year and more. And in a tantalizing, shimmering instant—a glimpse into a love that transcends . . . A love that shakes you. That expands your heart beyond the boundaries of air.

—

WE ARRIVED home at six o'clock in the evening on that pleasantly warm Wednesday. Patrick was in and out of a kind of tired lucidity, and it was difficult for him to concentrate on anything. He was also very weak, and though he was still somewhat mobile, he needed a lot of assistance and guidance. It was *quiet* in the house. So quiet . . . Like the whole world had gone away.

I settled him in and discovered the bag that sat waiting on our fireplace hearth in the bedroom. As promised, it was the bag of supplies delivered by the hospice people. I opened it and found a stash of *new* drugs, with *new* instructions; Haldol, an antipsychotic, for anxiety, nausea, vomiting, Atropine, 1 percent solution, three to four drops in the mouth, Acetaminophen suppositories, for temperatures greater that 101, Ativan, to be administered sublingually or rectally . . . things I hadn't heard of or seen before and instructions that were new to me. And I was flooded with a panic and fear that I had just made *the biggest mistake of my life by bringing him home.*

How stupid could I be? How incredibly stupid? I am completely out of my league here. I'm a fool! Panic was rising into my throat.

I forced myself to remain calm. With regret, I harkened back to my cavalier response earlier that day, *"No, no, I don't need the hospice people to meet me tonight. Just have them come tomorrow at noon. I'll be fine tonight."* I'm sure that some of my panic was due to the nature of the situation and feeling so all alone, and not just the new drugs. But my being frightened that I'd make a mistake made me hypervigilant. I fretted that I might do something that was not in Patrick's best interest, or that my lack of knowledge might make things painful for him. *I had all these strange new drugs* . . . And because he was not completely cognizant, he was not of much help in letting me know what was going on with him. I weighed whether I should make a mayday call, and I decided to "hang tough" for the moment. I thought I could get him through the night without mishap, then I would have all answers on his care and the strange bag of drugs tomorrow.

And the night did pass without incident, except that Patrick got up and wandered around while I was still asleep. And that was cause for concern, since he hadn't been able to walk without assistance for days. But somehow, he found the energy. It was early in the morning as Donny prepared to go to San Diego to run an errand he'd been putting off for a long time. Donny figured he'd zip down there for the day and make it back by early evening . . .

when suddenly, Patrick was standing outside his door, leaning against the hallway wall, his eyes bright!

"Where are you going?" Patrick asked emphatically, as if he was immensely perturbed.

"I've got to go down to San Diego," a surprised Donny said. "Why??"

Donny carefully explained the trip he had to make and that he would be back after that . . . he felt like he was talking to a little kid, all the while wondering how the hell Patrick had gotten up the three steps out of our bedroom by himself!

Donny helped him back into the bedroom and to bed before he left.

Me? I slept through the whole thing. And when I heard about Patrick's early morning stroll, I was even more concerned than ever that he'd run afoul of some trouble in the middle of the night. But the ladies who were about to visit had some ideas about that.

—

TINA, THE hospice nurse, and Sharon, the RN who oversees all the nurses in the hospice's organization, arrived. Tina, a large, beautiful black woman, was a little surprised to find Patrick Swayze waiting for her care. She was totally warm and professional while she was here, but after she left, she turned to Sharon and said, "You could have *warned* me about who we were seeing." To which a flustered Sharon replied, "I thought I *did*!"

I was grateful that these two ladies showed up. They were warm, loving, sensitive, and knowledgeable. Sharon in particular was to help me navigate these new waters. Both were to teach me things I didn't know yet.

There is a huge difference between "trying to make better" and "trying to make comfortable." It's like leaving planet Earth, with its hospitals and doctors, and moving to a whole new planet with a new country, rules, and languages. Don't ask the doctors how this part of the journey will go. Unless they've gone through it themselves, they don't know and they can't tell you. These women who were visiting Patrick and me could.

This part of care is its own art form. And the transition to learning this was a little tough and jarring for someone like me, who had battled for the last twenty-one months so fiercely to help make the one I loved better. First came removing any last treatments. This entailed stopping the antibiotics that Donny and I were still hooking up for him. Not giving him the Albumin that he had needed to replenish the protein levels in his blood after his last drain/paracentesis, and some of the drugs and supplements that had always been on his daily list of treatments. These items were about making him "better" and would only get in the way of letting his body do what it needed to do—move into its process of shutting down. Why would I want to give him something that would make this process more difficult for him, that would possibly make him suffer longer than he needed to? This was a hard thought to wrap my head around, but not impossible. It was another learning curve.

I was also told that to give him IV fluids was not a good idea. His body could drown in them, his lungs could fill . . . "The body can't handle it," said Sharon. "It's why people stop eating, stop drinking near the end . . . their body is saying, 'Leave me alone, I've already got so much I'm doing.'" If you drizzle water down their throat, they can choke on it if they are unable to swallow. But you can moisten the gums, the lips . . .

"But dehydration?" I asked.

"Dehydration is actually a preferable way to go," Sharon said calmly and evenly, "it's painless."

There was also learning their tips on the more basic care: feeding, not feeding, drinking, not drinking, lips, eyes, and new supplies and instructions to take care of hygiene. Like I said, it was another art form, and they did things quite differently.

Oh, and the wandering at night?

"Put some little bells or something on his tray table," said Sharon. "When he moves it out of the way to get out of bed, they'll ring, and it'll wake you up."

I couldn't believe it! I felt like a bonehead. I'd agonized about this for almost a year without coming up with any solutions. Bells! Of course!

I worried about Patrick's heart. It beat so strongly. I was afraid his heart would not let him go when he needed to. That it would keep beating, keep hanging in there, and hurt him. And I believe if his heart had been weaker, he would not have lasted the extra days that he did. *But damn, even now he was so strong!*

It was strange to suddenly have to learn the finer points of how to not interfere with death, but step in enough to make sure that the person you're caring for is comfortable. And if he wasn't lucid, how did you know if he was comfortable or not? They had tips on that also. "Grimacing. Grimacing was one of the ways to know." And Patrick did his fair share of grimacing. They wanted to "up" his base dosage of Dilaudid by almost four times, not just for his pain, but also to keep him calm. But I was wary of the effects of too much Dilaudid on Patrick and opted for a lower base rate, but with a higher bolus "press the button" dose that we could press every twenty minutes if needed.

After two hours of instructions, much discussion, and two pamphlets dealing with various physical and emotional situations, and one on the nuts and bolts of the dying experience, Sharon and Tina left. They'd be back again tomorrow.

You're going? I wanted to say incredulously. Somehow I had thought they'd be there all day. I resisted the urge to grab their arms and firmly guide them back into the room. But after they were gone, I was okay. *I had a game plan now.* Whereas before, I had done my best to help Patrick to live, I now had to focus on being the best I could be at helping him in these last days. I was armed with some knowledge now. That, and a cell phone number. And this new focus gave me a purpose. A purpose that was filled with the unconditional love and care that I felt for him.

—

THAT THURSDAY, Patrick and I sat outside for much of the day enjoying the fresh air. I went into the kitchen to get some soup and as I was going back outside, through the windows I could see Patrick sitting, looking out over the yard and pool, the dogs lying around him . . . I knew I had made the right decision in bringing him home, even if it was only for a few moments that he was truly aware and could enjoy his time here.

When the sun was going down and it was getting cold, I helped him back into the house and into bed. He was in and out, sometimes talking slowly but clearly, sometimes mumbling, mostly quiet and gentle. When we were ready to go to sleep, I moved the tray table next to his side of the bed and hung small, light chimes on it so that when he got out of bed, I would hear them and wake up. And after I set him up in bed, I lay next to him, the bolus/button clamped in my hand. He had looked uncomfortable, and I ascertained that he really did need the extra Dilaudid. So, throughout the night, every twenty minutes, I pressed the button. And I pressed it every twenty minutes until Sharon and Tina showed up the next day.

—

"WE NEED to reprogram the pump," I sighed tiredly. "I spent all night pressing that thing. But who knows how many times I might have missed during the night because I was sleeping."

"Well, we can see just how much," Tina said as she accessed the memory on the pump. She peered at the numbers, "Oh . . . You didn't sleep at all last night, did you?"

I hadn't missed a single dose.

"Did he get out of bed last night?" they asked.

I shook my head. "No." And I was a bit sad about that . . . for so long I had been afraid that he'd get up in the night without my knowing and always prayed for him to have a long, restful sleep and *stay* in bed. And now, I would have given anything for him to be up and around and worrying me. I wasn't going to need the chimes after all.

—

MY MOTHER-IN-LAW, Patsy, was the first to visit from the family. Patrick was sitting on the edge of the bed with Tina assisting him when he heard her voice call from outside the bedroom door. He shot me a look of pain and anguish . . .

"Why? Why did you bring her here?" he whispered.

How could I not? I had always been on Patrick's side, but . . .

"She's your mother," I said with as much compassion as I could, "You have to. You know?"

I could see Patsy pacing outside the door, nervous, like a long-tailed cat in a room full of rocking chairs, as we say in the South. I decided that I was going to nip this in the bud right now and try to make them both comfortable.

"Patsy!" I called out to her.

"What?" she called back tensely.

"Buddy's afraid that he's going to upset you seeing him like this. He doesn't want you to feel bad."

"What?" Patsy had the perfect opportunity, and she moved into the room and to Patrick, "No . . . noo," she cooed, "I don't want to upset you. I'm just happy to see you."

Patrick slowly put his hands by his side to push himself up.

Tina was there to help, asking gently, "Do you need to go to the bathroom?"

Patrick didn't respond, but stood up, and once on his feet, he took one step forward, and put his arms around his mom to give her a big hug.

And then all was fine.

As the day went on, more family came by to visit. My sister-in-law Bambi's husband brought the barbecue they were planning for a party. And my amazing friends Kay and Lynne dropped everything to bring food and to serve in whatever capacity was needed . . .

During the trail of visitors, I stepped outside Patrick's door to privately ask Sharon for advice about something that was bothering me, really bothering me. It was difficult, and it hurt to ask. But I didn't know what to do.

"I haven't . . . Patrick and I haven't talked about what's going on," I told her. "I haven't brought up about him dying . . ."

She just looked at me. "He knows."

Of course he does. Of course he does . . .

—

PATRICK SPOKE his last words on Friday evening. My brother, Eric, and his wife, Mary, came through the bedroom door, and a woozy Patrick looked up, pleased to see them . . .

"Heeeyyyy, Eric and Mary . . ."

My last words with Patrick? "I love you." And he to me. I never stopped saying it—when I would leave the room, or when I came back into it. And he said it to me until it was only the movement of his lips without sound, and then . . . only his soft ears that my words would fall on.

After I brought him home, things went very fast.

He had already been in something of a semicoma, but late on Friday night, he slipped fully in. We still talked to him. Sat with him. I ended up limiting the number of people and the amount of time they could be in the room with him so it wouldn't get too raucous. I chuckled to myself, because I knew that if Patrick had been able, at a certain point in these raucous times he would have jumped up and said, "Hey, would everybody get the f★!k out of here?" There *are* advantages to knowing someone so well.

In the evenings it would get quiet again when everyone left, and I cherished the alone time with him . . . holding his hand, listening to music, sleeping with my arm around him, my head on his shoulder, wordlessly.

I had been told what to look for that would tell me when the end was near: a weakening in the pulse, a change in the skin color, a gurgling in the breath . . . His pulse was strong, but clearly the rest of his body was not in good shape.

We kept on through the weekend. And in the quiet of Monday morning, September 14, Donny walked into the bedroom and stood next to the bed. Donny was horrified that he'd overslept by almost two hours and missed his turn to give Patrick his IV Ativan. As soon as he approached the bed, I surprised him by sitting up quickly, not panicked, but eyes open and alert as if I had never been asleep.

"I know," I answered the question he hadn't asked yet, "he's been breathing like that for two hours."

Patrick's breathing was odd. It was shallow . . . incredibly shallow.

Donny looked worried and bemoaned that he had overslept, excusing himself to go prepare the Ativan in the kitchen.

I felt Patrick's warm pulse. *Still strong.* I looked at his face and listened to the tiny sips of air he was taking. Tiny, light sips of air . . . There was something . . . delicate . . . childlike about it.

I knew it was time. I didn't want to leave the room, but crazily, I wanted to be thoughtful of Donny. Also, I didn't know what *I* would or might do. I was afraid that suddenly I'd be afraid, or . . .

I raced quickly out and called to Donny that he should come. And went to lie back at Buddy's side. I held his hand, and felt his pulse again . . . *was it?* . . . *was it?* . . . listening to the childlike breath . . .

And then he didn't breathe anymore.

—

IT WAS ten o'clock in the morning. And he'd used that body. He'd used every last bit of it. That much was clear to me. He didn't need it anymore. It was no good to him and he needed to leave it behind.

It was the way it needed to be. And I thought that maybe I'd have a hard time being with him as he, or his body, died. But it wasn't creepy at all. It was a body that had used up its purpose. There was an acceptance. It was realistic and clear. And what was in the air transcended any puny little thoughts I might have dreamed up during my little lifetime about what this moment might be.

Donny came back into the room with the Ativan syringe in his hand and stopped at the side of the bed.

I looked up at Donny and saw that he knew. And then I suddenly had an urge and I lifted the bolus/button and pressed it, delivering one extra dose of Dilaudid. I had the strange thought that maybe Patrick needed just that little extra bit of comfort as he left. That maybe there was one little part that might have been having a hard time letting go in his body and needed help.

And I looked up at Donny and said, "Just in case . . ."

Donny put his hand out and pressed it over Patrick's heart, and I heard him sniff back a tear. "That's okay, big brother, you don't have to take another breath."

After a moment, I looked at the syringe Donny was holding . . .

"Guess he won't be needing that anymore."

In an hour or two, family started showing up. I sat outside the double bedroom doors that opened to our yard for a moment while family came in to visit and view Patrick's body. Kay and Lynne sat down beside me.

"Oh, my God, yesterday when you were taking a nap in there with him," Lynne said, "you had your head resting on his shoulder the whole time. You looked just like an angel."

"Like you were *his* angel." Kay nodded.

"And now he's mine," I said.

As more and more family and close friends came around, Lucio, our groom, brought Roh, Patrick's favorite horse, down to the house. The same brilliant, white horse that Patrick had rode in on during our wedding vows renewal. I had straightened up the covers around Patrick's body, hung a gorgeous coral, turquoise, and crystal amulet above his head that befitted his Warrior Spirit, and placed the most perfect white rose on his chest. Lucio and our friend, Steve, brought Roh right up to the double doors that opened into the bedroom, so close that the horse was almost inside, standing, towering, vibrant. Lucio gave Roh the cue, and this powerful horse bowed to Patrick.

—

OUR SECURITY, Bill, was on hand to help get Patrick to the mortuary safely and privately. And late in the afternoon, when his body finally started to grow cold, a small SUV van showed up. I was glad that it was so late in the day, glad that Patrick was no longer feeling warm to my touch. I don't think I could have let them take him earlier. The car that showed up, a smaller, family-style SUV, was so nondescript you would never know its purpose if you were driving on the freeway next to it. The vehicle would take Patrick, and then at the precise time he arrived safely at his destination, we'd release the statement that he had died. It would be perfect timing.

The family stood in the living room as the body was lifted and wheeled through and out the front door to the vehicle. I followed closely along with family, but stopped away from the car as they loaded Patrick's body in. The door slammed shut, the two men started the car and it rolled up the drive to the gate. And that's when it hit me. They were taking him away. He would be gone. Like seeing your loved one board a plane and take off into the big, blue sky. But this time, he's not coming back. You reach out, but you can't touch him, you feel . . . severed from him. It was an awful feeling, one I hadn't felt quite yet, and I couldn't watch the car drive away. I turned to bury my face in my mother's shoulder and started to sob. Deep and heavy and awful sobs. Sobs that weighed a ton. And when I had cried for a while, I lifted my head, blew my nose, and started to walk back into the house, unsteadily. Kay and Lynne moved in to flank me, each holding an arm to support me. But after two or three steps, I had to say through the blur that had settled over me, "I have to sit down." My legs were wobbling and losing strength. "Okay," they said, "we'll find a place in the living room." I took another step. "No . . . I have to sit down—now," I warned them. And I sank to the ground into a crouched position, my head doubled over as I started to sob again. And when I could feel my legs again, I stood up to move back into the house. I know everyone was there . . . but I couldn't tell you where they were or what they were doing. I was isolated in a small universe of fog. And they, and everything else, were mere shadows around me. And it didn't matter. Nothing much mattered.

Chapter 24

THE IMMEDIATE AFTERMATH

*At Rancho Bizarro, nine of our trees died suddenly
in August/September 2009.*

AFTER PATRICK DIED, I sat outside with family and close friends gathered around a lit fireplace that evening, sharing stories, some of them funny. At a certain point, I'd had enough. I stood up and went back into the house. Everybody stood up with me and departed soon after . . .

Hard to imagine that little more than twelve hours ago I was listening to my husband take tiny puffs of breath that were his last. That he was lying in our bedroom growing cold, his beautiful countenance frozen into a crisp. Twelve hours ago that I cried as they were driving his body out the gate. Twelve hours since I entered a nightmare I was afraid of because I believed it would be terrible, and I believed it would be only as terrible as a small portion of how terrible it really is. And in the last four hours I got to see what it's like to laugh as if he wasn't lying breathing his last breaths in my bed. I got to see how bad it hurt to have laughed when it was only this morning I was left with devastation.

Early morning, September 15, 2009

I wish I had something good, or enlightening, or even remotely encouraging to say about the process of losing someone. But I don't. There is nothing fun about it, nothing good, nothing hopeful. It's like the world is twisted like a wet rag until all the color, all the poetry in life is squeezed out of it.

Sorry to say, I feel a little let down.

I can launch into cynicism. The cynicism that has come up since I lost my Buddy. I can talk about how the naïve thought that I'd always had—that life will reward those who are kind and do good things—how that's not true, and just a man-made notion to ensure that in our society we just don't all kill each other. Right? There's no art here. Even the sad stuff is just made-up fantasy. Just stuff invented to make the real emotions of life bearable. When the fact is—there's nothing romantic about life at all.

Hah! Case in point . . .

Yes, there are the songs about how I "Can't Live Without You." How about songs about breathing? "I Can't *Breathe* Without You." There are a number of titles with variations on that same "can't breathe" theme. All beautifully composed, expressing loss in such a lovely and heartfelt way . . . Can't breathe without you? Well, yes, that's true. Losing someone you love so much *does* make you feel like you can't breathe. But not because of some longing and lyrical sadness. It's because you feel like someone is literally *sitting on top of your chest.* Try it. Say, "Hey Tim! or, Gladys . . . Come sit on my chest so I can feel what it feels like to lose someone I love so m—Ah!! Ah!! I *really* . . . can't . . . breathe! Ah!" Seriously, this would be an accurate recreation of what it feels like. So much for poetry.

What else?

Four days after Patrick died, my wonderful girlfriends suggested we have a PJ party. It was great. The next night everyone showed up in their pajamas, we had a poker game (I had just started to learn Texas Hold 'Em), and in the spirit of "girls' night," I wore a dime-store rhinestone, pink and white princess crown, just thinking maybe it'd make me feel better somehow. We all sat outside around the fire later, one of Patrick's favorite places on cool evenings in the past months, and one of my friends opened the big can of worms by asking, "How *are* you doing . . . ?" I cried, which was something I did many times during the day anyway, so what else was new. And had to point out that Patrick and I had been married over thirty-four years. Thirty-four years with the same person . . . always there . . . always in your life, in the morning, in the day, and the night. "Face it," I reasoned, "even if I hated his guts I'd be having a hard time." And I cried a little more . . .

"You know, in all of our relationship," I managed between tears, "I don't think there were more than three times that we went more than one day without talking to each other . . ."

And it was true. No matter where each of us was in the world, we talked, we touched every day. India, Nepal, Russia, Africa, Illinois . . . It didn't matter. We could have loved each other, hated each other, been drunk, not drunk, couldn't wait to tell a story, couldn't wait to get off the phone, mad, or delighted. Working on a scene, working on our lives, working on making dinner, looking at the stars, feeding the dogs and cats, driving home at night, lying in bed, watching a movie, crying, laughing, sighing, smiling, rolling our eyes . . . we did it all. And somehow we managed to do it together.

That night by the fire—it was Day 5.

—

ON DAY 2, I had spilled out of bed because I heard his voice. Out of a deep sleep, I heard him say, "Lisa!" It came from inside the bathroom, and had an intense, needy urgency to it. *It sounded just like him.* And it was a tone that I'd heard before from him when he needed my help, and quickly.

I tumbled to the floor out of the bed onto all fours, and sprang up to race into the bathroom to see what he needed. As I was scrambling, I was aware that he was dead. But maybe . . . maybe . . .

I rounded the corner, half desiring to see him, half afraid . . . He was not there . . .

> *Dark night.*
> *If I imagine, I can feel your hand*
> *I hope that you are here with me*
> *Because I am feeling so very alone without you.*
> *This is harder than I thought*
> *It's beyond physical*
> *Beyond a simple ache*
> *It's sickening and an attack on my being*
> *On a cellular level*

Like a life of its own
Like illness
Like disease
The wave catches me and does with me what it will
Plunging me down
Drowning me at a moment's notice
My will is not my own anymore
It is lost in my love and connection to you.
Inexorably and forever
intertwined

Yeah . . . for me . . . Grief is something that happens on a cellular level. It's not an emotion. It's something that worms into your DNA. Splitting your nuclei. Grief is like little worker bees streaming through your blood, buzzing and working overtime at paralyzing bits of your life. I can see why spouses sometime follow their mates into death. It's not a choice. Your body either survives the onslaught, or it doesn't. It is meant to be, or not. It's not your choice. Things are happening inside you. Things you have no control over.

As much as my world is rocked, or maybe because of it, I can sit for long periods of time not moving. No, really . . . not moving. I breathe. That's about it. Otherwise, I'm as still as a rock. If there were radar out there, it would not pick me up on its screen. If there were people passing through, they would not see me.

I could think of a lot of other, happy things to say. But . . . I won't. That's the unfortunate truth. Sorry to disappoint.

Let me think of something that I can say that might have some redeeming value . . . Something that says something other than *"Life sucks."* Uhm, can't think of anything.

Well, one more thing . . . I found myself blaming myself. Blaming myself for taking him *to* the hospital, taking him *out* of the hospital, being the one to "give up," for not making him well . . . And if that wasn't enough, I started to blame myself for everything I ever did wrong in our relationship. Every time I was unreasonable, angry, grumpy . . .

And after that—I blamed him.

For what, you might ask? Hey. We were married for thirty-four years—trust me, I have a list. And I'd yell at him. I'd yell into the air. And I'd be *very* angry.

—

ON SEPTEMBER 29, little more than two weeks after Patrick died, his autobiography, *The Time of My Life*, was released and became an immediate *New York Times* bestseller. It had been hard doing the book at times in the last year, like a fish trying to swim upstream against a strong current, but I was glad we made the effort. It was something tangible that I could hold in my hand. It represented him in the world. It said, *"Don't forget me!"* We were proud of how the book came out. It's a good read, and you see what an incredible life Patrick had, how hard he and I worked, and also how we had a few laughs. A few laughs . . . that's one of the things that always worked its way into our lives.

We were always up to something crazy. It's why we named our ranch in Los Angeles "Rancho Bizarro," because you never knew what we might be cooking up. Early in our ownership of Rancho Bizarro, we threw a "Rock" party, which was merely a disguise for the true agenda: Those who showed up would literally be picking up rocks out of our horse arena. And then there were the swordfighting lessons that were used to hack the weeds out the back door. Every movie, every job, was reflected in what we added to the ranch; *North and South* brought the pool that Patrick reasoned we had to have *before* we added on to the house so our family-workers could cool off. *Dirty Dancing* bought the new master bedroom, bath, and closet, a solarium and dance studio, and the next movie converted our old root cellar into a music/recording studio for Patrick. And then there was adding a barn and arena . . . converting the old tack room into a guesthouse . . . new garage and carport . . . landscaping . . . If you read the autobiography, you will know that both Patrick and I are accomplished carpenters (from our lean days as dancers in New York). And actually, every stick of moulding in the house was done by my hand. And one day, I *will* putty in some of those nail holes.

Anyway . . . The book!

The book was released, and our press agent, Annett, and I began talking with our publisher about what I could do to promote it. I still could function great when called upon! I would just pay for it by crashing back down pretty hard later. The only concern I had about interviews was being able to control my emotions. Of course people were going to ask me about Patrick's death. A little emotion was okay, but if an interviewer asked a question and I careened off that cliff into full-blown, ballooning sobs . . . that was *not* okay as far as I was concerned. I found out in one trial run, an onstage discussion about grief at the Women's Conference in Long Beach, that I might skitter to the edge of the cliff, but I was able to throw a rope around myself and rein myself back in to safe enough ground.

Going out and doing press on the book may have been asking a lot of myself, but I was goddamned if this book wasn't going to do well. As much as people loved Patrick, I knew—if they didn't know about the book, they couldn't buy it. And I wanted *everyone . . . everyone . . .* to know what a fantastic life he had. So, I got myself together and in early November, I went on a press tour.

I found that every time I had to leave a hotel, get on a plane to go somewhere, I felt like my world was being torn apart. I felt like I was digging my nails into whatever I could find as life and schedule dragged me to somewhere new. I wanted to say in the most nonsensical, childish way, *"Nooo . . . pleeease don't make me gooooooo!"* It didn't matter where I was going and where I was leaving from . . . I just didn't want to move. But, in a kind of stunned way, I kept my thoughts to myself and went ahead and did it. I was talking to my friend Kay about this later. How crazy this feeling was that I didn't want to leave anywhere. How pain-ful . . . And you know what she said?

"I know why you didn't want to leave." She nodded. "It's because you're moving on with your life without him."

. . . It was so true.

After Patrick left, everything was a series of "firsts." The first time I pulled onto the freeway. The first time I left town. The first time I walked into a restaurant, my yoga class . . . And they all hurt.

—

EVERYONE AROUND me tells me how incredible I've been. How well I've been handling this. And what a strong woman I am. And I smile and thank them, but inside *I think they're freakin' nuts!* Because inside, I do not feel strong and courageous. I feel like a puny, sniveling, whiney mess. This is not pretty. And I am at the opposite end of the spectrum from glamorous. Although I put on a pretty good show for moments at a time, the moment the need to *perform* for people is gone, I become a clump of wet, muddy, wilted grass.

And months later, when the being stunned after his death and the deer-in-the-headlights look wear off . . . just when you think it can't get any worse . . .

It gets worse.

—

AFTER THE initial release, *The Time of My Life* is released internationally. And I'm called to do some more press. That's okay . . . it helps me to have something to focus on. It helps me *a lot*.

This interview is via satellite to a live, London morning show. Which means that I need to be ready to go on around eleven o'clock at night. So, I show up at an address in Culver City, where there are probably only two to three other people in the entire building since it's so late. I have my hair and makeup done. And then I wait . . . and I wait in the darkened building for my cue to go one. It feels like when I was performing in the theater. The times when I've waited in the dark wings, listening for my moment to go on . . . the dazzling lights beyond, onstage . . . And I wait. And you know what? It strangely feels like my life . . .

> *Maybe I'm waiting for him.*
> *Like his stuff, his toilet bag, brush, toothbrush, cologne is*
>   *waiting at his bathroom sink. It looks so natural there.*
>   *And it looks like he'll show up any second to use it.*
> *As if nothing bad has, or ever has, happened.*
> *Maybe I'm peering into the darkness to find him.*
> *And then, just waiting. Patiently for a sign. For my cue.*
> *They say that I'll always have him with me. Well, what I*
>   *have right now is a piss poor version of that.*
> *They say at some point I'll be able to go on with my life.*
> *And I have. Heck, I'm working, taking care of business and*
>   *the ranch, etc. But that's all just going through the mo-*
>   *tions. Is it really moving on? No, it's just functioning in*
>   *spite of myself. Something I'm pretty good at given the*
>   *drama I've experienced in my life.*
> *But I have faith that what they say is true.*
> *That the loss of the one I love will become an asset in my life.*

That I will cherish what we had and I'll be happy because
    of it.
That I will move on.
I wait patiently for all those things to come true.
Then I can step out of this darkness.
And into the light.

That is my wish.

I have been a romantic at heart. But I'm a realist . . . And I'll wait to see if what they say is true. That I will heal, find a way to manage. And . . . maybe I won't. That's possible, too. But I have the wherewithal to wait and find out. As long as I have breath, I can keep putting one foot in front of the other. Because in my Finnish roots, I have my "Sisu."

So . . . I'll wait.

EPILOGUE

Me, with my fabulous cowgirl cake.

A S I WRITE this, it's mid-May 2011, and it's been one year, eight months, and one day since I lost my Buddy. I have a birthday coming up at the end of this month, and it's funny how all the anniversaries have changed for me. There are always those milestones, those benchmarks that note and mark your passage through life: birthdays, wedding anniversaries, Christmas, New Year's . . . I have added the date that my Buddy died. And that has strangely altered all the other dates and occasions—it's the Christmas without him, the New Year starting, the birthday for myself that I really tried to ignore last year (unsuccessfully), our wedding anniversary, *his* birthday . . . The date of his death changed everything, because everything is now without him.

It's no small wonder that I've tried to ignore all those holidays and anniversaries. I busy myself and hope they'll slide by like any other day. That's hard to do. It's like hiding from myself, pretending (with my finest acting ability) that God cannot see me. And of course wouldn't you know it, it's usually my tender friends who call my attention to the day. They call to check on me, to ask what I'm going to be doing that particular day; they invite me out. The ones who showed up with a surprise birthday cake complete with cowgirl figurine and chocolate frosting two weeks before my actual birthday. Two weeks before because I was planning to *be out of town for my birthday!* Agh! Foiled again. I burst into tears when this cake came out of hiding, with lit candles, and I had to walk away for a few minutes. *I just didn't want to have my birthday without him.* And my picture is taken with the amazing cowgirl cake before we cut it. And I've kept that picture propped up in my kitchen in New Mexico. And I think I've kept it there this past year, where I can see it every day, because, as curiously full of pain as I know I am in the photo, I look at it and I know I am still loved.

No one told me how hard it was going to be living without my husband. It's like learning to walk again—but with only one leg now. And beyond the grief, there seems to be a never-ending barrage of financial and organizational repercussions that have accompanied his death. My widow friends and I laugh about how being a widow (a term that I hate) is like being blood in the water. You know . . . the sharks can smell you for miles away, and they come after you. *Why do they think I'm so weak? I mean, I'm in pain, deep pain. But don't piss me off right now, or you're gonna get a whole can of whoop-ass!* But I *am* weak. My life roars in my ears and is spiraling out of control much of the time, but that doesn't make me stupid. But the sharks and the challenges just keep coming. And I know that I'm *probably* not being persecuted *personally,* not in *every* case, although it *sure looks like it to me.* It's just that every change, every attack, every complication is a lot to handle. It's a lot to handle on my own.

I see now how I always felt protected by Patrick. We had our hard times, and challenges that were towering, but I felt . . . safe. It's crazy, 'cause Patrick wasn't always the one protecting me, much of the time I was doing the protecting, and sometimes, even protecting myself from him. But after I lost him, I suddenly lost that feeling of being safe, and I didn't understand why.

"I know why," Kay offered. "You felt safe because he loved you."

Ah . . .

Yes. And his love was like an umbrella. It covered me, kept me from the storm, and safe in his arms. And now, as I mentioned earlier in this book, I'm out in the cold, looking for a life raft anywhere, and finding none.

In addition to feeling like I've lost one of my limbs, that umbrella has snapped shut and I've been shoved out into the rain, and on top of that, I have to look at the world through different eyes now. Patrick and I saw the world together for over thirty-four years. *And this world looks different without him.* Even the things that haven't changed at all look different. It's like the planes of the earth have slid to an angle and shaken loose bits and pieces. And some of them are good, and some of them are bad, and all of it has changed.

There have been a few friends who have been left along the way since Patrick's death, mostly because I realized they were *not really our, or my, friends.* But mostly, there are the many fantastic friends who have stuck by me. I have to say that somehow, someway, Patrick and I chose our friends well. And their love and support has meant the world to me. And yes, there are a few who just don't quite know what to do with me right now, and that can be uncomfortable for them. But they don't go away, and they will wait out this storm.

And then I have my new "widow" friends. I was lucky enough to meet two wonderful women after Patrick died. Both had lost their husbands to pancreatic cancer, one a year earlier than me, and the other six months behind me. And when we get together, *the sh*t can fly!* Meaning, we can short-cut all the small talk and get right down to it. There's a lot of anger that accompanies the loss, also blame and other unpretty emotions that you cannot go around expressing to people who don't understand what you're going through. With each other, we can let it rip, and the other one will just keep responding in agreement, *"I hear you, I hear you."* The three of us are very different people, with different lifestyles. But it's amazing how similar our experiences are in dealing with our husbands' deaths. Until the fall of last year, I felt protective toward my widow-friend who's six months behind me in her loss. I didn't want to tell her what lay ahead of her in this terrible journey, because I knew how much pain she was already in. To think that you would have *more* pain could be a reason to . . . *just not go on.* And that's another thing we widows share with each other—that we tinker with the thought of suicide.

I stopped being so careful with my friend last fall. I believe it was right around the time that I actually had a good day. (Up to that point, I had seriously thought that I would not survive.) And I told her, "It *can* happen!" And, slowly, it has. I can have a few days strung together when I actually *feel pretty good.* And sometimes, *feeling good* feels like euphoria. I can only think that this is because my body has been wracked with pain for so long that, when it gets a chance at relief, it interprets it as nirvana!

But if I can have one good day, I can have another, and another.

And I have.

It's just taking a long time.

—

I HAD the hardest time starting to write this Epilogue. Because part of me thinks, "I should be over this by now." It's been one year, eight months, and one day since I lost my Buddy. "I should be doing better by now." It's almost like an embarrassment. In addition to feeling like a broken girl, I feel like a broken record. It's only just recently that I started talking to a grief counselor. I got sick of hearing myself say the same stuff in my head and to the friends I share with. And depression seems to have become a permanent fixture in my life. Like it's stuck inside me and won't unclog. I'll have some wonderful days, and then I'll crash and it feels like nothing has changed at all. I still miss him as terribly as I ever did.

I was just sitting at Sunday breakfast with my friend Lynne. It's one of her and my favorite places and it was a beautiful, cool morning as we sat at the café table out on the sidewalk talking about our out-of-control lives (she's having a challenging time herself right now). We were sharing about how much we are overburdened, stressed to the max, and are having to do the work of what seems like a small army when it's only just one person—us. And I found myself desperately searching for some kind of answer (because I am desperately sick of feeling this way), looking for some way out of the feeling that I might buckle under this weight, and I broke in, "You know, maybe . . . maybe all this stress isn't just about . . ."

And I stopped suddenly, and retreated.

"What? What? You can't just stop there!" she exclaimed.

I gathered myself because, in the midst of our girlfriend camaraderie as we complained on this beautiful day, my heart had suddenly slipped through the cracks. And the pain was fresh again. And this hurt feels like falling. Like falling through air with nothing to hold on to.

And I bore down and did my best to force the tears back down and step back to reality.

"Okay. I got a little choked up," I said, getting it under control, "I was just going to say that maybe we wouldn't be so overwhelmed, that it wouldn't be so hard to take if we weren't *hurting*. Maybe it's really about, you know . . . the hurt."

Lynne pursed her lips. It was not somewhere she wanted to go at that moment.

Me neither.

I was told by my widow friend with the one-year seniority that it's not so much that the pain gets better as that it gets more "manageable." And so far, that's true for me. But I describe it a little differently. It's like what I said about losing a limb, the "losing a leg" scenario—suddenly, a world I have always shared with someone, I'm left to carry on my own. I feel the weight of this burden. It's just me, little painfully compromised me, who's carrying the weight that two people carried before. But when I carry that weight every day, I get stronger, and I find little tricks to better bear it. So, you're missing a limb? Get twice as strong. And you don't want to, you have no motivation . . . you're not even sure you want to live. But every day that you get out of bed, it's going to make you stronger. Whether you like it or not.

My out-of-control life?

Change is hard. And this kind of loss forces you to change. It's *enforced change*. And loss doesn't lie still after you lose your loved one. It tumbles and tumbles, and becomes a series—loss, after loss, after loss. I'm keeping the faith that any good ground-work I lay now will pay off later. *It's got to get easier than this!* And I am working hard. Very hard, in every way I can.

In the meantime, I'm strong enough this year to think about celebrating my birthday. I'll just have some of my friends over, and we'll laugh.

May 15, 2011

ACKNOWLEDGMENTS

I LAUNCH INTO THESE acknowledgments knowing that, like every invitation list I've ever made for a big party, I'm going to forget someone accidentally. I apologize in advance to them. There are also people who were mentioned in the book that I may not mention here, but there are some I will.

There are so many wonderful and talented people who made such a difference in the last two years of my husband's life and my own. Many of those people I've never even met, or spoken to. I send out my love and appreciation to all of them.

Haapaniemi / Niemi Family

Dr. Maria Scouros and Ed and the kids; Eric and Mary and Will; Paul and Jessica and Valerie; John, Alex, and Carol; and Mom.

Swayze Family

Donny, Patsy, Bambi, and Don; Sean and Jami and the kids.

Stanford Hospital and Cancer Center

Drs. George Fisher, Jeff Norton, Elwyn Cabebe, Jacques Van Dam, Albert Koong. The great people in patient relations: Judy Kinsberg, Michael Granneman, Julia Vitenberg, Pam Huggins.

Ex-CEO Martha Marsh, along with the experienced and wonderful gals in the trenches during chemotherapy, nurses, Cathy Krum, and Mary Salom.

Cedars-Sinai Hospital

Drs. Simon Lo, Mark Ault, Geemee Chung. Patient Services: Madeline Lehrman, Yuri, and Lidia. Della and all the fabulous RNs in the procedure center, and the staff in the hospital.

Northwestern Hospital

Dr. Mary Mulcahy and all the heartfelt help provided by their cancer and GI department. Thank you, Dr. John Martin, for getting that new stent in. Whew!

Tower Oncology

The wonderful Dr. David Hoffman, our main man Jose Ramirez, and Pia Chantravat, and Bill Such. John Rice at Premier Infusion Care.

Loving Friends

Lisa "Above and Beyond" Dickey, Kay "Always There" Lenz, Brian Braff, Warren and Jale "There's Nothing a Pair of Red Manolo Blahniks Won't Help" Trepp, Lynne Butler, Joe and Sandy Bourdeau, Whoopi Goldberg, Cash and Monica Schoch, Randi Barnes, Dwight Rhoden, Desmond Richardson, Stacy Widelitz, Griff Griffis, Travis Fimmel. Kenny and Joanne Gordon, Mark Smith, Steve Diamond, and so many others.

The Beast

A&E and Sony TV for taking a chance on both Patrick and me. Michael, Roy, Vincent, Bill, and the entire production crew—you're the tops!

The Team

Our hard-working, caring publicists, lawyers, agents, managers: Annett Wolf, Jayme Phillips, Fred Gaines, Mel Berger, Richard Solomon, Nicole David, Jenny Delany.

Atria Books

My fantastic editor, Sarah Durand, and her assistants, Sarah Cantin and Alex Arnold. The wonderful Judith Curr. Paul Olsewski and Yona Deshommes. And the special Elisa Shokoff and Matt Cartsonis.

And ...

Our Beloved Animals—the ones I lost in the year after I lost Patrick—Tina the cat, Patrick's sleeping buddy, who died herself exactly one month later, at the same hour, from her own cancer. My beautiful filly that was born at 5:30 A.M. August 2009, and perished six months later during colic surgery. And our magnificent stallion Roh, who died from mysterious complications in August 2010. It was a rough year.

And the Beloved Animals who have survived with me, and love and protect me. Canines: Lucas, Murphy, and Kuma. Felines: Possum and Lupe. Equines: Bint Bint Subhaya, Zahra Galila, Shirin Jewel, Assirah, Nadra, Shamrock, Nation, Rabba, Emir, La Dior. My two bad-boy colts: Faris Al Ahlam and Malik al Malouk. And my beautiful new filly, Farah Jewel, born June 2011.

LIST OF ILLUSTRATIONS